MW00414342

THE DUMBEST KID IN GIFTED CLASS

by Dan Ryckert

Foreword

by Tim Turi

"Dan is a liar."

I remember the first time I heard someone whisper those words to me in the *Game Informer* vault, surrounded by a treasure trove of video games numbering in the thousands. I hadn't paused to consider that Dan might be a compulsive fibber before that moment, but that explanation to his bombastic persona suddenly seemed so obvious.

Dan Ryckert and I signed our papers to join the Game Informer team and begin our dream jobs on the very same day. The ink was barely dry before he began regaling the staff – unsolicited – with myriad stories about his adventures growing up in Kansas. His unassuming demeanor made each yarn even more unbelievable. Dan's an average dude with glasses, a Thin Lizzy shirt, and a worn pair of Adidas. But somehow, at age 19, he was savvy enough to con GameStop businessmen into paying him to create an in-store commercial – all so he could fly out to GI's offices and plant the seed for his eventual employment while running around in a shark suit.

Dan would begin talking, wide-eyed with enthusiasm and gesticulating wildly as he recounted story after story. The hits kept coming: The time he found himself in a car next to funk mastermind George Clinton and Eddie Winslow from *Family Matters*. How he had uploaded a compromising video of Kansas City Royals legend George Brett talking about shitting his pants, which became an internet phenomenon.

Over time these tales were met with amusement, inquisition, interrogation, and eventually disbelief. I can practically hear *Game Informer*'s Joe Juba murmuring "uh huh" in his dry deadpan and walking away with his arms folded across his chest after hearing Dan's latest.

How could this Dan guy, whose culinary peak was a bottle of Mickey's and cheap Fettuccini Alfredo somehow have had more excitement in his life by age 25 than most find in a lifetime?

I admit, even I had my reservations, despite Dan and me quickly bonding over classic rock, a shared appreciation of awful video games, and the mutual understanding that *Terminator 2* is perhaps the perfect film. But my doubts about Dan's raucous Kansas past faded to the background as we became close friends. Coming out of a bad breakup, I discovered a source of much-needed kinship and distraction in him, as I ended up in situations uncharacteristic for me.

Suddenly, I found myself standing at the open hatch of an airplane, wind whipping through my hair as I wondered how he had persuaded me into skydiving. I watched in disbelief as an office argument we began over boneless vs. bone-in buffalo wings erupted into a global Twitter debate – all thanks to Dan's knack for spin – culminating in culinary tastemaker Anthony Bourdain concluding that boneless wings are "a sin against god" (he's right, #TeamBoneIn 4 life).

I sat in bewilderment as Dan led rap artist/reality TV star Riff Raff out of a hotel and crammed him and his hulking bodyguard into my tiny Toyota Corolla so we could all play ToeJam & Earl in Panic on Funkotron.

The point is that I think it's natural to see someone like Dan – a fiercely "normal" guy – and wonder how his life could be so chock full of extraordinary events. Anyone who tunes into Dan on Giant Bomb, has heard him on old episodes of *Game Informer*'s Replay, or listens to his stories over a beer or two, would be within their rights to question what they've heard.

The thing is, as I learned through firsthand experience, if you stick with Dan long enough you see these things happen before your very eyes. Whether you live some of these remarkably lucky encounters alongside Dan, like I have, or see the zaniness pop up on your Twitter feed, enough evidence mounts to reinforce Dan's crazy, charmed life.

One crucial factor separates Dan and I when reflecting back on our weird antics: Dan has a special way with words. He is perhaps the best storyteller I've ever met, making a conversation about the most mundane facets of life – scrambling egg whites, for example – enthralling and hilarious.

So it stands to reason that a collection of his stories will undoubtedly entertain. My recommendation after over 8 years with this guy as one of my best friends: strap in and enjoy the ride.

Oh, and remember one thing: It's true. All of it.

Dedicated to Bianca

THE DUMBEST KID IN GIFTED CLASS

Blood on the Sand

Elementary school kids typically don't have strong opinions regarding their choice of deity. A couple of folks give birth to you, and your early years come with an assortment of grandfathered-in opinions on religion and politics and everything in between. At Holy Trinity Elementary School in Lenexa, Kansas, this led to an entire building filled with kids who proudly wore Catholicism on their sleeves and *really* hated Bill Clinton.

I was by no means a hard-nosed atheist growing up—that period took place during an especially obnoxious six months or so in college—but I didn't have strong opinions when it came to the big questions of the universe. Considering that Holy Trinity was an expensive private Catholic school, not a lot of parents sent their kids there unless the whole God thing was particularly important to them. My parents and I were not weekly churchgoers unlike virtually all of my classmates. I attended Holy Trinity solely because my grandparents had money and they were adamant about me being raised Catholic. When they offered to bankroll the tuition costs, my parents shrugged their shoulders and went along with it.

Kids at this school were 100 percent invested in the religion thanks to their parents' status as devout members of the church. I felt like I was the only one who didn't genuinely enjoy going to school Mass every Tuesday, saying full rosaries during class, and confessing sins to priests several times a year. It's not that I hated these activities; I just viewed them in the same way I viewed any other avenue of schoolwork: it was boring and I couldn't wait for it to be over.

THE DUMBEST KID IN GIFTED CLASS

I once overheard a group of my classmates swearing up and down that communion wafers would bleed if they were cut in two. These magic wafers were made up of the literal, for-real corpse of Jesus; surely this made sense. I was skeptical, so I ran a little experiment after one of our Tuesday Masses.

When it came time for the priest to place the wafer on my tongue, I quickly moved it between my teeth and did my best to keep it dry. I performed the sign of the cross and headed back to my seat in the pew. There, I retrieved the mostly dry wafer from my mouth and stealthily moved it to my front pocket while pretending to be deep in prayer with the rest of the class. Once Mass was done, I shifted the wafer to the middle of my spiral notebook to make sure it stayed intact until I got to my grandmother's house that afternoon.

In the 25 years I spent with my grandmother, I can barely remember any instances of her being even slightly mad at me. There was that one time she yelled at me in the car for being a little shit while sledding with my cousins, but that's about it. When she walked into her kitchen to see me holding a knife over a split communion wafer, she ranted and raved and yelled enough to make up for a quarter century of total benevolence toward me.

It didn't bleed, by the way.

My father never talked about religion at all during my youth, and I can only remember one time that my mother and I discussed anything on the topic. After catching myself muttering "Jesus Christ!" in vain while dying in a video game, I went downstairs to ask her if I'd be irrevocably condemned to hell as a result.

"Eh, I don't think so," she said. "You'll still go to heaven if you're a good person, but I don't think there are a bunch of dead people walking around and talking to each other."

That was the first time I had any questions about religion, which was a subject taught right alongside math, science, and English at Holy Trinity. As I got older, questions started bouncing around in my head more frequently. During one religion class, I caught myself ruminating on one thought. I approached my teacher after the school day was over.

"Mrs. Herding, I have a question."

"What's that, Danny?"

"We know for sure that Jesus Christ is the son of God and that everything we learn about in class is how things really are, right?"

"Yes."

"But what about the other religions? People that believe in those probably believe that their god is the real god just as much as we believe ours is, right?"

"Yes."

"We can't all be right, though. So we know for sure that we're the right one?"

"Yes."

"Alright, thanks!"

I wasn't particularly sold, but her confidence assured me that the conversation wouldn't progress past that point.

Despite my questions about religion, my lack of opinion on the subject was far from the biggest reason that I didn't fit in at Holy Trinity. Put as generally as possible, I was a weird-ass kid. Video games and professional wrestling were the two things in the world that I cared about, and it seemed impossible to find anyone who wanted to discuss either topic.

I hit a brick wall at recess when I wanted to talk to *anyone* about how crazy it was that Diesel won the WWF title from Bob Backlund at a house show. Blank stares were the only reaction when I excitedly relayed the information that Chuck Norris helped The Undertaker at Survivor Series by kicking Jeff Jarrett in the chest. Nothing in the world seemed cooler than this, so why did everyone prefer to talk about boring stuff like the Kansas City Chiefs or Jesus?

In third grade, I became aware of another amazing thing that was roundly ignored by most of my classmates. My grandmother would pick me up every Wednesday after school and take me to my uncle's gas station. He had a rotating selection of games in the building, usually consisting of two arcade cabinets and one pinball machine. I spent a lot of time with classics there: the *Simpsons* arcade game, *Teenage Mutant Ninja Turtles*, the *Terminator 2* and *Addams Family* pinball cabinets, and others. After a few months of this weekly tradition, a new game arrived at the gas station that was unfathomably cool to my eight-year-old brain.

My grandmother sat in the car while my cousin and I went into the gas station with our quarters. As I walked in, I saw two teenagers standing in front of a cabinet that I didn't recognize. The fact that they were teenagers was scary enough, and they became even more intimidating when one of them complained that they lost due to "fucking computer shit." These weren't just teenagers. They were *cussing* teenagers. They might as well have had shivs and assault rifles strapped to their chests as far as I was concerned.

I found a table that was far enough away to feel safe from the teenage menaces, but still close enough to see the screen. Witnessing blood erupt out of the fighters' heads every time they were punched was immediately captivating, but what really made me lose my mind was seeing a man's head get punched clean off his shoulders. Afterward, the deliverer of the punch pumped his fist in celebration, put on sunglasses, and crossed his arms triumphantly. I didn't know what I was seeing, but I had no doubt that it was the newest, coolest thing on the planet.

My cousin Matt noticed my open-mouthed reactions to everything I was seeing and expressed surprise that this was my first encounter with the game.

"You haven't played *Mortal Kombat* yet?" he asked.

"No! How long has this been out?"

"About a month. I know all the secrets if you wanna see the fatalities."

We had about an hour to play before my grandma took us home. I told Matt that he had to teach me absolutely everything he knew about this magical game. During my crash course, he taught me how to throw Scorpion's spear, bombard enemies with Liu Kang's fireballs and flying kicks, and spam Sub-Zero's freeze-uppercut-slide combo. As great as those moves were, nothing compared to the moment after the fight was over. Whenever the "Finish Him!" prompt appeared and the screen darkened subtly, I felt like I was about to see something that I wasn't supposed to see. Video games weren't about heads being punched off and bodies being burnt to their skeletons; they were about jumping on some things and collecting a bunch of other things. When Matt was inputting a button sequence for a fatality, I felt like I should glance over my shoulder to ensure that my grandma or any of the gas station patrons weren't within line of sight of the dark arts playing out on screen.

Each of the seven fatalities (well, six if we're not counting Liu Kang's bullshit cartwheel) burned into my

5

brain. The next day, all I wanted to do was spread the good word of *Mortal Kombat* to everyone at school. I'd surely be a celebrated messenger, opening the eyes of my classmates to this amazing secret that none of them were aware of.

As soon as recess started, I bounced around from the basketball court to the kickball area to the kids with jump ropes, regaling them with stories of the glorious things I'd seen.

"Kano punches through the other dude's chest, then pulls his heart out and holds it up and blood drips everywhere!"

"Scorpion is a teleporting ninja and he pulls his mask off and it's just a skull underneath, and then he can breathe fire!"

"You can rip a dude's head off and see his *spine* hanging out!"

Reactions ranged from apathy to revulsion, making me feel like I was surrounded by insane people. Were they hearing what I was saying? The spine was attached. You can pull a guy's head off and his *spine dangles down from the neck hole*. This was all a real thing that could happen in a video game. How were my classmates not immediately abandoning recess and marching en masse to my uncle's gas station?

No amount of enthusiasm could properly relay my excitement to others, squashing my desire to convert them into fellow *Mortal Kombat* devotees. During religion class that day, I ignored my teacher entirely as I pulled out my colored pencils and spiral notebook. I drew Raiden first, arcing his lightning toward a blank space that used to be Johnny Cage's head. After filling in Cage's legs and torso, I broke out the red colored pencil and drew a geyser of blood that made the actual game's spray seem modest. With roughly 40 percent of my page covered in red pencil, I looked up to see my teacher standing over me with a very concerned look on her face.

By the end of the day, I found myself in the office of Principal Weber for the second time in my elementary school career. He wanted me to know in no uncertain terms that it wasn't right to be drawing images like that, and he was concerned about my interest in something so violent. Enjoying *Mortal Kombat* must have been heresy to the staff of Holy Trinity, considering that a class meeting was called the year prior to inform us that we were forbidden to discuss "a popular television program with Beavis in the title, and another part of the title that will never be said within these walls."

My reputation as a weird kid persisted throughout my kindergarten-to-fifth grade history in Catholic school. As time went on, I felt increasingly different from everyone else my age. I thought I was being funny when we practiced singing "Silent Night" for the annual Christmas program, but I sang it in Bob Dylan's voice. It didn't take long to realize that few children in the early '90s had any idea who Bob Dylan was.

I grew to resent and dislike my peers because of how different they were from me, and I was certain that everything they liked was wrong. Things came to a head in fifth grade as my behavior, interests, and sense of humor continued to be at odds with the rest of the class.

I was far from athletic and had no interest in sports. Understandably, I was always picked last for any team-based physical challenge. I never knew what I was doing when a ball came my way or when it was my turn to kick a thing. This was a conservative Catholic school in Kansas, so my classmates concluded that I clearly had to be gay. In that environment in that time period, "you're gay" was the only insult that boys gave to other boys. Occasionally, you'd hear someone call you an idiot or a weirdo or whatever, but "you're gay" was the clear favorite among Midwestern Catholic kids. I liked playing *Super Mario Kart* more than I liked talking about football, so obviously this meant that I was sexually attracted to men. Whenever I missed a free throw in basketball or let another goal whiz by my uninterested head while playing goalie in soccer, there were always three or four classmates ready to yell "faggot!" When I couldn't finish the mile run before class was over, it was probably because I was too busy thinking about all the penises I'd get to see when I was older.

This was confusing to me for a few reasons. The first is because I'm straight. The second is because I didn't think that sexual orientation was determined by athletic prowess. The third is because I hadn't gone to church enough to hear about how being gay was supposedly evil, so I didn't even understand why it was an insult.

Unsurprisingly, I had learned about homosexuality as a result of watching professional wrestling. My education happened during a match between a sexually ambiguous character named Goldust (who resembled a living Oscar statuette, gold face paint and all) and Razor Ramon, a traditionally macho dude who talked like Tony Montana and had phrases like "Oozing Machismo" emblazoned on his merchandise. Goldust was "playing mind games" with Razor by grabbing his crotch and being overtly sexual, and Razor would react with horror whenever a golden gloved hand would come within a foot of his genital area.

"What's going on here?" I asked my mom.

"Oh, Goldust is gay."

"What does gay mean?"

"He wants to kiss guys instead of girls."

"Oh, okay."

That was the extent of it. No condemnation of Goldust's lifestyle or sermons about Leviticus, just "he likes dudes" and that was that. As a result, I never attached any negative connotations to homosexuality, even when I was surrounded by the total opposite mindset every time I stepped on the playground.

Most of my classmates were content to call me gay once or twice per recess, but no one seemed to relish the opportunity more than Jake. In a class filled with mean, privileged Catholic kids, Jake was the absolute worst. It didn't seem like he called people gay because his religion forbade it; it just seemed like calling people gay was the only thing fueling his entire existence. He was a Catholic robot who ran on calling people gay instead of on gasoline or electricity or whatever fuels robots. I'm struggling to think of Jake doing anything besides calling someone gay during the six years I went to school with him.

Jake sucked. In fact, he still sucks if a recent Facebook search is any indication. I clicked past the frat memories and beer pong pictures and landed on "Details about Jake," producing the following text verbatim:

I am an Asshole. But I am one of those rare lovable assholes that once you get to know, you just can't help but like me. So, if you meet me and you think I am the biggest Asshole, that you've ever met, wait a while, we'll probably end up as friends. (By the way if that doesn't sit well with you that sucks. And if you think that you'll always hate me and think that I am a dick you've got the odds stacked strongly against you so good luck with that.)

THE DUMBEST KID IN GIFTED CLASS

Based on my memory of Jake, he's being far too nice with that description of himself. I also apparently have the odds stacked strongly against me, whatever that means. Jake's Jake-iest moment came during a fifth-grade field trip to Skateland South, a roller-skating rink in Shawnee, Kansas. This place was exactly what you'd picture from a roller-skating rink in the mid-'90s: Lots of neon lights rotating around a blacklight-drenched skating surface, with various claw games, arcade cabinets, and shoe lockers surrounding it.

I was—and still am—absolutely terrible at skating in any form, so I probably would have fallen down numerous times without any outside interference. However, Jake wanted to speed up the process. Whenever I stepped onto the rink and worked myself into something resembling an actual skating motion, I'd quickly get tripped or shoved to the ground. I expected to see Jake whenever this happened, but was surprised to see a revolving door of other classmates instead. Several of them were among my quieter classmates, ones who hadn't bullied me nearly as much as Jake or the other main offenders. On one occasion, the fingers on my left hand were skated over immediately after I was pushed to the ground. I clutched my arm to my chest and looked up to see Josh, a classmate of mine who had never bullied me before. In fact, he would even come over to my house to play video games on occasion.

"Sorry, Dan," he said. "Jake's telling us all to push you over."

In almost any other situation, I'd want to make sure that I did my due diligence and got my facts straight before seeking revenge. Considering my long history with Jake and my knowledge of how much of an irredeemable dickhead he was, I wasn't too worried about it at the moment. I got back to my feet and scanned the area, spotting Jake talking to two girls on the other side of a waist-high wall on the edge of the rink. Giving myself enough time to actually get my footing and start skating semi-properly, I worked up some speed and beelined directly toward him.

When I reached the edge of the rink, I lunged forward and threw the first punch of my life directly into Jake's dumb face. The actuality of what happened probably looked significantly less cool than the Stallone-caliber punch I envision in my head, but it felt amazing nonetheless. Jake was on skates, so not only did he get punched in the face in front of two girls he was chatting up, but his legs flailed around like he was a Looney Tunes character as he struggled to remain upright. He made a valiant effort, but his skates slipped out from under him and he fell directly onto his back.

Several of my classmates, their parents, and some faculty members witnessed this, and Jake was helped to his feet and left the field trip. The school called my mother and she arrived shortly thereafter to take me home. That weekend, the principal of Holy Trinity called my house. He informed my parents and me that he was going to hold a class meeting to discuss the incident. Days later, I found myself in a room with Principal Weber, my fifth grade teacher, Jake, the kids who shoved me down, the kids who witnessed it, and all of their parents.

We were organized in a big circle with the children sitting at desks and their parents sitting or standing behind them. To my surprise, most of the kids that had shoved me down had no issues with placing all of the blame on Jake. Some of them even defended my retaliation, as did some of their parents. One mother seemed terribly inconvenienced by the meeting, constantly rolling her eyes and saying "Why are we here? This is just boys being boys."

THE DUMBEST KID IN GIFTED CLASS

In the end, nothing was accomplished. The consensus seemed to be that Jake was a dick and my actions were understandable given the context. Regardless of the useless nature of the meeting, my mother and I decided that it was time to get out of the toxic environment of Holy Trinity. We were almost at the end of my first semester of fifth grade, and I could start the second semester fresh in public school. On my last day at Holy Trinity, the teachers held a little goodbye party and gifted me a bunch of POGs and a softball that was begrudgingly signed by my peers, who couldn't have been that sad to see me go.

With public school, I saw a chance to reinvent myself. This was a nice idea in theory, but it wasn't particularly useful in practice. I would no longer be forced to wear the red shirt and blue pants of Holy Trinity every day. Unfortunately, this proved to be more stressful than freeing considering I had absolutely no idea what I was supposed to wear. Based solely on what my peers wore, I should have invested heavily in gigantic JNCO jeans and wallet chains, but that seemed too stupid to me even back then. In this new environment, I could conceivably wipe away my previous reputation as the weird kid in school. I imagined myself starting fresh, learning from my past experiences and blending in with my peers for once, instead of feeling like an outsider.

This idealized version of "Fifth Grade, Part II" didn't come to pass. One of my first acts was an extremely ill-fated attempt to woo the most popular girl in class. My second genius plan was to ditch "Danny" and start going by my initials. For approximately two weeks, I signed my tests and papers as DJ Ryckert. Even in these years, before I irrationally hated all electronic music, I would see that name on the page and feel like it just wasn't right.

BLOOD ON THE SAND

In no time at all, I was an outsider again. I thought that removing myself from the bullies of Catholic school would be my saving grace, but it turned out that many of my peers were some shade of terrible, regardless of religious inclinations. In time, I would learn to accept and embrace the fact that I wasn't like everyone else. That would take years, however, and I still had one friend who wasn't tied to any school that I attended.

Larry was the one kid in my neighborhood that I hung out with, and I had hung out with him a lot ever since we met around kindergarten. Our neighborhood in Lenexa was home to a lot of young married couples, and most of their children were significantly younger than me. Larry was the only one within walking distance who was my age, and we shared a love of video games.

Larry was a "friend" by default, given the slim pickings of friend candidates in my neighborhood. On the one hand, he was my age and liked video games. On the other hand, he was pretty terrible in every other way. Imagine Cartman from *South Park* made flesh and you've got a pretty good sense of what Larry was. He was loud, foul-mouthed, mean, insensitive, and not particularly bright.

His propensity to freely cuss in front of his parents fascinated me and made me somewhat jealous. I always viewed myself as a wholesome, clean kid during my childhood, and seeing someone be so proudly foul-mouthed was alien to me. I bought Aerosmith's *Get a Grip* on cassette around this time, and one song featured a lyric about being "shit outta luck." I opened the liner notes, looked up the song ("Walk on Down"), and saw that Joe Perry wrote the lyrics. For a while, I considered myself a fan of Aerosmith but disapproved of that no-good Joe Perry.

13

THE DUMBEST KID IN GIFTED CLASS

Larry would lose his mind whenever I beat him at *Street Fighter II* or *Mortal Kombat*, frequently throwing action figures at me and screaming "Get the *FUCK* out of my house!!!" In one particularly dramatic outburst at my place, he threw one of my Ghostbusters action figures at my framed Ninja Turtles poster. The glass shattered, and he tackled me to the floor before punching away at my arm and chest. My RC car must have gotten crushed under one of us, because I noticed the antenna lying next to me as I tried to escape from under him. I picked up the thin, long piece of metal, and whipped him hard across the cheek. It drew blood, and Larry stomped home in a rage.

No matter how many times this kind of thing happened, we kept hanging out because of the lack of other options. We didn't talk much about school, but I got the sense that he didn't have many other friends either. One of the rare times that we were around other kids was on his tenth birthday. I saw this as a perfect opportunity to put on a live *Mortal Kombat* stage show of sorts. His parents organized a party at the house with several other kids, so I'd have a chance to cast them as members of *Mortal Kombat II*'s roster. This was a party filled with ten-year-old boys, however, and my script called for two girls to play Kitana and Mileena. I was still at least fifteen years away from being able to talk to girls without having a panic attack, so we asked one of the more socially capable boys at the party to help us out. He asked a couple of twin sisters from the neighborhood to wear maroon and blue handkerchiefs on their faces for our dumb video game play. They weren't interested for some odd reason, and Kitana and Mileena became victims of my last-minute rewrites.

Larry and I played the lead roles of Johnny Cage and Scorpion, respectively. My faithful adaptation of *Mortal*

Kombat lore was going about as well as you can imagine until a climactic scene in which Cage (Larry) hits Scorpion (me) with his trademark fireball (green Koosh ball). With a yellow handkerchief over my mouth and a black scarf around my head, I caught the Koosh ball against my stomach and tried to sell its devastating effects by doing a front flip. I decided to do this flip on the fly, failing to factor in my complete lack of athletic ability or threshold for pain. Also, I don't know why I thought the physics of a fireball hitting someone would cause them to flip forward, but whatever. Thankfully, I cleared enough of the flip to avoid landing on my neck. Paralysis was dodged, but landing on my back on a thin layer of carpet in Larry's basement was enough to cause pain every time I stood up for the rest of the night.

My mother picked me up early from the party and took me to the doctor, who said I would be fine but I probably shouldn't be flipping onto what amounted to concrete. This was the same doctor that had previously seen me for a different *Mortal Kombat*-related injury, as I once tweaked the muscles in my neck while straining too hard to complete a "Test Your Might" challenge in the Sega Genesis version of the game.

Our love of *Mortal Kombat* was one of the few things Larry and I had in common, as every other aspect of his life was inconceivable to me. His brother Harrison was 16 and worked at the grocery store that my father managed. When I stepped into Harrison's bedroom for the first time, the decor seemed borderline illegal to me. I'd only occasionally get a chance to peek in there, but every inch of the walls and ceiling was covered with Playboy centerfolds and various disembodied photos of breasts. I hadn't quite hit puberty when Harrison was still living at home, but I remember thinking "This kid seems like he's got it made."

Hindsight makes it pretty clear that Larry's home life might not have been ideal. His mom didn't seem concerned by his awful behavior, and his nearly silent father always gave me the vibe of a Vietnam vet who was about one bad DMV trip away from snapping and winding up in the newspaper.

Larry's parents were from Denver and they viewed Broncos football as the most important thing in the known universe. I didn't care about football, but I knew enough to know that the Denver Broncos were bitter rivals with the Kansas City Chiefs. Thinking that I'd playfully irk them during breakfast one morning, I did the "Tomahawk Chop" motion and chant that was frequently done at Chiefs games. Larry's mother responded by standing up, calmly walking over to me, and twisting my arm behind my back hard. When I went home and told my mother about this, she told me that I wasn't allowed to hang out at Larry's house for a month.

I had no intention of disobeying my mom's ruling, so I spent more of my free time that month swinging and playing by myself at Kickapoo Park, a small park between Larry's house and mine. One day, I spotted Larry walking on the sidewalk toward me as I sat on the swing. We hadn't had any contact for the last few weeks and I didn't know what to expect from him. As he got closer, I stopped swinging and noticed that he had something in his hand.

"Does your mom think you're too good to be hanging out with my family?" he asked.

"I think she's just mad about your mom twisting my arm," I replied.

Without another word, he cocked his arm back and heaved something at my face. A sharp pain shot across my cheek as I instinctively put my hand over it. Larry ran back toward his house, and I pulled my hand away from my face to see a red streak across my palm. A bloody shard of green glass sat in the sand by my swing, and it looked like it came from a bottle of Heineken or Rolling Rock.

My mom upgraded the Larry Warning Level to critical when I got home, cleaning my wound and bandaging it up. She told me that I was never to be around him under any circumstances. I understood her reasoning, but I wanted to see him get some form of comeuppance before we officially ended our friendship.

The next day I put my plan into motion, but it required a little setup. With my cheek bandaged, I grabbed my stepfather's shovel and several paper bags, and headed back to Kickapoo Park. Three swings hung from a metal structure there, and I dug a hole about fifteen feet in front of the middle one. It was probably two feet deep at most, but it seemed massive to me back then. Trees surrounded the park, so I went around breaking off long twigs that I crisscrossed over the hole. Next came the paper bags. I tore several of them at the creases and laid them flat over the twigs. Once the hole was adequately covered, I concealed the entire thing by shoveling a layer of sand over the top of it.

I walked over to Larry's house and knocked on the door for the last time in my childhood. He answered in his pajamas and asked me what I wanted. I told him that I wanted to race him, and he was too stupid to wonder why I'd want to do such a thing. A quick change into his shorts and sneakers, and we were heading back to Kickapoo.

"Okay, the starting line is here," I said. "We go on three, and the first person to touch the swings wins. Mine is the left one, yours is the middle."

Larry agreed to the terms and we lined up for the race. With good reason, I never went into anything resembling an athletic event with any sense of confidence. This one was different, however. I wasn't going up against my peers at recess; I was going up against *Larry*. Put simply, Larry was a big fat kid and I was not worried about outrunning him.

We counted down together and started sprinting. Sure enough, I immediately pulled ahead of him and reached the swing first. Upon making contact with the goal, I turned around just in time to hear twigs snap and see Larry disappear into the ditch with the most satisfying guttural yelp I've ever heard. I peeked down into the hole to see him covered in sand, looking about as pissed off as I'd ever seen a kid.

That was the last time I'd see Larry as a child, because shortly thereafter I moved to the nearby town of Olathe. Both Jake and Larry were asshole ghosts of my past for several years, until I ran into a drunken Jake as he was leaving a house party during college. With our skating rink incident being ancient history at this point, I thought it would be fun to reminisce a bit about our childhood at Holy Trinity. He slurred his way through a brief conversation, then hopped into a car with his frat brothers.

Our little reunion was a non-event, but it got me thinking more about my childhood and wondering what Larry was up to. I hadn't driven by my old Lenexa neighborhood since my family moved prior to sixth grade, so one weekend I decided to pay a visit. My old house looked the same, with mulberries staining the driveway and my basketball goal sitting just as unused as it had been when I lived there. Kickapoo Park had been renovated with new slides and swings, and Larry's house looked exactly how I remembered it.

It had been long enough for me to wonder if Larry's family still lived there, but I went up and rang the doorbell anyway. He would have been about 20 or 21 by then, so I assumed that I'd encounter his parents if anything. Sure enough, his mother answered the door. I was about a foot taller and six years older than I was when she twisted my arm, so I had to remind her of Danny from down the street. My Tomahawk Chop was apparently forgiven at this point, as she gave me a hug and invited me into the house. To my surprise, she told me that Larry still lived there and was asleep in his room. She led me down the hall to what was once Harrison's room, meaning that at some point Larry had graduated into the vaunted Boobed Room of Adulthood.

After rapping at the door and unsuccessfully yelling at Larry to wake up, his mother told me to go ahead and walk in. Larry was groaning in bed and rubbing his eyes as he tried to get his bearings. I noticed that the disembodied breasts on the wall had been replaced by dozens of Japanese anime posters. Wearing a *Dragon Ball Z* shirt, Larry finally woke up enough to have something resembling a conversation. He relayed plenty of information in a short amount of time, including how he had been experimenting with a lot of drugs and had just received his second DUI as he drove home from a 311 concert. Also, he had lost his job doing something stupid that I don't quite recall.

After this enlightening conversation, I got in my car and drove back to my dorm, feeling pretty good about my life choices. Larry would resurface later in my life via Twitter and Facebook. I learned that he spent several years following 311 across the country and becoming extremely vocal about Illuminati conspiracies. We eventually had a second falling-out when I made a post about going to New York City for a Nintendo 3DS event that I was covering for my job at Game Informer. He failed to convince me that I was a government pawn, blindly falling into President Obama's plot to control citizens' minds through new technology, so he took the next logical step and blocked me on all social media. After all, I was probably reporting his activity to the FBI.

I have no idea what Larry is up to these days, but I'm confident that you can find a big guy at a 311 concert who would love to have an impassioned chat with you about chemtrails.

Squeaky Wheel

Outside of an 18-month stint after college in which I worked at a sports-based TV station and a company that made GPS devices, my resume could effectively double as my "Hobbies" section in a dating profile. I've worked at McDonald's, a video game store, a liquor store, a video game magazine, a video game website, and as a professional wrestling manager. For a guy who has spent most of his life thinking about fast food, video games, and wrestling, it's been a pretty great run, and I consider myself very fortunate.

I was also a fanatic about movies when I was younger. During the mid-'90s, I'd frequently go into video stores and beg them to give me their promotional cardboard standees when they were done with them. Sometimes they'd let me write my name on the back as a reminder to call me instead of throwing them away. Eventually, my bedroom was filled with these large displays dedicated to movies like *The Rock*, *Broken Arrow*, and *Face/Off*.

My mother also enjoyed these movies, and we'd often watch them together. They were usually R-rated, which ran the risk of featuring an errant boob or tame sex scene. To combat being in the same room as her if anything sexual was happening on screen, I always had my bathroom breaks timed out. A sudden urge to pee (or poop, depending on the length of the scene) would conveniently overcome me during specific parts in each movie. Stanley Goodspeed having rooftop sex with his fiancée. An animated woman shaking her breasts on the screen of Castor Troy's bomb at the LA Convention Center. Kyle Reese and Sarah Connor having sex to an acoustic version of the *Terminator* theme (this scene in particular is what taught me what sex was in the first place).

I eventually found a book at Borders that listed fan mail addresses for various celebrities. I'd cut out pictures of Nicolas Cage, Michael Biehn, and Bonnie Bedelia in *Entertainment Weekly*, put them in a package along with a note and a self-addressed stamped envelope, and hope to get anything in return. Cage signed a picture from *Face/Off* with a "To Dan, Best Wishes." A picture that I sent to 30 Rockefeller Plaza in New York intended for Conan O'Brien came back with signatures from both him and Andy Richter. I was thrilled to get a Jim Carrey one-sheet with a "Spank You Very Much" note, until I realized that it was a facsimile that his people sent out to every fan who wrote in.

In junior high, I devoted an hour a day to an independent study course that tracked box office results. My school's gifted class allowed me to pick whatever independent study subject I wanted to focus on, which proved to be great for learning more about the things I was passionate about. From studying box office results to pro wrestling to video production, being able to say "Here's what I like. I'm going to make sure that most of my schoolwork revolves around it" was fantastic. During ninth grade, I decided that I just wanted to watch movies and write papers about them. I told my teacher I was interested in films that had a psychological angle. She recommended *A Clockwork Orange* and secured a VHS copy of it for me to watch at school. Within a few minutes of sitting in a classroom and seeing bare breasts and a graphic rape scene, I found myself looking over my shoulder wondering if she had made some terrible mistake.

SQUEAKY WHEEL

Transitioning from junior high to high school made me more ambitious when it came to learning about movies. I was previously content with watching a bunch of films and tracking their success at the box office, but now I wanted to make them myself. My dream job was always to cover video games for a living, but I figured that "Hollywood director" would make for a solid fallback option.

In high school, I was allowed to sign up for several hours a day of the independent study program. One of these hours was dedicated to studying the professional wrestling industry. Each day started with the school's official video production class and ended with three consecutive hours of video production independent study. During these hours, I had no oversight. There were no assignments or lectures, just a room full of cameras, tripods, and iMacs with Final Cut Pro installed.

I had all the time in the world to do whatever I wanted, and I referred to my camera as my "universal hall pass." If you were a student who happened to be walking the halls of Olathe East during class time, a faculty member would almost assuredly ask you about why you weren't in class. However, when I had a little MiniDV camera strapped to my hand and a tripod over my shoulder, no one ever gave me any flak.

This was the only period in my life in which I seriously considered focusing my career on something other than the video game industry. Shooting videos was so much fun, and it was easy to stand out considering how bad everyone else was at it. When other students in my production class were assigned a video announcement, they always phoned it in with dry, information-driven pieces.

I was always more interested in flash than I was in information, so I took that approach whenever I received boring assignments. Cross country running sounded like the most boring thing in the world to me, but making a parody of the Beastie Boys' "Sabotage" video starring the OEHS Cross Country team was a blast. One assignment required me to raise awareness for our team of janitors, so I made a full *Fight Club* parody starring our quiet, awkward custodial team. Making parodies of popular music videos and movies isn't exactly high art, but considering the dry, by-the-books work my peers were making (and the fact that I was 16), I might as well have been Stanley Kubrick by comparison.

One person who wasn't particularly amused by my approach was our school's guidance counselor. After receiving an assignment to make a video announcement about her services, I talked to her about a variety of ideas I had. She was adamant that this announcement be strictly about the facts and her role in the school, and refused to play any kind of character. I told her that I understood and that I'd just need some footage of her working in her office. I set my camera on a tripod and captured a minute or two of nearly silent footage of her leafing through papers. Then I thanked her and went back to the edit room.

It's a good thing she didn't request to see the video before it aired, because it never would have made the announcements if she had. The announcement began with Jimi Hendrix's "Purple Haze" blaring, accompanied by text that read "DO YOU WANT A CAREER THAT'S..." followed by a series of adjectives in loud font, set to the timing of the guitar riff. "EXCITING?! SEXY?! REWARDING?! FUN?! LUCRATIVE?!"

Immediately after the text montage, I cut the music and replaced it with thirty seconds of crickets chirping as I rolled raw footage of the counselor staring at paperwork in a sterile office. A painful amount of time passed, and then a final slide popped up as Hendrix's "YEAH!" signals the return of the music: "BE A GUIDANCE COUNSELOR!!!"

Later that day, my video production teacher informed me in no uncertain terms that the counselor was not a fan of the finished product. It wouldn't be the last time that an official class project got me in trouble with my teacher.

Like every other teenage idiot film dork back then, I was a big fan of Quentin Tarantino. I didn't know how to write clever or believable dialogue to save my life, but I could try to ape his trademark moments of sudden violence. Of course, mine were free of character development or style, and just boiled down to "wouldn't it be crazy if this dude just got shot all of a sudden?"

One project was called "The Aviator." It featured a cheery guy in aviator goggles and a bomber jacket playing on a jungle gym (set to U2's "Beautiful Day") before getting shot down. Another was "Lex Talionis," which I wish I had done as parody but was probably made in earnest back then. First off, I did the cliché "let's take a cool-sounding phrase but translate it into *LATIN* to make it sound super badass!" thing that every film student or crappy local band has done at some point. Also, it didn't make any sense and existed solely as a dumb vehicle for me to include a bunch of random deaths.

"Lex Talionis" starts with dudes in suits sitting in a dingy basement, smoking cigars and playing some indeterminate card game. Not long into college, I learned that every single student filmmaker makes the dumb move of casting their barely post-pubescent white buddies as fucking Yakuza godfathers or whatever, and it always looks super dumb. It looked super dumb here.

Three of the guys win the card game and celebrate, causing the other two guys to get sad for a second and pull guns on them. The three winners split up and run away with their cards, because I guess the cards themselves were the prize for winning this card game? The rest of the short film features the losers hunting them down and taking their cards back. One guy tries to hide in the woods, but gets discovered and killed after he farts loudly. Great stuff. The second hides out in a bathroom. A gunman finds him, puts his head into the toilet, and blows his brains (ketchup and hamburger meat) into the water. Top-notch material.

The last of the three gets gunned down in the street, but not before I utilized my first celebrity cameo. You gotta start with something big, so who could be bigger than 1991-1992 Kansas City Royals pitcher Mike Boddicker? Most people, it turns out. Not being a sports fan, I had heard his name on TV a couple of times, but had no idea if he was well-known and/or good at baseball. I still don't. Regardless, my friend Bret told me that Boddicker lived just around the corner from where we were shooting that day.

"Hey, baseball players are famous!" I figured.

We walked over to Boddicker's place and knocked on the door. A middle-aged and presumably famous guy answered. I explained that I was a student shooting a short film, and was curious if he'd be interested in doing a very brief cameo. I just needed him to nod his head and then point down the street when the bad guys came to his door. He agreed, and the most uneventful and celebrity-devoid cameo of all time was filmed.

With the hot tip from Boddicker, the bad guys track down the final target and take him out. The villains stand tall, with all three of the sought-after cards in Bad Guy #1's hands. In a "shocking," "Tarantino-esque" turn of events, Bad Guy #2 interrupts #1's gloating by shooting him in the head and taking all three cards for himself.

That was the foundation for a lot of my short films back then. I bought prop guns from Walmart, downloaded a few songs on Kazaa or Morpheus that I thought would be cool in a video, and then assembled some bullshit that would serve as a loose excuse for people to shoot each other to music. In these pre-YouTube years, I'd dump the videos to a VHS and physically mail them (along with a submission fee) to a website that showcased student films. Feedback was hard to come by, as few people spent time on a site that was composed mostly of idiot 17-year-olds trying to make Reservoir Dogs on 1/1,000th of the budget and 1/1,000,000th of the talent.

One form of feedback that I did receive during this period was from my video production teacher. Mr. Snozek was a wide, towering, Catholic man who resembled a living refrigerator, and he was very concerned about any student project that featured violence. Inserting fistfights into a video was enough to get yourself pulled into his office, and here I was trying to find the right raw meat to best resemble bloody brain particles.

During this semester, each school day included four hours in Mr. Snozek's video production lab. I had a lot to lose if I pissed him off, but I continued to make videos that focused on gunfights. Considering that these usually involved intentionally stupid elements like farting and guys in monkey suits and U2 songs, I hoped that they'd come off as silly enough to keep me out of trouble. Mr. Snozek only saw the guns, however, and eventually banned me from his video production classroom outright after several warnings.

This left a huge void in my daily schedule. My mom assumed I was at school and my gifted class teachers assumed I was in the video production lab for over half the day (Mr. Snozek failed to inform them of the ban). With no one to hold me accountable, I did the only reasonable thing that a high school student would do: egregiously skipped class.

Three of my four video production hours were piggybacked at the end of the day, meaning that I had nowhere to be starting at noon. My personal MiniDV camera would serve as the key to my escape, since I wasn't allowed to use the school's cameras any more. When the bell rang at the end of my fourth-hour history class, I'd grab the camera from my locker and head out to my 1994 Ford Taurus. If anyone tried to stop me, I was always ready to hold up the Canon and say I was shooting something for the video announcements. If my own gifted class teachers didn't know about Mr. Snozek's ban, the school's security guards sure as hell wouldn't.

No one ever tried to stop me from leaving. That wasn't going to keep me from feeling like I was some school-skipping rebel, breaking my way out of the confines of Olathe East and peeling out into freedom (actually, I never knew how to make my car peel out and probably wouldn't have done it anyway, since that would be loud and rude). With a total lack of self-awareness, I'd put on Rage Against the Machine or, more frequently, the theme song of the wrestling group D-Generation X. This was *rebellious stuff.* I was breaking the rules and getting the hell out of Dodge. It seemed only fitting to blast songs about Che Guevara that I didn't understand or theme music for a bunch of wrestlers whose defining character trait was "wearing neon green and gesturing toward their penises."

In hindsight, this high school view of myself clashes somewhat with the reality of a socially awkward wrestling dork leaving school to go to the FuncoLand that he works at to play a Dreamcast game with fake maraca controllers because he's too nervous to tell his mother that he got kicked out of class. It was less "sticking it to the man," and more "getting pretty good at *Samba de Amigo*."

In those days, I had a couple of great options if I needed to stay out of the house. My two jobs at the time shared the same parking lot and centered on two of my favorite things. One was a FuncoLand video game store, and the other was a newly constructed 30-screen AMC movie theater. For a kid who didn't like to socialize but loved video games and movies, it couldn't have been a better situation. Both positions paid barely over minimum wage, but I saved a ton of money thanks to unlimited free movie tickets and the ability to rent games from the store whenever I wanted.

About six months into being 14 years old, I left my first job at McDonald's to work at the theater. My age prohibited me from performing most functions at AMC, but I was allowed to work the concession stand register as long as I didn't venture anywhere near the popcorn popper (this was deemed too dangerous for our young brains and hands). Concession was the starting point for virtually every employee and everyone hated it. If you could prove to be reliable there, you could start ushering. Do well there, and you might get bumped up to the box office. Then, you could go to Guest Services, the projection booth, or start working toward being a manager.

I wanted to move up the ladder quickly, as I hated working the long concession lines during the frequent rushes. This desire was at odds with my even stronger desire to do the least amount of work humanly possible. Better shifts, more power, and higher pay sounded fantastic. Working hard? Not so much.

Avoiding work entirely was impossible at my lowly position, but I assumed that it would get easier if I moved up the ladder. I constantly badgered my managers about being promoted to supervisor.

"We don't move 14-year-olds up to supervisor," one of them said. "But keep asking...the squeaky wheel gets the grease."

That advice stuck with me for years because it made sense. You rarely get anything if you don't ask for it, so I made my desire to become supervisor known to everyone who outranked me. When these decision-makers were around, I was the most gung-ho, take-charge employee anyone had ever seen. If a rush ended, you couldn't put a broom in my hand fast enough to enthusiastically clean up all of the popcorn kernels.

When the higher-ups were out of sight, I was no better than a loiterer. In fact, I was actively impeding the theater's ability to properly serve customers. I'd hang out behind the soda machines, dipping popcorn into nacho cheese and trying to get it to stick to the ceiling. Batches of popcorn turned into dumb social experiments as I'd see how many spoonfuls of radioactive-looking orange salt I could put into a batch before customers complained en masse. I'd dare coworkers to drink horrible concoctions that consisted of soda, popcorn salt, nacho cheese, chopped-up hot dogs, and our "butter-like" substance. This escalated until a coworker vomited during a shift.

After a solid seven or eight months of "working hard" at the right times and bugging the right people, I was finally bequeathed the green epaulets of an AMC supervisor. With my newfound power, I graduated from useless to insufferable. Here was a cocky 15-year-old kid who managed to weasel his way into a supervisor role, and he was running around telling people twice his age what to do. Every time I asked some 30-something coworker to grab a pushbroom, I felt like it took everything in their power not to chokeslam me onto the hot dog rollers.

Hypocritical as this was, I couldn't stand the laziness of my coworkers. Couldn't they at least *pretend* to want to work hard when higher-ups like me were around? Their constant smoke breaks infuriated me to no end, and I frequently complained to my managers about how employees shouldn't be granted bonus time off just because they picked up a stupid habit. Considering that most of my managers would smoke by the dumpsters with the same employees I was complaining about, I didn't get a lot of traction in this area.

In any situation that would allow it, I took full advantage of my supervisor status. During the weekend that *Toy Story 2* was released, it was featured in all four of our biggest theaters. Our concession stand was cursed with nearly day-long rushes that were composed mostly of children. This meant a lot of indecision, a lot of noise, and making a ton of annoying-to-assemble Kids' Packs. I wasn't even on the front lines (the registers), but I still needed to get the hell out of there.

No one would expect you to just abandon your post as a supervisor. If a supervisor wasn't visibly doing something in the stand, it was usually a safe assumption that they were off doing Important Things somewhere in the back or with management. I knew that everyone would assume that of me (although any of them who actually knew me shouldn't have), so I used my supervisor's key to escape into the stockroom. This was my favorite place to go AWOL, as the standard employees had no access to it and therefore could never discover me. Second on the list was the tool closet, which also required a key. It was a fantastic place to just lie flat on your back for 30 to 45 minutes while actual work was being done outside of this mop- and hammer-filled sanctuary.

My coworkers would constantly steal hot dogs and nachos for lunch and never get busted for it. I was too mortified of the potential consequences to even try. Cameras were everywhere, so I was happy with paying my $2 employee price for our concession items. The stockroom was a different story, as it was easy to snag a quick bag of candy or bottle of soda without any prying eyes catching you in the act. During the Great *Toy Story 2* Rush of 1999, I holed up in the hot dog freezer with three bags of Sour Patch Kids and several bottles of Fruitopia to weather the storm.

When things got too chilly, I moved to another safe haven: the soda syrup room. This area was open to all employees, but no one would catch me slacking off, thanks to the insane rush keeping them busy out front. A few of the syrup boxes were low, so I justified my existence back there for a minute and replaced them with fresh supplies. As I was carrying a box of Mr. Pibb into the closet-sized room, I estimated that it probably weighed a solid 50 pounds or so. Behind "Video Game Journalist" and "Hollywood Director" on my list of viable careers was "Professional Wrestler," but I always doubted its likelihood based on my complete lack of strength or athletic ability. What better way to test my current strength than with a box that weighed about a fifth of an average professional wrestler?

One of my favorite wrestlers as a kid was Kevin Nash (aka Diesel). His finishing move was the Jackknife Powerbomb, which involved lifting his opponent until he was horizontal at eye level, then slamming him down to the mat on his back. I guess if we're being specific, a Kevin Nash powerbomb was more of a drop rather than a forceful slam, but that's beside the point. It seemed like a natural move to attempt at the time, so I stood in the center of the syrup room with the Mr. Pibb box in position. I raised one fist into the air, surely looking as cool as Big Daddy Cool himself.

As it turns out, it's not all that hard to lift a 50-pound box to eye level even if you're a scrawny teenager. Once it was there, I released it and took a step back before it hit the floor—I wouldn't want to hurt my toes, after all. I'm not sure what I pictured happening at this point, but I didn't expect the cardboard to split. More importantly, I didn't expect the syrup bag to split. It wasn't like I actively considered the possibility and determined that it was statistically unlikely; it was a matter of not putting any forethought into the situation at all. If someone had shoved a microphone in my face just before to ask my prediction, I probably would have said that the box would kinda thud on the ground and get dented at worst.

It didn't thud on the ground. Everything immediately split open, and viscous, delicious Pibb syrup crept out until it covered the entire floor. Panicking, I hopped out of the way and escaped the syrup room without any evidence slopping its way onto my uniform or shoes. A slight lip separated the syrup room from the rest of the area, so there was a well-defined stopping point to the goopy mess. Everything on my side of the line was pristine, and everything in the small room on the other side was wading in an inch of pure, sugary syrup.

If this had happened in the supervisor-only stock room, the Pibb incident would clearly be on my hands. But thanks to the soda room's accessibility to any employee, I had some plausible deniability. Sure, all of the concession workers were hawking Kids' Packs at hundreds of screaming *Toy Story* fans at the time, but it was at least conceivable that one of them had found their way into the syrup room and done something stupid.

If there were ever a time to put on the facade of a responsible, attentive AMC employee, it was now. I'd get out there and do my job with vigor, proving that I couldn't have been the careless employee who royally mucked up the soda room. Fleeing the scene of the crime, I reemerged in the concession area and started working like I was gunning for another promotion. Need a new batch of popcorn over here? I'm on it. Hey, let me sweep up these kernels for you on the way. You guys can just focus on the registers; I'll be back here filling your sodas so you don't have to. Whoa, looks like you're running low on Cookie Dough Bites! I'll grab a few from the stockroom without even stopping for a quick Fruitopia.

In my mind, I earned enough goodwill in the later stages of that rush to deflect any suspicion. People would hopefully remember only my most recent whereabouts, not the fact that I was wholly absent for the majority of the madness.

"Oh, Dan?" I imagined my coworkers saying from an interrogation room later on, management shining a light in their faces. "He was right here on the front lines, keeping the customers moving swiftly along! He surely couldn't have been performing powerbombs on any items in the back room, no sir."

Once the rush was over, I was in no rush of my own to "discover" the worsening mess behind the scenes. I was perfectly willing to let anyone else stumble upon that atrocity. When all four of our main theaters had moved into their runtime of the movie, the crowd naturally thinned out. A handful of patrons trickled out from time to time for refills, but this was our best chance to get the concession stand restored to 100 percent before the next wave hit. Everyone hustled around, stocking their registers with candy and making sure they had enough bills and coins for change.

For reasons I don't remember, everyone referred to one of my fellow 15-year-old employees as Roly Poly. It was probably me who came up with the nickname, but I'm unsure of my logic, considering that his spiky hair made him resemble a hedgehog more than those weird little ball-like insects. Roly Poly wasn't particularly bright and didn't have much in the way of personality, but he wasn't a bad guy. I didn't wish the Syrupocalypse upon him, but fate wasn't kind to him that day.

While everyone was performing their duties up front, Roly Poly approached the soda fountains to do a routine check of their levels. My eyes were frequently scanning this area, as I wanted to know who would have the ill fortune to venture toward the back. Pressing all of the soda buttons to check the color of the liquid, Roly Poly didn't see anything immediately suspicious. To check the Sprite, he put a spritz into one of the courtesy cups that we gave to customers who wanted free water. When he raised it to his lips, I could tell by his face that he tasted carbonated water and was therefore destined to a really rough remainder of his shift.

Roly Poly slowly waddled to the back, innocently expecting to swap out a quick box of Sprite and move on with his day. I stayed in the concession stand, mentally picturing him stumbling upon the goop and letting out a sad little sigh. Sure enough, he reemerged about a minute later and approached me.

"Dan, there's a really big mess back there."

"Oh yeah?" I feigned surprise. "What's the matter?"

"There's syrup everywhere."

"Yikes, let me go take a look!"

After going through the charade of walking to the back and pretending to see the mess for the first time, I approached Roly Poly in the stand.

"Boy, you weren't kidding! I hate to do this, but we're gonna have to get that cleaned up ASAP. Why don't you grab a mop and a bucket and start getting to work on that?"

He seemed understandably bummed about his assignment. I unsuccessfully tried to make him feel better by telling him that he could stay on mopping duty rather than attend to customers for the next rush.

"The next rush" turned into the rest of the day. Roly Poly had to go through cycle after cycle of mopping, cleaning the syrup out of the mop, mopping some more, changing the water out of the bucket, and so on. With the rushes being so big, I couldn't even put any additional employees on mop duty to help him out. After he spent six hours of his day mopping up sugar goo because I wanted to powerbomb a box, I don't think any court in the country would convict him if he decided to murder me.

It wouldn't be the last time I broke something at AMC because of wrestling-related experiments. I once broke a table in the back because I wanted to see how much force it would take to get slammed through one. My research proved that a 15-year-old jumping up and landing butt-first on the middle is more than enough to permanently damage one, although the real deal never broke quite as cleanly as the ones on *Monday Night Raw*. Naturally, I told my manager that I had no idea which one of my mischievous employees would be so reckless as to break a table.

My ability to slack off only intensified once I turned 16 and was allowed to work in different positions. Ushering was a mostly solitary job, and my supervisor status didn't grant me as much authority there as it did behind the concession stand. Despite this, I was more than willing to sign up for these shifts, based on how easy they were. Instead of having to deal with lengthy rushes prior to a movie's start, it was just a matter of working for quick bursts when movies let out.

Cleaning the theaters was actually pretty relaxing. It required no interaction with the patrons and the dark theaters made it easy to seem like you were working. I didn't forgo my duties entirely, as I found it pretty fun to sprint up and down the aisles with a wide pushbroom. Picking up people's half-finished troughs of popcorn and buckets of soda wasn't something I enjoyed, so I found a way to greatly cut down on how much of that was necessary. I found that if I wheeled trash cans into the theater and placed them by the exit just as the end credits started rolling, a large percentage of the audience would toss their own crap away instead of leaving it at their seats. It helped if I stood there facing the crowd, putting a face to the poor AMC employee that would have to handle their trash (aka "do my job") if they didn't do it themselves.

Ushering was the only position in which I was able to watch movies while I was on the clock. Each of my shifts would naturally contain chunks of time in which no movies were letting out. This gave me a chance to step inside a theater and absorb whatever was playing for 20 or 30 minutes at a time. With 30 screens, there was never a lack of variety when it came to my options. This led to me seeing a lot of movies (or at least parts of movies) that I'd have zero interest in otherwise. I'm not gonna tell you that *Held Up* starring Jamie Foxx or *Love Stinks* starring French Stewart are excellent movies, but sitting in those theaters several times a day was still a better option than doing actual work.

One aspect of my job as an usher was extremely tantalizing: I had the power to kick people out. This power was not to be wielded recklessly, as kicking a customer out without good reason could come back on me in a bad way. A few things were guaranteed grounds for ejection. Bringing alcohol into the theater, doing anything involving nudity, helping others get into the theater via exit doors, or being obnoxious after a warning could justifiably get someone kicked out.

More than anything in the world, I wanted to kick rowdy teenagers out of movies. As a socially awkward kid who didn't drink, I envied and somewhat resented my peers that were confident enough to bring booze into a theater or talk to the opposite sex. Naturally, this made me want to ruin their party by shining a flashlight in their face and telling them to get out. I imagined high school delinquents seeing my green epaulets, recognizing the vast authority that they represented, and begrudgingly grabbing their plastic bottles of vodka while leaving with their heads hung low.

At the beginning of each usher shift, I'd scan the list of what was playing and single out the movies that would most likely draw teenage no-gooders. I'd stalk the aisles of *Fight Club, South Park, Scream 3,* and *Final Destination* just chomping at the bit for a chance to let out my best big-boy "hey!" and point at the culprits. After pointing, I imagined that I'd make a cool "get out of here" motion with my fist and thumb so they'd know I meant business.

It never happened. Those kids surely existed, but they were probably savvy enough to tone things down and hide the drinks when they saw the 15-year-old in an AMC uniform—green epaulets or no—repeatedly prowling the staircases and scanning the audience with the focus of someone looking for a dropped contact lens.

Whenever the week's schedule was posted, I looked forward to usher shifts and dreaded the concession ones. A third option, the box office, started popping up more and more as my time at AMC went on, and my opinion on these shifts fell somewhere in the middle. Selling tickets in an air-conditioned box was certainly more comfortable than the hustle and bustle of the concession stand, but it didn't allow for as much goofing off and movie-watching as an usher shift did.

The box office certainly had some advantages. With a glass rectangle surrounding the employees, rushes didn't come with the overwhelming roar of impatient customers that was par for the course in concession. It was also the best position for me at AMC from a social perspective. It allowed me to frequently work alongside two of my best friends at the time, Chris and Bryan. We were in video production classes together, and all of us were into video games and wrestling. Chris was the quietest of our trio, but had a goofy sense of humor that shined once you got to know him. Bryan was a mostly good-natured guy who would get irrationally angry back then whenever the topic of gay people came up. He's now a happily married gay man.

Repetition was the killer during box office shifts because there was no real variance in activity. Concession had a variety of duties and ushering allowed for some time to watch movies, but with box office it was only "keep selling tickets." We did our best to remedy the boredom by being as stupid as possible.

Customers seemed entirely unfazed no matter how ridiculous we got. Our box office was separated from the lines by a glass wall with embedded speakers, and the employee headsets were the only way to communicate between the two sides. For the duration of one shift, I had Chris wear a disconnected headset as I ducked out of view while wearing the one that spoke to the customers. When they approached Chris's window, they'd see his lips move but hear my voice. On the customer's side, it looked just like a badly dubbed Japanese movie with my words not at all matching Chris's flapping mouth. The only reaction we'd get was some staring or pausing. If my head had sprouted wings, separated from my body, and flown around the line spitting tickets at customers, I bet they'd all just pick them up off the ground and head into their showing of *Road Trip* without batting an eye.

Management was rarely seen in the box office, so I didn't worry about getting in trouble there. My bosses could have been the least of my worries if I had followed an idea that I learned from a customer, however. At the end of one shift, we were closing our registers out when Bryan made a discovery. Somebody had bought a ticket to the Kirk Cameron vehicle *Left Behind* with what appeared to be a $100 bill, and thus received over ninety dollars in change. I don't actually remember if this customer saw *Left Behind*, but it's a safe bet because I feel like we sold at least four billion tickets to that movie. This was Kansas, after all. In the chaos of the rush, Bryan didn't notice anything suspicious as he slipped the $100 bill under the plastic part of the drawer, as we were instructed to do with anything over a twenty.

Once we were closing out and Bryan had a chance to actually inspect the bill, he realized that it was actually a $10 bill that someone had altered with a pen. In the most slapdash, broke-ass case of counterfeiting that I've ever heard of, the customer had simply separated the zeros in each "10" into what looked like two zeros. As easy as that, $10 had become $100. It was such a boneheaded attempt, but if it worked on Bryan, who's to say it wouldn't work elsewhere?

Plus, I was just a teenager. If I tried the same trick and some cashier caught me in the act, I'd just act surprised and pretend like I hadn't noticed it.

I had pulled some dumb tricks in the past to save money, but I certainly never had the nerve to attempt straight-up counterfeiting. I'd buy a game at Walmart, beat it, delete the save file, then use the shrink wrap machine at FuncoLand to make it look new again before returning it, but never counterfeiting. I'd Photoshop a fake Circuit City ad for a video game that made it look like they charged $19.99 instead of the standard $49.99, then take that ad to Walmart for them to price-match, but never counterfeiting. I'd go to Walmart at 3:00am and get games prior to their release date by finding the most checked-out, uninformed employee there and saying that the new game that had arrived in their back room was already being sold nationwide, but never counterfeiting. I guess what I'm saying here is, if you want to do some shady-but-not-technically-illegal stuff to get games earlier or cheaper, go to a Kansas Walmart in the middle of the night in the early 2000s.

I took my pen to a $10 bill the next day, telling myself that it probably wasn't counterfeiting. After all, counterfeiting was all about printing your own money, right? I was just drawing some little lines! Surely the law would see this as no different than drawing a cigarette in Abe Lincoln's mouth or sunglasses on George Washington. This was destined to go well, and I'd be paying for Skittles with a ten and getting $99 in change for the rest of my days.

As I always did with things like this, I planned on attempting the transaction as late at night as possible and from the employee who looked the least invested in their job. I continued to overthink things like this years later once I was buying condoms in college. Buying them from an attractive girl who was close to my age seemed scary to me, as I was afraid it would come off as "boy, I can't wait to put these condoms on my penis and have all sorts of sex!" bragging. As such, my condoms were always sold to me by self-serve Walmart robots or old men who seemed to be on the brink of death.

The stakes for counterfeiting were a bit higher than some social embarrassment. Scouting the available cashiers at Walmart that night, I found myself thinking that I should have researched the penalty if I got caught doing something like this. My confidence came from the fact that I was 16 years old. What was the worst thing that would happen to a 16-year-old for drawing some lines on a piece of paper? Teenagers have literally murdered people and been out of kiddie jail in time to celebrate their first legal drink. I was just trying to get (way) too much change for some damn Skittles.

Only a few cashiers were present at this time of night, so I did a quick scouting run before I took the plunge on one. Some looked borderline lucid and that just wouldn't do for these purposes. I landed on a girl who couldn't have been much older than me, and she was staring glassy-eyed at her nails. When she didn't even glance up to greet me or make eye contact when I entered her aisle, I figured that the ruse's success was a lock.

No matter how confident I was about this, it still felt like my heart was about to beat through my chest as I grabbed the red Skittles bag and placed it on the conveyor. I had received no verbal acknowledgment at any point thus far. Hopefully, her lack of interest would carry over into the process of distributing change. She grabbed the bag and scanned it, and I prayed that she wouldn't bat an eye as I handed her the "hundred."

Taking the bill from my hand, her eyes immediately locked onto its face.

"The fuck is this?"

"Uhh..." I stammered, not having any explanation preloaded in case this happened. "What do you mean?"

"Did you draw on this ten to make it look like a hundred?"

I feigned shock as she showed me the poorly altered numbers on the bill's corners.

"Oh wow!" I said. "Nope! That's crazy, I didn't even notice someone had done that. Go ahead and ring that up as a ten, please. Because that's a $10 bill, obviously."

Opening the register, she counted out my nine dollars in change while occasionally pausing and giving me the eye. In my mind, she was debating whether or not to call a SWAT team in to haul me off to Fort Leavenworth. A far less dramatic result occurred; she silently gave me my change and I scurried out the door. I didn't want to look like I was sprinting to my car because that would look suspicious. Instead, I did one of those gliding walk-runs that you do when you need to poop but you don't want to fully commit to a run in fears of bouncing a turd out.

I needed to sit in my car until I calmed down, but I also wanted to be as far away from the Walmart as possible. Pulling into a nearby bank lot, I shifted into park and turned off the engine. My breath and heart rate were racing like I had never felt before, and this was all thanks to a complete nonissue. A girl took a bill from me, gave it pause for three seconds, and then did her job and handed me the correct change. No managers were called, no lights were shined in my face in an interrogation room, and no heavily armed SWAT teams arrived via helicopter. Even still, it took me the better part of a half hour to compose myself enough to drive home.

This was the point in my life in which I realized where my "line" was. Slacking off at work and making managers and coworkers hate me was no problem. Skipping class and risking disciplinary action didn't faze me. It was the prospect of *actual* trouble, jail time, that I couldn't handle. I had seen *Face/Off* too many times, and those magnetic prison boots looked really uncomfortable. My blood wasn't hard enough for actual crimes, so I'd be sticking to perfectly legal mischief going forward.

My final bit of trouble at AMC was perfectly legal and even had management's express permission, but it was the one that had the most lasting ramifications. It involved our break room, where almost nothing of note ever happened. Outside of the time that the mushroom-dealing usher kicked in the glass of the vending machine to retrieve a stuck tube of Rolos, the break room was a historically uneventful area of the theater.

I'm not one to care about the decor of a room, but even I noticed that our break room was clinical and cold. White paint covered the walls, and there was a healthy amount of nacho cheese and ketchup splattered around. Two vending machines sat on one end, a video camera was perched up in the corner, and the computer that served as our time clock was stationed near the door.

At some point, management decided it was time to paint the break room to make it more inviting. AMC had yet to discover e-mail technology despite this being in the early 2000s, so we were informed of this the way we were informed of everything: on a piece of paper tacked to a corkboard. They were taking suggestions from employees about how the room was to be renovated, such as what color it should be painted and whether it should have a theme.

I didn't care about the colors or what the room looked like, but I did care about having a good excuse to do something stupid. My idea wasn't simple enough to write into the provided spaces for color suggestions, so I went downstairs to talk to a manager.

"Hey Jackie, I have an idea for the break room."

"What's that?"

"How about we buy a few buckets, a ton of tennis balls, and a bunch of different colors of paint. Then, anybody who's interested can join up after work one night and dip tennis balls in paint and throw it super hard at the walls. It'll leave a big colored splat and might look really cool by the end."

The correct answer would have been "no," but Jackie said she'd float the idea to her higher-ups. Somehow, they wound up approving this. I was given a company credit card and told to go to the Home Depot to get supplies.

As I write this, I'm trying to think of what gave me this idea. My first instincts are that it had to be something I saw on *Jackass* or in a *Mario Tennis* minigame. After some research, I found that neither of these things ever had a "throw a paint-dipped tennis ball at a wall" segment. *Mario Power Tennis* for the GameCube included a minigame called "Artist on the Court" that had a similar theme, but that didn't come out until 2004. Perhaps word of this break room incident spread to Nintendo and they stole the idea.

Home Depot was by no means an establishment that I frequented back then, and my knowledge of the store's goods hasn't really grown in the years since. I have a decent idea of what a two-by-four is (a wooden plank, and I believe the numbers refer to inches); I know the difference between

45

a Phillips head screwdriver and the standard variety (one's a plus, one's a minus); and I learned the hard way about what a wall stud is after I had seven separate wall-mounted wooden DVD racks collapse and take down a good portion of my living room.

Corporate credit card in hand, I hopped in my car and sped over to the cavernous, confusing, and very orange store. A thorough knowledge of its merchandise proved unnecessary, as it was simple enough to find a bunch of paint cans and empty buckets, although I had to make a separate run to Target to pick up the tennis balls. Management updated its corkboard notice to explain what we were going to do and when, and every employee was invited to take part.

Once the night of the painting arrived, I noticed the only people who showed up were the young employees with nothing better to do on a weeknight. We now had a room full of two dozen teenagers, close to fifty tennis balls, and enough paint to cover an entire room and then some. Jackie brought in some tarps and asked us to cover the various electronics in the room before we started. Then she told us to have fun and she stepped out of the room. No goggles, no safety instructions, just "hey, put this thing over the clock-in computer so it doesn't get messed up" and she was out the door. To be fair, I was the guy who came up with the idea and was tasked with getting the proper items from Home Depot, so maybe I should have thought of goggles.

With Jackie out of the room, it was time for the paint to fly. Sure enough, a tennis ball covered in orange paint was whipped directly into Bryan's eye within ten seconds. Through the bright blobs that were whizzing across the room, I clearly saw him staggering toward the door, arms outstretched, with his face looking like the Nickelodeon logo.

Getting paint in your eyes is no fun, but I also learned that a tennis ball can hurt quite a bit if a 16-year-old football player throws it full speed into your temple. All of us were constantly getting pelted in every location—I thankfully avoided any crotch shots—and we weren't the only victims. Our hastily placed tarps wasted no time in sliding off the various items in the room, so everything that was supposed to be protected was now fully exposed.

A plastic bubble was supposed to protect the security camera in an upper corner of the room, but it shattered easily. Like a bank robber spraying foam over a camera's lens in a movie, one of my coworkers beaned the exposed camera hard and obscured it. Vending machines made for a large target, and their exteriors and windows became completely covered. Once the tarp was knocked off of the clock-in computer, the keyboard only had a few seconds of life before multicolored paint seeped between every key and rendered it unusable.

Everyone was in pain or at least half-blinded by the time Jackie re-entered the room. She had run into Bryan in the hallway as he walked out of the restroom with bloodshot eyes. After he informed her of what happened, she must have realized how ill-conceived this idea was and ran back to stop it. I'm not sure how long she was yelling for us to stop before any of us heard it, but we eventually turned and saw her as the tennis balls stopped bouncing and slopped to the floor.

Every inch of that room was covered: walls, ceiling, floor, vending machine, camera, computer, as well as over 20 young AMC employees. Surveying the room, you could tell that Jackie immediately understood that this was a bad idea. She told us to clean ourselves up and go home, and said we'd later figure out what would happen to the break room.

By the end of that week, Jackie was moved to another theater. I'm still not sure if this was a direct punishment for allowing the break room painting to take place, but it seemed suspicious that she was gone so quickly afterward. Someone had to be punished for the damage done to the items in the break room, and I wasn't spared. At the beginning of my next shift, management pulled me into a room and informed me that I was being demoted back to regular staff status.

I'm not sure why I put so much pride into my ill-gotten green epaulets, but I wasn't about to go back to being a grunt. Instead of reverting back to a position in which I'd be easily bossed around, I quit without the slightest bit of anger. After all, I had been getting away with nonsense for years by then. They could have fired me at any point along the way, and I'd have shrugged my shoulders and said "Yeah, that makes sense."

My friends who still worked at the theater told me that within two weeks of my departure, management painted over the tie-dye vomit that covered the break room with an inoffensive shade of blue. The security camera and computer were replaced, the vending machines were thoroughly scrubbed, and everyone did their best to forget the tennis ball incident.

I managed to cause residual trouble at AMC 30 even after I left. I had an usher friend smuggle out a walkie-talkie and we'd sit in the parking lot barking confusing orders to the staff until they realized what was going on. After buying a "TV-B-Gone" device that could turn off any TV, I'd stand in the concession line during rushes and stealthily turn off the screens that displayed all of the items and prices.

Management never asked me to give my uniform back when I left, so I'd put it on friends who never worked at AMC and have them show up to the theater unannounced. I gave them elaborate backstories about how they were supervisors who transferred in from Nebraska. From afar, I'd see how long they'd be able to bum around the box office or concession stand giving orders (with hidden microphones in their pockets) before management realized they weren't actual employees.

I haven't worked at AMC 30 for almost 15 years, but it's still the theater I go to with my sisters whenever I'm back in Kansas. When I go there now, I don't recognize any of the faces. A few of my fellow teenage employees went on to work for the company's corporate office in Kansas City, but the staff of my old theater is now completely new. It's still a great place to see a movie, but when I go back I can't help but hope that there's some insufferable teenage employee there that's keeping management on their toes.

Burying the Bucket

Several periods of my life have been marked by obsessions that came and went. Along the way, a few have stood the test of time. A lifelong love of video games began with my first console—the NES—at the age of four, and I've been fascinated by professional wrestling ever since I first saw it on my television screen in 1993. Another longtime love of mine that has never seen my interest waver is pranking people. My brand of messing with people has run the spectrum of scope and consequence, ranging from innocent fun to potential legal proceedings.

My early attempts at "pranks" make me think that I didn't fully understand what a prank was supposed to be. When the idea of April Fools' Day was first explained to me, I must have thought that it was simply an excuse to aggressively grief people rather than find clever ways to annoy them. Before each April Fools' morning as a kid, I'd get up late in the night and wreak havoc upon my mother's house.

Every plate, bowl, and tray in her kitchen was removed and laid end-to-end across the floor with a single tortilla chip on each one, maximizing how annoying it would be to clean up. The living room TV was unplugged, leading to the "hilarious" consequence of it not turning on when she pressed the power button. Fake cockroaches were placed in her tubs of butter. Confetti was heaped upon the ceiling fan, set to shower down across the room whenever it was turned on. Clocks were set to a variety of incorrect times, many with random alarms primed to go off throughout the day. Every single movie in her VHS collection was removed and put back in the wrong box (the same went for all the bags of cereal).

Incisions were made on the undersides of potato chip bags, and the packages were carefully slid back onto the shelf with all the chips still inside. When a bag was removed, the entirety of its contents would crash to the kitchen countertop or the floor.

My mother took everything in stride, dealing with the cavalcade of annoyances and frequently—and rightfully—calling me a "little shit." But one specific moment on April Fools' Day 1997 was the final straw for her. Along with the other random stupid things I did around the house, I had placed a full bunch of bananas in her oven. My thinking was that she'd open the oven at some point and see a bunch of bananas, and that would be hilarious for some reason. The concept of a prank continued to elude me as I still thought that "random = funny = prank."

Once she had restored the majority of the house to working order, my mother wanted to relax with a frozen pizza. Setting the oven to preheat for a while, she went upstairs to use the restroom and get ready for the day. On a normal day, she'd have used the one downstairs near the kitchen, but I had set off a stink bomb in there earlier and its effects were still extremely potent.

Ten or fifteen minutes later, she was halfway down the stairs when she noticed a strong banana scent overpowering the horrific stink bomb stench emanating from the bathroom. The bananas had fully melted in the 425-degree heat traditionally reserved for a delicious Totino's Party Pizza (I hope it was the Combination variety, but I can't be sure). This wasn't my intention, as I hadn't considered that she'd almost certainly preheat the oven before using it. She had, and she opened the oven door to see flattened banana peels bleeding goopy, yellow sludge, quickly hardening into a thick crust on the floor of the oven. Turning the heat off, she fruitlessly attempted to clean the solidified banana goop once it had cooled. Residue remains almost twenty years later.

I was at school while this happened, unaware that several years' worth of annoyance had reached a boiling point in that moment. My history teacher's words were falling on deaf ears as I mindlessly doodled scenes from *GoldenEye* in the margins of my notebook, wondering which of my "pranks" my mom was discovering at home. What I didn't know was that she finally had enough and was currently enacting some revenge only a few hundred feet away from me here at California Trail Junior High.

The bell rang to signal the end of history hour, and I grabbed my books and headed back toward my locker. My friend Afshin had the locker next to mine, so I always bored him during this walk with my current thoughts on the world of professional wrestling. ~~Sure, it was nice to see Randy Savage back with Miss Elizabeth, but it made no logical sense that he'd join the New World Order. After all, Hogan's betrayal of him via multiple leg drops (exposing himself as the teased "third man" joining Scott Hall and Kevin Nash) at Bash at the Beach less than a year earlier was the catalyst for the very formation of the villainous group. If the stable continued to expand at this rate without logical storylines to support the reasoning, WCW was running a risk of diluting one of the true phenomenons in the industry and could possibly squander~~ *(ED NOTE: STOP)*

Sorry.

From down the hallway I saw a cluster of classmates standing near the general area of mine and Afshin's lockers. I didn't imagine it had anything to do with me, but I was still nervous about the possibility of having to interact with a bunch of my peers. Unless the person was Afshin or one of the very few other people I regularly interacted with, I did everything I could to fly under the radar of anyone close to my age. Talking to these people was bad enough, but the reality of the situation proved to be even more terrifying. Like a scene from my most social anxiety-riddled nightmares, their eyes turned directly to me as I approached the locker.

One of the guys said "looking good!" as the group dispersed, still laughing. I glanced down to make sure I hadn't left my fly unzipped or worn my shirt inside out or something. Nope. Same old dorky stuff as usual, nothing to see here.

When the group cleared out, I was able to get a glimpse of my locker. It was covered from top to bottom with photographs and I stepped closer to get a better look. There I was, wearing a shiny green vest from a Christmas program I had to sing in during Catholic school. Next to it was another picture of me, shirtless while wearing my grandfather's fishing cap and oversized eyeglasses. Yep, that's definitely a young me in a bathtub.

In retrospect, none of these were particularly damning. They were innocent, silly photos, but even the most minor and harmless attention focused on me in those days was *way* too much attention. I took the pictures down with the haste of a teenage boy closing internet porn windows when he hears footsteps coming up the stairs, a feeling that I was very familiar with at that particular time.

Afshin good-naturedly ribbed me as I scrambled to hide the photos, but it's not like the school was buzzing about it for the rest of the day. All the other kids went back to their usual seventh-grade business, which at my school usually meant "quoting Ma$e interludes while wearing JNCOs." Still, I wanted to scour the back room of tech class for a rocket ship that would blast me off into orbit until the day's final bell rang.

Riding the bus home felt like it took even longer than usual on that April Fools' Day. It always seemed like an eternity, because I hated being "peers" with these idiots who sniffed rubber cement in the seats next to me and—far more damningly—preferred Saturn to PlayStation. Looking back, I'm not sure why I hated them while simultaneously putting so much worry into whether or not they'd make fun of me. Oh, right, it's because they could all beat me up if they decided they didn't like me.

To clarify, I never got full-on "beaten up" in junior high. Jocks would punch me hard in the arm a couple of times a day in the hallway, but it's not like they were beating me with socks that had bars of soap in them. One thing they did do that consistently infuriated me was this little "game" that always ended with me getting punched.

"Hey Ryckert," one of them would say in the hallway or locker room.

I'd glance at them, then notice that they were trying to get my attention with one of their hands. Every time, they'd be making a tiny circle with their index finger and thumb. Sometimes they'd be holding this hand signal on their thigh, other times on their forearm. If I glanced at it, that meant I got punched. If I flinched during the punch, I'd get punched again. This recurring song and dance drove me insane as I never understood the logic behind getting punched for looking at a hand signal that they were clearly trying to get me to notice. Then again, I was in no place to question logic, considering that I had spent my morning putting a bunch of bananas into an oven.

The bus finally got to my stop after a 20-minute trip that felt like three hours, and I prepared for some mild gloating from my mother. When I arrived home, I walked in to find her in the kitchen looking awfully proud of herself.

"Still feel like fucking with me?" she grinned.

"I'll admit, that was a pretty good one."

"Just wanted to let you know that I can always fight back. I hope you don't have any big plans for the rest of the night."

I asked what she meant by that, but she wouldn't elaborate. Fearing that she was hinting at more to come, I ran upstairs to make sure everything in my room was in its proper place. My bed, computer desk, and gaming systems were all exactly where they always were, but thousands of additional items had found their way into my room.

Seemingly every square inch of real estate on the floor was covered with pennies and nickels. This seemed like an annoying thing to clean up, but the sudden appearance of a large amount of free money—regardless of the denomination—is rarely a bad thing. I paced through the room for a bit, sweeping at the floor with my socks to form little mountains of change. Despite there not being any single coin worth more than five cents, the sheer volume of them made me think that there must have been hundreds of dollars resting on my carpet.

There was. After her photo escapades at my school, my mother had gone to the bank that held my savings account. As a co-owner of the account, she was able to drain it entirely in whatever way she wished. When I went to school that morning, my bank account was nothing more than the number 500 in a computer system. When I got home, that intangible number was now very real and spread out across my bedroom.

I've never worked at a bank, but I used a coin rolling machine enough during that week to get good at one aspect of the job. It was the perfect comeback. She didn't take a single cent from me and she was able to create a monumental headache without actually harming anything. More importantly, it permanently got her off the hook as the target for my pranks. I knew she might not strike back every time if I continued to target her, but I was now aware of just how capable she was at striking back in a major way when the time was right.

Going forward, I started to audition new targets like a sitcom producer dealing with a departing star. My grandpa was a good first choice, so I started rigging his house with traps when I'd stay over. Late into the night, I'd cover hallway entrances with Saran Wrap and create web-like obstacles around his living room with numerous spools of yarn.

Barely anyone had a cell phone back then, so I'd utilize a trick in which you could make a home phone call itself. Knowing that he'd come out to investigate as soon as the phone started ringing, I'd turn off all of the lights and pretend to be asleep on the couch. I've always been good at keeping a straight face when I really want to laugh, but it's never been harder than when I'd hear a steady stream of "goddammit" and "what the Sam hell?" coming from my confused and sleepy grandfather as he flailed through layers of plastic wrap and yarn.

His reactions always made me laugh, but it seemed like he got genuinely annoyed at the pranks without seeing any humor in them. I didn't want to torture my poor grandpa with something that he didn't even find funny, so I moved onto my sisters.

Katie and Kayla were eight years younger than me, and they certainly had the same propensity for mischief that my mother and I possessed. As a result, they'd surely see the comedic value in the various pranks I'd pull on them. While this seemed like a good fit, I had to worry too much about their nearly immediate retaliation. At one point, Katie fell asleep on my bed while watching me play *Silent Hill*. Naturally, I responded to this by putting shaving cream into her palm and tickling her forehead with a towel. Instead of slapping her own face with a palm full of shaving cream, she woke up and immediately smeared the shaving cream all over my sheets.

After running everything through the wash, I went to bed assuming that we were even. She thought otherwise, shoving handfuls of Cheez-Its in her mouth and swishing them around with water as she chewed. When I woke up to my sister spitting a mouthful of soggy Cheez-Its into my face, I knew that it was time to move on to the next candidate.

As a popular athlete at my school, Tom Saltzman was an unlikely candidate for me to mess with. Unfortunately for him, he was a heavy sleeper and was seated next to me on a flight from Kansas City to Washington, D.C. for an eighth grade field trip. Less than an hour into the flight, he fell into a deep, snoring sleep. I tapped a few nearby classmates on the shoulder to get their attention and went to work making Tom look stupid. I grabbed his limp wrists and flailed them around, putting on a little puppet show as people snickered. This graduated to making him slap himself in the face, which surprisingly didn't wake him up.

Tom wasn't stirring in the slightest, so I started elevating things to see how much he could sleep through. Napkins and magazines were balanced upon his head followed by a number of ice cubes. After another game of unconscious "quit hitting yourself," I rested his fingers in a glass of orange juice.

He was the heaviest sleeper I'd ever seen, but everyone has a breaking point, and his was rapidly approaching. I was running out of implements of annoyance and a quick inventory of my surroundings yielded nothing but literal peanuts. Always resourceful, I ripped a bag open and grabbed a few. Without even thinking about it, I instantly shoved a peanut in each nostril and each ear.

All of my classmates in the nearby rows were laughing at Tom by now, with his magazine head, orange juice hand, and peanut ears. I reached for his forearms for another round of my puppet show, but I sensed him starting to rouse. Tom's eyes fluttered as his breath attempted to squeeze past the peanuts in his nostrils. One forceful exhale later, both peanuts flew out of his nose and onto the tray in front of him.

Slowly opening his eyes, he first saw me laughing hysterically and then noticed the eyes of the people in front of us peering over the top of their chairs. With peanuts still in his ears, he turned around, surveyed the nearby rows of classmates, and noticed their growing laughter. Not wanting to cause a scene on the plane, he casually removed the items from his head, wiped his hands off on the drink napkin, dug the peanuts out of his ears, and sat in silence for the remainder of the flight.

At no point during the flight or the rest of the trip did he acknowledge that any of this had happened. If he complained about it, it wasn't within earshot of me. Instead, his response would be prolonged and consistent, and would last until the end of high school. Every time Tom saw me in the hallway, he punched me hard in the arm. I'd been mad at classmates for senselessly punching me in the past, but there was no way I could blame Tom for this. Whenever I was walking down the hall and suddenly felt a blow to my shoulder, I'd wince, look up to see Tom, and think "Yeah, I can't really be upset about this."

With Tom permanently crossed off the list of potential targets, I needed someone else. Before I settled on a particular target, something fell into my lap that virtually demanded that I use it to prank random strangers. My friend Shawn's mother enjoyed making costumes and she had crafted an adult-size, realistic gorilla costume for reasons that I've wholly forgotten. I do remember my utter joy when Shawn told me about its existence, and my immediate pleas for access to it.

His responsible, adult mother had no recurring need for a gorilla costume for some reason, so it was bequeathed unto me. For weeks, my friend Chris and I would rampage around the suburbs of Olathe, getting kicked out of numerous Borders bookstores and Targets. My favorite recurring gag involved going to various 24-hour drive-thru places in the middle of the night. Chris would order four large waters at the intercom, then intentionally pull up to the window with his car uncomfortably far away. As the poor late-night fast food employee attempted to stretch the tray of gigantic waters out of their window, I'd emerge from the bushes in the gorilla suit, sprinting past while slapping the tray high into the air and disappearing into the night.

Looking back, I'm glad that Shawn's mom asked for the gorilla suit back before somebody freaked out and put a bullet into whoever was inside of it during one of these pranks. I had somehow survived high school without anyone kicking my ass too badly; now it was time to bring my "talents" to college.

The whole time I was in high school I should have realized that the perfect target for griefing was right in front of me. Despite my father's seemingly permanent college-aged state of mind, I've never once seen him attempt anything resembling a prank. He's past the age of 50, and he'll still stay out all night drinking, laugh at fart jokes, and turn into a Tex Avery cartoon character whenever he sees a picture of Pamela Anderson. Pranks always seemed to be too juvenile for him, however. What made him an ideal target was the fact that he was far too lazy in these matters to muster any kind of meaningful retaliation. Like an ineffective, dumb version of a Terminator, I locked onto my new mark and planned for a full-blown attack.

At this time, my father was knee-deep in one of the dumbest decisions he's ever made. Despite his disdain for rich people, religious people, "fancy" things, children, and dogs, he had married a devoutly Catholic multimillionaire who associated with only the fanciest and most pretentious of company. She also had three children and about fourteen dogs. He lived with them all in a veritable mansion in Leawood, a city so up its own ass that its residents would return correctly delivered mail if the envelope read "Overland Park" instead of "Leawood" (Overland Park was the also-rich, but-not-quite-as-rich, neighboring city). Sharon, his wife, refused to set foot in restaurants like Applebee's or Chili's because she was afraid of someone recognizing her in such a "low-class" establishment and dropping her a few ranks in the Leawood Status Weekly publication that probably exists.

My dad's marriage to Sharon was his sixteenth or seventeenth, if I'm remembering correctly. She and I got along all right—or, at least, as well as a pretentious millionaire and a perennially farting college student could. She seemed keen on the idea of griefing my father, so I reached out to her before one April Fools' Day to help me organize an elaborate prank on him.

The prank involved getting to his house early in the morning, covering the floor of a necessary hallway of his house with over 800 cups of water, and watching him deal with it as he tried to leave the house to get to work. I also covered his car with Post-it Notes and filled it with balloons for good measure.

While there's a video documenting the water cup incident, the next elaborate prank I attempted to play on him didn't end with a tidy YouTube clip. The water cup video blew up online and received hundreds of thousands of views at a time when I wasn't yet publicly known for being an idiot on the internet. Naturally, my next goal was to top that one with an even more intricate plot.

April Fools' Day was out of the question; after the water cup incident, he'd clearly be on high alert during that time of year. I settled on a winter break while I was home from college. These trips home were extremely laid-back and stress-free, at least for me. I'd have a few solid weeks in which I didn't have to work or even pretend to go to class. My father was in a trickier situation, wanting to go out to bars with me every night while still having to wake up and deliver mail during the busiest time of year. However, this didn't stop him from joining me for almost nightly trips to the Red Balloon. He'd show up complaining about being tired, but then a few Red Bull vodkas would perk him up and fuel him until our traditional post-bar Taco Bell trip.

Halfway through one of these nights, I realized that it was a rare instance in which he didn't have to work the next day. Putting together an elaborate prank to grief him gives me great joy, but I didn't want to risk him actually getting in trouble for being late to his job at the post office. He was drinking hard that night and I knew that he'd be asleep in no time once we got home. It seemed like the perfect time to rig up whatever I managed to think of.

God knows what got me started on this train of thought, but I concocted the plan sometime after midnight. Here's how I imagined that I'd pull it off:

- wait for Dad to fall asleep
- put his car/house keys in the microwave
- get a gigantic bucket
- fill bucket with cooked spaghetti, maple syrup, and salsa
- bury bucket in his backyard
- stick a shovel in the freshly dug mound of dirt, so it sticks straight up
- place a note where his keys used to be that reads "Check Backyard"
- Dad wakes up, sees the note, sees the shovel in the backyard
- He digs up the bucket, then sifts through tons of goopy crap to get to the bottom
- He finds the note at the bottom that reads "Your keys are in the microwave, dummy"

It seemed foolproof. If Dad wanted to leave the house, he'd have to take a shovel to his backyard and spend a bunch of time getting his hands and forearms all sticky just to find out that his dumb keys were right there in the microwave the entire time. I'd have cameras set up to capture the action, and boom, there's another successful prank and YouTube hit. He wouldn't know it, but I'd be hiding in his house, peering around corners and through windows to watch his frustration firsthand.

Thrilled with my plan, I texted my sisters from the bar and asked them to prepare a ton of spaghetti. I'd also need them to bring shovels, a bucket, syrup, and salsa to my dad's house. They weren't his daughters, but they knew him fairly well. Katie and Kayla were always game to screw with people, so they accepted and started getting the supplies ready.

As was the case with most things involving my father, the rest of the night played out as I expected. His Red Bull buzz started to wear off as last call drew closer, and he shifted into the phase of Drunk Dad in which the only phrase he's capable of uttering is "I'm so tired." Last call kicked the next phase into gear, which usually consists of a brief surge of energy as he realizes that Taco Bell is imminent.

Instead of calling a cab like we usually did, I planned on having my sisters show up as our ride home. Whenever my father is drunk and something is either saving him money or making something more convenient for him, he doesn't tend to care about logic. My wholly unrelated-to-him sisters had magically shown up at two in the morning to pick us up and he didn't bat an eye as to why they were suddenly our ride home. He didn't glance into the back of their SUV as he stumbled in, but he probably wouldn't have questioned the shovels and bucket at this point, either.

We quickly replaced the suspicious smell of freshly cooked pasta with an influx of Double Decker Tacos, Triple Layer Nachos, and Chili Cheese Burritos once we got to Taco Bell. At least, those are the actual names for the items. Drunk Dad's order typically consists of him mumbling "I wanna bunch of beefy crunchy cheesy thingies," and then our driver or the poor late-night drive-thru employee has to decipher what that means. Thankfully, several dozen of Taco Bell's menu items could classify as "beefy crunchy cheesy thingies," and all of them would satisfy my father in this state.

BURYING THE BUCKET

Arriving back at his place with the Taco Bell bounty, my sisters and I sat down on the couch with our food while Dad took up his usual post-bar spot on the floor. Now, it was just a matter of waiting out the next step in the process. It starts with him repeating things like "Taco Bell is the best food" and "if you don't like Taco Bell, you're an idiot" in between bites of beefy crunchy cheesy thingies. Next, he starts to pat his stomach near the end of the meal before lying face-down on the carpet. He then mumbles about being tired for a solid 15 minutes in which he's too tired to actually stand up and walk to his bed. This process can sometimes be expedited with a little prodding, frequently involving throwing things at his face or poking him in the stomach. When it's time for him to actually make the move to the bed, he temporarily stands upright before crawling up the stairs at a sloth-like speed, using his hands to support himself on each step. After he disappears at the top of the stairs, the sounds of snoring emanate from his bedroom within seconds of his taco-filled body collapsing on the mattress.

Katie, Kayla, and I took some time to clean up the living room while we waited for him to enter a deep sleep. Once the snoring started, we got to work. My sisters had taken my request seriously, making enough fresh spaghetti to fill the majority of a ten-gallon bucket. Before we dumped condiments into it to make it a sticky mess, I put clear shipping tape around the "YOUR KEYS ARE IN THE MICROWAVE, DUMMY" note and wiggled it down to the bottom of the pasta. The fresh pasta smelled great, but it became less appetizing when we took the bucket into the backyard and sullied it with full containers of salsa and maple syrup. Forks and spoons wouldn't do the trick when it came time to stir, so we did our best to mix everything up with one of the shovels. This ensured that on top of the salsa and syrup that he'd have to paw through, there would also be plenty of dirt sticking to everything.

With everything properly gooed up, it was time to put this thing in the ground. We probably should have considered checking into the placement of power cables before we started hacking away at the dirt, but we somehow managed to avoid electrocuting ourselves in the dumbest way possible. Outside of my revenge on Larry as a kid, none of us had much experience in the field of digging holes. Everything took longer than expected because of our inexperience. After working our way through some roots or skeletons or whatever it was that was blocking our path, we finally wound up with a hole big enough for our pasta bucket. We heaved it in, covered it up with dirt, and then stuck two shovels into the mound like the American flag on the surface of the moon.

My sisters and I said goodbye, and they headed back to my mother's house. When my dad woke up and found his house empty, he'd probably think that I went back with them. After all, my mother actually has extra pillows and blankets and beds at her place. By contrast, my dad has a terribly uncomfortable fold-out couch, no blankets, and a stained old pillow with no case. Also, from time to time, his house is known to be filled with wasps. Deciding where to sleep when I'm back in town is like trying to decide between having some nice Kansas City barbeque for dinner or getting stung by a bunch of damn wasps.

On this particular night, I'd have to stay at his place if I wanted to document the results of the prank. His morning routine is predictable, so I set my alarm for 5:45 a.m. to have enough time to set up a camera before his went off at six. Minutes after his alarm goes off, he emerges from the bedroom like a hungover groundhog and ambles down the stairs in his robe and baseball cap. Next, he grabs a gigantic energy drink, a lighter, and a pack of cigarettes before spending what feels like 45 minutes sitting on his front steps, smoking and playing Words With Friends (At least, that's what he does now. Maybe it was Snake back then?). Most mornings, he'll spot a squirrel that he deems is "up to something" and then text me updates about its suspicious behavior.

On this particular morning, I knew his routine would go off the rails before he had a chance to light his first cigarette. You see, his brain shuts down entirely if he is not aware of the exact location of his pocket-sized necessities at all times. This consists of his cigarettes, lighter, phone, gum, and keys. With the last link in that chain nowhere to be found, his routine would have to wait until those keys were safely in his robe pocket where they belonged.

When my alarm woke me, I immediately grabbed my still camera and placed it on the floor of his back deck. I adjusted its location so it had a clear view of the dirt mound in its viewfinder while still remaining inconspicuous. All of my stuff in the living room was moved to the basement to keep with the illusion that I had gone back to my mother's house. With a couple of minutes left before he'd be performing his majestic robed morning shuffle, I perched myself at the top of the basement stairs and prepared to stealthily film him with my flip phone.

As soon as I heard the deliberate, slow steps coming down from his bedroom, I hit record and anxiously awaited his reaction. My vantage point didn't allow for much of a view, but I caught a glimpse of him heading toward the kitchen to grab his smoking accessories. He stopped in his tracks once he reached the spot where his keys usually were. Despite not being able to see him, I could definitely hear him.

"Oh, god *dammit*, Dan..."

His tone was the one that he reserves for when he's genuinely angry about something. Considering that he thought that he was the only person in the house when he said that, I had little doubt about his anger's authenticity. "Check backyard" was the note sitting where his keys should have been, and he immediately stomped to the back porch.

The first sign that my plot wasn't working came as soon as he stepped outside.

"WHY IS THERE A CAMERA BACK HERE?"

Well, shit. There went my plans for a candid shot of him digging for his keys. I barely had time to be disappointed by that thought before I saw the camera fly into the living room and land face-down on the couch. Well, there went my plans for *any* usable footage of this prank.

"DAN, I FOUND THE CAMERA!" he yelled into the house. "I know you're here! I'm not in the mood for this shit today! Where are my keys???"

Even without being able to capture any good footage, I stayed silent so that I could watch the prank play out until the bitter end. YouTube might not be able to see it, but I'd be close enough to hear all the grunts and cursing as he voluntarily plunged his arms into the disgusting pasta bucket.

"All right, Dan, I know you're here," he continued to yell. "Now *this* is happening until I get my keys back!"

What was happening? I was out of sight and all of my belongings were down in the basement. At least, that's what I thought, until I saw him walk past the basement doorway with a grocery bag full of my newest Xbox 360 games.

Shit. I had left my 360 plugged into his TV, and at that point I was working as a video game reviewer for a local college newspaper and website. As the only gaming editor, I still had a ton of holiday releases to catch up on over winter break. They were now literally walking out the front door to face some unknown fate.

After the door closed behind him, I could hear him yelling things from the front porch but I couldn't quite make out what he was saying. A quick moment later, I clearly heard the sound of a game case hitting concrete. What was he doing? Was he just throwing my games into the parking lot?

It didn't take long for me to realize what was actually happening. His roof was slanted, and he was unsuccessfully trying to throw my games onto it. One by one, they were hitting the shingles and then sliding off until they free-fell to the concrete below.

THUD, SLIDE, CRACK

There goes Left 4 Dead.

THUD, SLIDE, CRACK

That was probably Banjo Kazooie: Nuts & Bolts.

Sliding off the roof and dropping onto concrete was actually worse than if they had stayed up there. One option required a ladder; the other could render the games useless. Dad had my number. I wanted to see my quickly deteriorating prank play out, but not as badly as I wanted to save my games from an undignified, gravelly death. Biting my lip, I stopped recording on my cell phone and ran outside in my socks and pajamas as more cases hit the pavement.

"ALL RIGHT, ALL RIGHT, STOP," I pleaded.

"Aw, look," he said. "Looks like it's not that fun being on the other side of this, is it?"

"This is totally different. I was trying to prank you and you're just breaking my shit."

"And I'm gonna keep doing it until I get my keys back," he said as he pulled another game out of the bag. "Gonna give them to me or is this one going too?"

I glanced down to see *Sonic Unleashed* in his hand, and my unspoken thought was, *well, that wouldn't be much of a loss*. Seeing him with the upper hand was killing me, however, so I relented. With no need to keep up the bucket charade, I walked into the house and anticlimactically grabbed his keys from the microwave. We made the games-for-keys trade and I dejectedly picked up the rest of the cracked cases off the pavement.

My attempt had failed miserably, so I explained the original plan to my father and offered to extract the bucket from his backyard. He declined on the basis of it being too dangerous because of the possibility of severing underground cables. Now that I think about it, he might have just been worried about temporarily losing cable TV and having to deal with a repairman.

To this day, the bucket sits underground exactly where my sisters and I buried it. I've offered to exhume it on numerous occasions, but my father never has any interest in getting his yard dug up again. After almost a decade, I can't help but imagine what the bucket's contents look like. It was a mess of goo, pasta, and dirt back then and I'd love to see what the years and an assortment of underground creatures have done to it.

As it stands, it's an unmarked grave commemorating many years of annoying my family. By that point in my life, I had found a more fruitful and varied assortment of people to mess with who were in no way related to me. Surrounded by like-minded idiots of the same age, it was time to narrowly avoid getting my ass kicked in the college dorms.

Hashinger

After a very comfortable and private adolescence consisting of playing video games, watching wrestling, and copiously masturbating—rarely at the same time—in the comfort of my childhood home, moving into the college dorms was exactly what I needed. I had just turned 18, and I was destined to live a very boring life if I didn't find some kind of kick in the ass that would force me to coexist with others my own age.

Knowing that college would be a dramatic change of pace, my mother recommended that I enroll in something called the Freshman Summer Institute at the University of Kansas. This involved living on campus for a month and attending classes, but its primary purpose for me was purely social. I couldn't stand most of my peers in high school, and that was back when they were forced to pretend to be civil human beings under the watchful eyes of their parents. I was dreading what they'd be like once they were let loose for the first time in their lives.

A four-person suite would be my living quarters for the month, featuring two rooms containing bunk beds, and a common living room area and bathroom in between them. Bryce was my roommate, and I wasn't particularly concerned about him. We weren't close friends—he tended to hang out with the jock crowd—but we had gone to school together since sixth grade and there had never been any problems between us.

One of our suitemates was a kid named Lucky who was the son of a literal oil tycoon. Even for our one-month stay, he brought enough electronic equipment to launch a space shuttle. He fancied himself a DJ, and the small common area between our two bedrooms didn't exactly muffle the day-long electronic music that he'd be playing or attempting to make. These were the days when I militantly rejected any music that wasn't classic rock from the era between Chuck Berry and the end of Led Zeppelin.

I had heard next to no hip-hop in my life, and I dreaded waking up every morning to Bryce's alarm clock, which blared Outkast's "Bombs Over Baghdad." This period actually led to me becoming more open-minded about rap and hip-hop. As the weeks went by, the constant Notorious B.I.G., Wu-Tang Clan, and Jay-Z that Bryce played in our room started to grow on me. While I got used to his musical preferences—and certainly preferred it to Lucky's techno/electronica/ house/whatever it was—I could never quite get used to the girls that he'd bring to the room. I'd leave while they were messing around, obviously, but I had to overhear some truly mind-numbing conversations as Bryce tried to woo these future sorority recruits.

Most of these exchanges have been successfully scrubbed from my mind. I'll never forget Alyson, though. Like Lucky, Alyson had come from a very rich family about two hours away in rural Kansas. Her father had bought her several cars, but had neglected to teach her how to fill them with gasoline. Back in their hometown, he would drive her car to the station and fill up its tank whenever it was empty. Within days of Alyson arriving at the dorm, she broke into a crying fit about how selfish her father was for not wanting to drive two hours to put gas in her car. One pouty phone call later, her dad was on the highway to save the day as he always had. This continued for the entire month.

Bryce's frequent trysts served as a reminder of my lifelong lack of activity in this arena. Still a virgin who had never kissed a girl, I viewed college as my chance to wash away my reputation as an odd, awkward kid. Never mind the fact that the University of Kansas was about a half hour away from where I grew up and that the "odd, awkward" reputation came as a result of my actually odd and awkward personality at the time. This was college! Things would be totally different, and I'd seen enough movies to know that I'd be getting laid left and right as soon as I stepped into the dorms.

Under wildly different circumstances, I'd actually had a chance to lose my virginity a couple of years before this. At the time, my mother's boss was a former NFL player named Geoff. This was back when I believed I could become a pro wrestler if I just got into good enough shape. Geoff heard about this through my mother and offered to help me with my workout regimen since his enormous house featured a personal gym.

A few times a week, I'd head over to Geoff's to perform sloppy bench presses and almost pop blood vessels in my head while trying to do a single pull-up. To this day, I've never successfully performed a pull-up, and I'm convinced that any you've ever seen has been an optical illusion. This gigantic dude would do his best to give me tips here and there, then inevitably get frustrated and go back to doing curls with barbells that outweighed me.

Geoff's NFL days left him with more money than he knew what to do with. This led to him becoming a highly valued customer of an armada of Kansas City strippers. Whenever I'd go to his house, it wasn't unusual to see one or more strippers lounging around his living room. I guess I can't prove that they were all strippers, but they certainly fit the profile. If someone put Geoff's girls in a police line-up and asked you "Which one is the stripper?" you'd point to all of them.

Sometimes he'd bring one of the girls along as he gave me a ride home to my mom's. The stripper would usually sit in the back, looking bored and smacking gum. On one occasion, a busty blonde sat in the passenger seat while I sat in the back. Geoff pulled up to my mother's driveway and before I could say thanks and get out of the car, he stopped me.

"Hey Dan," Geoff said.

I glanced at the front seat to see him slowly running his hand up the blonde's thigh, sliding under her short skirt. As he darted his eyes back and forth from me to the girl's crotch, he was clearly trying to draw my attention to what was happening down there.

"This is my girl, Dan. Do you understand that?"

"Yes," I said, understanding exactly zero of what he was trying to imply. During this, the girl was staring blankly at me.

"You get that? This is my girl. What do you think of that?"

"Uh, that's cool! Welp—thanks, Geoff!" I blurted out as I scampered from the car and ran into the house.

To this day, I'm still not sure what he was going for with that. Did he think that I was checking her out and he had to assert that she was "his" or something? Was he bragging in a "hey, check out this stripper that I get to have sex with!" kind of way?

Based on what he asked my mother the next day, I think he was probably gauging how comfortable I was around women. Geoff asked her if I had ever had sex, and I'd have to assume that my mother responded with at least ten solid minutes of laughter.

Armed with the knowledge that I was a virgin, Geoff offered a proposal to my mother. He owned several businesses in the area, one of which included a limousine service. His plan was to combine his access to limousines with his network of strippers to create the most fucked-up Make-A-Wish loss of virginity story imaginable.

"I'll get one of our biggest limos and fill it with the wildest girls I know," Geoff told my mother. "I'll tell them that Dan's got cancer and he's only got a few months left. They'll fuck his brains out all night."

My mother isn't a maniac, so she rightfully responded with something along the lines of "What the fuck is the matter with you? I'm not letting you put my 16-year-old son in a limousine with a bunch of your coked-up stripper friends."

I was crushed when she relayed this story to me. For an incredibly sexually frustrated teenager, the laws of logic and safety took a major backseat to "I would like to touch a vagina as soon as humanly possible." Why wouldn't my mother just loosen up and let her underage son partake in a drug-fueled limousine orgy that came with an almost certain risk of contracting several STDs? What a prude.

Since I didn't lose my virginity to a bevy of strippers while speeding down a rural Kansas highway—and I'm really glad I didn't—I'd have to figure out how to make it happen the old-fashioned way: quietly existing in a college dorm and hoping that some girl would have pity sex with me. For a week or two during my summer program, it seemed like it might actually happen. Most of the participants were strangers to each other, so there was a revolving door of people coming in and out of almost every dorm suite in an effort to socialize.

One night, Bryce smuggled bottles of McCormick's vodka and a case of Keystone Light into our room. We were on a floor filled with 18-year-olds who had just left home for the first time, so this proved to be a highly effective way of getting most of them to hang out in one place. Lucky made sure that a variety of identical-sounding electronic tracks played from his absurdly expensive speakers. Bryce put a DVD of *Spy Game* on the TV for some reason.

With very little drinking experience under my belt, I felt uncomfortable in situations like this. This wasn't because I was uncomfortable with drinking. On the contrary, the idea of getting drunk sounded really fun to me. It was because I never knew what to *do*. I didn't like the music that was playing and I had no idea how to dance. I was too shy to approach a girl, even in the rare instance that one would be looking at me and smiling.

On this night, a girl named Rebecca made it easy for me. Among the various posters of rappers and Hawaiian Tropic models that Bryce and Lucky decorated the room with, there hung my large Led Zeppelin tapestry. I was also wearing the "Led Zeppelin 1977 Tour" t-shirt that every teenage classic rock fan had back then.

"Oh cool, you like Zeppelin?"

The voice came from my left and temporarily snapped me out of worrying about where to stand and what to do with my hands. A girl had actually approached me, and she was cute.

Maybe all those college movies were right! This is *how it works!*

Also, she liked Led Zeppelin? College seemed great.

Well, maybe she didn't like Zeppelin all that much considering that she responded with "'Stairway to Heaven,' 'Free Bird,' all of their stuff!" when I asked about her favorite songs. I absolutely wasn't going to let a lack of classic rock knowledge get in the way of my enthusiasm. She was cute and she was talking to me. That was basically third base for me back then.

We spent an hour or so in a basic "whoa, it's crazy that we're in college now!" chat before the crowd started to dissipate and head out of our room. Looking back, it didn't seem like Rebecca and I had an awful lot in common, and I don't remember the conversation being particularly noteworthy, but it seemed promising at the time.

Over the next couple of weeks, we occasionally hung out in the dorms. When Rebecca came to my room, I assumed that the best way to impress her was to show her a bunch of my stupid short films and constantly complain about how I had never had sex or even kissed a girl. If there's anything girls love, it's guys who have no idea what they're doing sexually and spend their time making a bunch of short films about homicidal gorillas and armless hitmen.

For some reason, she continued to hang out with me. She laughed at my movies—in a good way—and assured me that there was no reason to feel bad for being an 18-year-old virgin. As we talked about this in the lobby one night, she assured me that "most guys don't even have the slightest idea how to finger a girl the right way." I assumed this train of thought would conclude with "...and now I'll take you to my room to teach you." At least, that's what would have happened in those college movies that were starting to seem less accurate by the day.

No fingering occurred that night, but I started to feel more comfortable with Rebecca, and asked if she'd want to see a movie. She said yes, so we made plans to see *Minority Report* when it opened over the weekend.

I don't remember an awful lot about the movie. What I do remember is spending 145 minutes wondering if it would be alright to lean over and kiss her. My confidence wasn't high enough for such a bold move, so we silently watched the movie and headed back toward the dorm afterward.

As I started to pull into a prime parking spot right in front of the dorm, she stopped me.

"Hey, park a few rows back."

"Why? There's a spot right here."

"Trust me."

Any sane, horny teenager would have realized what was going on here, and sped to the most secluded spot in the lot. Instead, I was baffled.

"But there's a spot right here!" I said.

"Seriously, trust me. You'll like it."

"There couldn't *be* a better spot than this one! It's right in front of the door. I don't understand why we'd park further away than we need to."

"Dan, do you want your first kiss or not?"

"Oh..."

Feeling suddenly dumb and also horny, I drove to the back of the parking lot and kissed Rebecca. It wasn't a spectacular, passionate, tongue-filled kiss but I was thrilled nonetheless. We weren't "making out" as much as "pecking at each other for about 45 seconds with the slightest perceptible hint of tongue." It didn't matter. For the first time, something was happening in this area of my life.

It didn't take long for the reality of the situation to become evident. I thought that this would be a step toward my first relationship, but it fell apart within a week. She'd alternate between being thrilled to see me and completely ignoring me, sometimes several times a day. After we had lunch one afternoon, she told me that when we got back to the dorm, I was to enter the building long after her so that no one would see us together. Naturally, I asked her why.

"I don't want my boyfriend to see us together."

Oh! Okay!

I never found out who this boyfriend was. Similar stories involving Rebecca's erratic behavior became a recurring theme among most of the guys on our floor. To this day, I don't know if the boyfriend existed, or if it was her way to end things with one guy and move on to the next. It confused the hell out of me for the remainder of the month, but I moved on, happy to finally get the "first kiss" monkey off my back.

One month of living in college dorms didn't end all of my social woes, but it did make me more optimistic about the next four years of my life (it wound up being closer to six years, but I didn't know that yet). I finally had my first kiss, I loved the KU campus and the town of Lawrence, and I could definitely see myself getting into the whole "drinking alcohol and being social" thing.

Since I was still heavily into video production, I made the decision to major in Film Studies. I landed on Hashinger Hall as my living quarters for the year because of its reputation as the "creative" dorm. I assumed that the artsy dorm would be the easiest one to find collaborators and actors in for my short films and comedy sketches.

I wasn't completely wrong. During my time at Hashinger, it was rarely difficult to grab people who were enthusiastic to show off their acting chops or appear in a stupid comedy bit. What I didn't bank on was the sheer amount, and intensity, of eccentric personalities. Some of them seemed very legitimate while others felt like a college persona that was chosen and donned like a suit prior to moving in.

Students at Hashinger viewed themselves as true individuals, not like the business majors, communications students, and future frat and sorority members at Lewis and Templin Halls. Its reputation came with plenty of behavior that you'd expect from the artsy dorm. Entering the building meant avoiding eye contact with patchouli-drenched bongo players. Walking through any of the floors' hallways forced you to brave a gauntlet of incense smells barely masking the copious marijuana smoke that lingered beyond most doors. No matter where you got off the elevator, there was an 80 percent chance that you'd be met with the sounds of at least one acoustic guitar playing in the lobby.

Other dorms would host presentations for students that focused on how to navigate the crowded fields of their chosen professions. Hashinger hosted exhaustingly bad slam poetry nights with themes that rarely strayed from "Let me spit some truth about 9/11" and "I do not like President George W. Bush." That same stage also hosted a tribute to *The Rocky Horror Picture Show*, which summoned an entirely different (and far more genuinely despicable) element to the dorm. Hashinger was an easy target for the foot soldiers of Fred Phelps' Westboro Baptist Church (the "God Hates Fags" people) because it was a stone's throw from Topeka. On more than one night I had to make my way through a crowd of hyper-religious bigots before walking through a smelly hacky sack circle just to get into the building.

"I need to get the hell out of this place" was a frequent thought.

Once inside, I actually enjoyed a lot of my time there. I lived on the top floor and the variety of personalities (good and bad) ensured that no night was boring. I could dedicate a chapter to almost everyone I met on the eighth floor of Hashinger Hall, but I'll opt for a few highlights from this rogues' gallery:

- **Andy:** A short guy with a lazy eye who was almost always on some kind of psychedelic drug. He was kicked out of the dorm for doing mushrooms; putting a Chipotle burrito-sized piece of human feces in a Pringles can and delivering it to the sixth floor; and then lying on his stomach in the lobby and repeatedly slapping his own bare ass. All three of these things happened in the span of about five minutes.

- **Ben:** Smart but socially awkward, Ben was always wearing a *South Park* shirt and looking for new ways to get high. This usually involved homemade remedies because he never wanted to spend the money for actual drugs. I watched him eat several tablespoons of nutmeg, snort crushed Halls cough drops, swallow a mouthful of liquid air freshener, and eat full packets of Morning Glory flower seeds from Walmart. Sometimes these message board recipes worked, and other times he'd be pale as a ghost and vomiting all night.

- **Peter:** A stocky hippie with a robust beard and long, shaggy hair. In a dorm filled with pretentious stoners, his genuine demeanor was a welcome relief. He was always the first to answer any kind of silly challenge, whether it was chugging a gallon of milk or breaking into a snobby scholarship hall to steal economy-sized containers of nacho cheese from their fridge. His time at KU ended after cops caught him having late-night sex with his girlfriend in an apartment complex's swimming pool.

- **Evan:** If Peter was the happy-go-lucky stoner, Evan was the stoner who got a little too deep into the drug scene. I considered him a friend, but his behavior grew worse until he was kicked out of the dorms due to lack of attendance in class. On one occasion, he became angry at me because I refused to drive him to his first attempted heroin pickup after he found a "promising" Craigslist offer.

- **Eric:** Our floor's quietest resident, who surprised everyone by taking mushrooms and sailing a canoe onto Clinton Lake in the middle of the night. We found him in a panic, rambling about how his hair was penetrating into his brain and making him lose his mind. When we got back to the dorm, he immediately shaved his entire head.

- **Finch:** While most of the dorm residents wanted to come across as tortured artists, Finch was all about flaunting how much of a sensitive soul he was. On the first day I met him, he was wearing a backpack adorned with pins and patches of every social cause I'd ever heard of, and many that I hadn't. Within five sentences of introducing himself to me, he said "I want you to know that I won't even say the word 'retarded.'"

- **Pearboy:** A strict and sober Christian, Pearboy always seemed like he wound up in the wrong dorm by accident. We knew two things about him: He was shaped like a pear, and based on his foot positioning under the bathroom stalls, it seemed like he pooped while somehow facing the back of the toilet. This mystery was never solved.

My roommate was Adam, an oaf of a man who towered above everyone else on the floor. He had been one of my video production classmates in high school and had attempted to transform himself into a misunderstood artist in the three-month span before moving into Hashinger.

High School Adam and Hashinger Adam felt like wholly different entities. At the end of high school, Adam wore polo shirts and jeans, kept his hair closely cropped, and listened to a lot of Godsmack. When he walked into Hashinger in August, he had grown a curly mop of hair that he partially hid under sideways baseball caps. His polos were replaced by hoodies that he covered in his own hastily airbrushed graffiti, and he loved to talk about how it represented "Phase One" of his new graphic design company. Godsmack and the like were permanently ousted from his music collection because he was suddenly an expert in underground hip-hop.

In high school, Adam was just a kid who shared an interest in video production with me. He was neither friend nor enemy, so I didn't hold any ill will toward him. Hashinger Adam was another story. I couldn't stand his obviously put-on persona and his behavior frequently made me want to deck him. I probably would have if he didn't have nearly a foot and a hundred pounds on me.

My tipping point with Adam came on the night when I hoped to get Kiss #2. During one of the regular "let's all drink beer in a dorm room" nights that occurred prior to anyone being 21, I had a conversation with a girl named Lily. We had a fun chat that ended with her saying we should watch a movie together. Since Adam was planning on going to a house party the next night, I asked if she'd be interested in watching *Die Hard* in my room. She said yes and I was optimistic about where the night would lead.

I was still nowhere near comfortable when it came to talking with girls, so it was time to acquire some alcohol. For those of us in the dorm, that connection was Malik. He was a tall, skinny, dreadlocked artist who was a regular in bongo circles at the front of the dorm. Rumors around Hashinger had placed him at anywhere between 21 and 30 years old, and some said he had lived in the dorm for many years. Others claimed that he loved the ease with which he could hook up with freshman girls, which kept him hanging around. I always got a shifty vibe from the guy, but that didn't stop me from throwing in $20 whenever he was running around the floor taking orders for the liquor store on Friday nights.

Malik returned early in the evening with a case of Milwaukee's Best, and I slammed a few in preparation for my romantic dorm room *Die Hard* date. When Lily arrived, we each grabbed a beer and sat on the small loveseat that Adam and I had barely squeezed into our tiny living quarters. Halfway through the movie, I was feeling good about the rapport between Lily and me. We had been laughing and joking and generally enjoying each other's company when Adam suddenly burst into the room, clearly drunk and home early from the house party.

Instantly, I was disappointed that this doofus had returned before I expected. My disappointment quickly turned into anger when he stumbled over to the loveseat and sat down on my lap with all 275 pounds of him. I struggled to push him off me as he put his arm around Lily's shoulders.

"Hey, who's this?" Adam mumbled at Lily, who understandably recoiled and stood up.

I wiggled out from under him and stood next to Lily, trying to keep my cool despite this idiot thoroughly ruining what had been a nice night up until his entrance. He became belligerent and defensive when I explained that he was acting like an asshole, and he refused to move from the couch. Lily saw that Adam wasn't budging—literally or figuratively—and said we should finish the movie another night before retiring to her room.

With no desire to put up with Adam for another seven months, I put in an official request to change roommates. Across the hall were Tyler and Logan, two kids who seemed mismatched from day one. Tyler was from rural Kansas and he leaned pretty far into the artsy side of the spectrum. Logan was a shy chess fanatic who stayed on his computer while Christian rock music played in his headphones. I correctly assumed that Tyler and Adam would get along thanks to their interests and pretension, and that I'd coexist more peacefully with a religious shut-in than with the drunken yeti who had sat on me.

All parties agreed to the move. Adam and Tyler were certain that they'd become the Jobs and Wozniak of crappy airbrushed hoodies, and I was excited about the prospect of sharing a room with someone whom I wouldn't want to punch in the face every time I saw him.

Logan and I got along fine despite our lack of common interests. He wasn't much of a fan of video games, but he'd occasionally take the headphones off and join me for a round of *Super Smash Bros. Melee* or watch me play *Grand*

Theft Auto: Vice City. Although we weren't close friends, I saw Logan as a good guy who fell outside of the pretension of the rest of the dorm.

Few things besides class motivated Logan to get out of the dorm room, and weekly chess club meetings were one of them. This group of enthusiasts would meet up at the student union building every Wednesday night and they usually didn't return until late. One of these Wednesdays coincided with new roommates and best friends, Adam and Tyler, getting higher and drunker than usual and bursting into my room.

"Ooh, is Logan at his gay chess meeting?" Tyler said as they sat down on the lower bunk to watch me play video games.

Their attention was quickly diverted when they realized it was a prime opportunity to mess with Logan's stuff. One of my roommate's favorite items was a fold-up chess board that he frequently played with in our lobby. Adam and Tyler grabbed it and excitedly mulled over their options.

"Dude, let's just take a shit in it and fold it up!" Tyler said.

While I'm all for a good prank if it's harmless enough, or if it targets someone who deserves it, I wasn't about to let something that gross happen to my harmless roommate. I grabbed the chess board, called them dipshits, and told them to get out. Before leaving to go smoke some more, they opened my room's mini fridge and took Logan's 12-pack of Cherry Coke (he was rarely without a can of it in his hand). I tried unsuccessfully to grab it before they left, then accepted that a few stolen Cokes were less damaging than turning Logan's favorite chess board into a turd sandwich.

With the soundtrack of Adam and Tyler's giggling and yelling coming from across the hall, I eventually turned my

GameCube off and hopped into my top bunk for the night. I'm not sure how much later it was when Logan returned, but I awoke to the sight of him gingerly holding the top of his twelve-pack with two fingers and asking me if I knew why it was dripping wet.

It didn't take long to process what had happened between the time Adam and Tyler took the Cokes and when I woke up. I had foiled their turd plan, so their minds clearly went from number two to number one. All dorm rooms in Hashinger could be easily jimmied open with a credit card, so they must have snuck into the room after I fell asleep and placed the soda box back into the fridge.

"I'm pretty sure Adam and Tyler peed on those," I mumbled from bed. "Sorry, man."

Logan sighed and stared at the ground for a brief moment before he stormed outside with box still in hand. I heard the door to the lobby area open, followed by angry shrieking that I couldn't believe was coming from my shy roommate. Adam and Tyler laughed uproariously as Logan broke down in front of them, screaming while on the verge of tears.

The laughter abruptly cut off as soon as I heard loud thuds emanating from the lobby. I sat up and considered running out to check on things as I heard several more thuds, followed by more yelling. Before I could leave the room, Logan shoved the door open, threw himself on his bottom bunk, and covered his head with a pillow.

He was clearly in no mood to talk, so I got back into bed and went to sleep. My suspicions were confirmed the next morning when I saw Tyler at the cafeteria with a large bandage over the right side of his forehead. Logan had thrown most of a urine-soaked 12-pack across the lobby and at least one can had squarely hit its mark.

Tyler eased up on his antagonizing of Logan going forward but this didn't stop him from being generally insufferable to everyone else on the floor. His abrasive personality was magnified whenever he was drunk, which was a regular occurrence. One weeknight, I was playing some form of indoor wiffle ball with other people from the floor. When the elevator doors opened, an obviously drunk Tyler stumbled out and made his presence known.

I was up to bat and trying to ignore him when he sprinted up and hopped onto me like a booze-soaked backpack. His weight caused me to lose my balance and I stumbled back toward the window. We didn't plummet eight stories to our unbelievably stupid deaths—thankfully—but his back did put a large crack in the glass.

Despite not being hurt, Tyler became furious with me.

"What the fuck's wrong with you?" he yelled. "You could have killed me!"

I informed him to the best of my ability that he wouldn't have almost fallen out of a window if he hadn't jumped on top of me. My attempt at using logic was lost on him. He continued to be entirely unreasonable until a sober Adam—a rare appearance—came out and convinced him to call it a night.

Our wiffle ball game continued until I decided that it was time for me to hit the hay. I wanted to take a late-night shower before bed, so I returned to my room to get pajama pants, a shirt, and a towel on the way to the bathroom. Logan was still awake in bed and wordlessly facing the wall. This was a common occurrence in the weeks following the pee soda incident. Talking to him in this state was nearly impossible, so I grabbed my stuff and went down the hallway for my shower.

As in most dorms, our showers were inside a bathroom that was unlocked and accessible to the entire floor. Four stalls lined the wall opposite the toilets, with tile dividers between them and thin plastic curtains to block visibility. I tossed my clothes on the hook outside a stall and draped my towel over the curtain rod.

As you do in a shower, I tilted my head up and rubbed shampoo into my hair. With the water running, I couldn't hear Tyler enter the bathroom and sneak toward my stall. My eyes were closed when I felt an oppressively heavy substance plop down over my entire face.

Slowly bringing my hands down, I attempted to assess the situation. All I knew was that I was shampooing one second, and now there was a bunch of stuff on my face, I couldn't open my eyes, and a horrible smell overcame the scent of the shampoo. I stuck my head under the water and shook it around like a dog coming out of a swimming pool, which cleared my vision enough to see what had happened.

Much of the alfredo sauce had rinsed off my hands at this point and was slowly seeping into the drain. Numerous long fettuccini noodles were still hanging between my fingers. Months earlier, Tyler snuck a huge Tupperware container into our buffet-style cafeteria in an effort to stockpile cheap food. He worked his way through all of the cereal, oatmeal, and mints that he had amassed, but this vat of pasta had been languishing in his fridge even before he moved in with Adam earlier in the year. I'm just thankful that my temporary blindness kept me from seeing most of the mold covering the fettuccini.

Immediately after the slop hit my face, I heard Tyler cackle as he ran back down the hallway and slam the door to his room. I did my best to avoid breathing through my nose as I repeatedly shampooed my head and scrubbed noodles off my torso. Rinsed pasta sat on the stall's floor as old alfredo sauce amassed near the drain.

Once I was certain that my body was cleansed of any hint of sauce and my hair was fully noodle-free, I turned the water off and prepared to confront Tyler. Reaching for my towel, I found nothing. I knew what was coming next, but I still sighed as I pulled the curtain back to discover that my clothes were no longer on the hook.

My options were limited, so I tore the shower's curtain down and wrapped it around my waist. Getting Tyler back in some way was my first order of business, but I wanted to get some damn pants on first. Me and my curtain skirt scampered down the hallway to my dorm room where I swapped my makeshift outfit for a pair of pajama pants. Logan was awake but in one of his usual catatonic states, so he didn't raise an eyebrow during this process.

Without any real plan in mind, I went straight to Adam and Tyler's door. Options spun through my head like a slot machine as I loudly knocked. I wasn't going to punch Tyler in the face because I was more annoyed than angry. After all, it wouldn't be sporting to get mad about an admittedly good goof after spending most of my lifetime messing with people. Removed from my alfredo-induced haze, I had no idea what my plan was when it came time for the door to open.

Tyler made sure that I wouldn't have time to do anything at all. With me standing shirtless outside of his room, he quickly opened the door, sprayed a generous amount of glue onto my chest hair, and slammed the door shut before I could even react.

Fettuccini Alfredo was something that I was very familiar with, but this substance was new to me. I didn't even know that glue came in spray form, but I learned quickly when I swiped my hand across my chest in an attempt to wipe it off. Thick, adhesive glue had matted my chest hair to itself and my skin. My palm swipe only ensured that I'd pull numerous hairs out as I assessed the situation. Back to the shower I went. My head and face may have been sauce-free, but now I had a sticky chest and hair on my palm. I threw another set of clothes on the hooks outside the stall, half expecting them to be missing when I stepped out.

No amount of scrubbing remedied the sticky situation on my chest. My hand was easy enough to clean, but trying to get my chest free of glue led to nothing but redness and discomfort. I turned off the shower and felt like I didn't have many choices outside of getting rid of the hair entirely. While mulling over my options for getting revenge on Tyler, I grabbed a razor from my room and fully shaved the area. A couple of floormates had heard about the night's events, and were laughing in the hallway as I walked back to my room with a freshly shaved red chest.

Even in my annoyed state, I couldn't help but appreciate the absurdity of the situation. It was really funny, but I knew I'd have to get Tyler back and I'd rather even the score sooner rather than later. An elaborate comeback would take a lot of planning, so I threw on some pajama pants and headed across the hall with a simple offer.

Knock, knock.

"Tyler, open up."

"There's no fucking way," he laughed.

"I'm not gonna do anything right now. I've got a proposal for you."

Peering through the peephole, he saw that I wasn't holding a pie or a boxing glove attached to a spring or anything obviously meant for revenge. He cautiously opened the door, and I explained my position.

"All right, here's the deal. I promise you that I'm going to kick you in the balls and it's going to suck. It might be when I see you on campus, it might be when you're getting off an elevator here at the dorm, or it might be out of nowhere at the cafeteria. I can do it that way when you don't see it coming, or we can get evened up right here and you won't have to worry about it."

Tyler could tell that I wasn't kidding. He considered my offer for a moment before stepping into the hall, biting the knuckle of his index finger. His eyes closed as he widened his stance.

"Just fucking do it. If you're gonna do it, just do it."

Fearing that he'd back out if I let him think about it too long, I didn't miss a beat. I reared my leg back and gave the swiftest, most perfectly placed field goal kick I could have possibly mustered. My leg swung straight up between his legs and my shin almost certainly struck the dead center of his scrotum.

I expected a pained yelp to be the first reaction, but this was a great underestimation. His body lurched forward as he projectile-vomited over my right shoulder. A night's worth of beer and whiskey soared through the air and splattered on my own door behind me. I glanced back to survey the disgusting scene as he slumped to the ground.

At the same time, Tyler and I started laughing uproariously. My laughter was out of pure joy. The whole situation was amazing and my door getting sprayed with vomit—with me remaining clean!—was an entirely unintended side effect. Tyler had fallen to the floor in equal parts laughter and pain, and the sounds coming out of his mouth made him sound genuinely insane.

Several people on our floor stepped out of their rooms upon hearing this commotion late at night. They saw me on the floor in my pajama pants, shirtless and sporting a newly hairless chest. They saw Tyler lying on his side, alternating between laughs that sounded like cries and cries that sounded like laughter. Behind me laid a puddle of vomit. Some of them stuck around to hear the story. Most retreated into their rooms and went back to bed as if it were any other night in Hashinger Hall.

The Dumbest Kid in Gifted Class

All things point to me being a pretty damn dumb guy: elements of my personality, things I've done, and plenty of things I've said. However, documented evidence from the past contradicts that notion! Teachers started to notice that I was different at a very young age. During standardized tests in first and second grade, I always landed on the extreme high end of the national average. After two years of this, Principal Weber and my second grade teacher asked my parents to have a meeting. They explained that my test results indicated a high level of intelligence, and that they didn't have the resources for a gifted program at this small Catholic elementary school.

They proposed the idea of bussing me from Holy Trinity to public school one day a week to participate in an "Enhanced Learning" program. My parents had no issues with this, and Monday instantly became my favorite day of the week. Watching WWF *Monday Night Raw* was the thrilling conclusion to the night, but I spent the day doing fun activities that fascinated me.

The Enhanced Learning room was filled with a variety of gadgets, chess boards, tangram puzzles, and building materials. We rarely had a set schedule. Students were encouraged to gravitate toward whatever interested them the most. Logic puzzles were my favorite. I'd spend hours reading clues and filling in grids with X's and O's to determine which color and breed of dog belonged to Fernando instead of Ginger or whatever.

Puzzles and problems based on numbers, shapes, and process of elimination always grabbed my attention. Other students took an early shine to Science Olympiad or political debates. I preferred puzzles based on pure logic that could be objectively broken down until you were able to reach a definitive solution. From my perspective, I was getting shipped away from the boredom of nuns teaching me about Jesus. For one day a week, I felt like I had won a contest that allowed me to have fun and play games instead of sitting through dry lectures.

I felt awkward when I started going to EL, because I'd still be wearing my Holy Trinity uniform (bright red polo shirt, blue slacks) while the public school kids were free to wear their Ninja Turtles shirts or whatever they felt like. Wearing the uniform at Holy Trinity was something I welcomed, as I've never had any sense of what I'm supposed to wear. By having a set uniform each day, I never had to worry about it. We'd have "dress down days" a few times a year, and I always defaulted to my Razor Ramon "Oozing Machismo" shirt that consisted mostly of a massive image of Scott Hall's face as he chewed on a toothpick.

Everything was better in public school. The kids were nicer, I actually enjoyed the "learning" part, and the cafeteria was on a completely different level. Compared to the bare-bones lunchroom at Holy Trinity, the one in public school seemed like something from *The Jetsons*. Students' meal balances were tracked via a computer system that utilized passcodes instead of paper punch cards. I didn't have to get milk every day, as vending machines allowed me to guzzle all the Coke and Mountain Dew I could stand.

About this time, I discovered my all-time favorite school lunch: a soft pretzel, french fries, and a gigantic bowl of nacho cheese. These items were found at an à la carte window stationed across from the main lunch line. Conceivably, it was put into place in case students wanted to get an extra item to accompany their meals. I learned quickly that I could make the à la carte window my primary destination and ignore the main line entirely. This window sold cookies and ice cream and plenty more, but I rarely strayed from my own cheesy Holy Trinity.

These Monday lunches were a blessing, and I felt like the luckiest kid in the world when I eventually made the permanent move to public school. I could eat these three items for lunch *every day*, and no one could stop me. I kept up with this tradition until I graduated high school in 2002. Concerns from parents would lead to less junk food in the cafeteria by the time my sisters went to school there. I was thankful to have attended during a glorious era that was rife with rivers of nacho cheese.

Mondays were amazing, which always made it disheartening to head back to the oppressive seriousness of Holy Trinity. There was a tension in the air there that I didn't see during my brief glimpses of public school. The nuns demonstrated a special breed of intensity. It wasn't quite "bending students over a knee and taking a paddle to them" intense, but they'd occasionally pull out a ruler for a quick knuckle rap.

My third-grade teacher was Sister Mary Ann Blackburn. She appeared to be in some nebulous area between 50 and 90, and the lines on her face formed a permanent frown. Despite spending nine months under her watch, I can't remember her attempting to teach us a single thing that wasn't Jesus-centric or at least Jesus-adjacent. I'm pretty sure math and science were subjects that third-graders were supposed to learn, but they were clearly not the priority in Sister Mary Ann's classroom.

She was militant about keeping kids in line and eliminating any kind of horseplay. As we were practicing for the annual Christmas program, she was furious when I sang "Silent Night" as Bob Dylan. I expected my classmates to laugh at the impression, but it turns out that not a lot of eight-year-olds in 1992 had even heard of him.

I wasn't yet in my glory days of enthusiastically causing trouble. That didn't stop Sister Mary Ann from coming down on me. The worst example still confuses me to this day. Holy Trinity was battling a scourge of boys' bathroom-related mischief at one point in the year. I was unaware of whatever had been going on in there, but the staff was apparently on high alert for the troublemakers.

After peeing into the urinal and washing my hands in a wholly unremarkable manner, I turned to see Sister Mary Ann standing in the boys' bathroom. She was holding her right hand up as if waiting for a high-five, and pointing at it with the other.

"I caught you red-handed."

This confused me for a couple of reasons. First, I wasn't doing anything wrong. Secondly, I had never heard the term "red-handed" before, and her hand was not in any way red.

She grabbed me by the wrist and yanked me out of the restroom. I asked her what I had done, but not in the belligerent, combative way that you see from a lot of guilty people. Rather, I was genuinely baffled as to why a nun was pulling me down the hall to the principal's office. My head was whirring through a variety of possible offenses, and I was coming up blank. I had woken up, put on my uniform, attended class, peed, and washed my hands. That was the extent of my day thus far, and I was about to face the principal for some unknown reason.

We entered Principal Weber's office and Sister Mary Ann acted like she captured Jesse James in the middle of a bank robbery.

"I got him," she said. "Caught him red-handed."

There was that weird phrase again. Principal Weber motioned for me to sit in front of his desk.

"So you think it's funny to horse around in the bathroom?" he asked.

"No... I just peed and washed my hands and then Sister Mary Ann yelled at me."

After talking for a bit, I learned the details of the heinous crimes that were plaguing the boys' bathrooms of Holy Trinity. It was just some kid who was jumping up over the stalls and throwing wet paper towels down on the heads of pooping children.

This made things even more confusing. Not only had I not been "caught red-handed," but *no one in the bathroom* was doing that when Sister Mary Ann made her dramatic capture. It's not like she witnessed someone mid-throw, then somehow got confused and thought I was the dreaded Paper Towel Bandit. She walked in on me washing my hands, and that was that.

"I know that you like going to EL class, don't you?" Principal Weber asked.

"Yes, it's great."

He stood up, preparing to drive home a final point for me to remember.

"I'm telling you right now, Danny: if we catch you doing this again...I'm *pulling the plug!*"

With those last three words, he made a way-too-dramatic "pulling the plug" motion with his arm.

"*PULLING THE PLUG!*"

He made the motion again. I stopped being confused by the whole situation for a moment, and tried to hold back laughter at this sweaty-faced German man standing up and yelling about plugs while repeatedly jerking his arm in case I didn't understand what he was saying. I held out for a second, but a small laugh escaped my lips as he glared at me.

"Do you think this is funny?" he asked.

"No, Principal Weber. I'm sorry."

I laughed again.

"He'll pull the plug, Danny!" Sister Mary Ann chimed in behind me.

"Yes, I understand. I don't think that's funny."

I promised the two of them that I'd never again do the thing in the bathroom that I had never done in my life, and walked out of Principal Weber's office. No plugs were ever pulled.

Thankfully, my experience in gifted class continued throughout elementary school, junior high, and high school even after I left Holy Trinity. With each passing year, it became more evident that I wasn't of the same ilk as the other students in gifted class. They all studied vigorously and grades were of the utmost importance to them. I opted to stay the course with the things I had always cared about—basically, video games and professional wrestling.

In sixth grade, I was the only student in gifted class who wasn't allowed to go to a "Treasures of the Czars" exhibit that came through town. Teachers had warned me about my mediocre grades and general apathy toward academics before, and they thought they'd reinforce their concern by forcing me to stay behind. My studious classmates walked around and stared at Fabergé eggs as I stayed back and ignored social studies lectures with the standard class.

THE DUMBEST KID IN GIFTED CLASS

Once I moved on to junior high, the structure and focus of gifted class—known as "Quest" in the Olathe School District—became even more open-ended. Want to learn about video editing? Sure, here's the equipment. Wanna have a structured debate with a fellow student about *Crash Bandicoot* versus *Super Mario 64*? No problem. Just be sure to bring your incredibly ill-informed ideas about processing power and how artificial intelligence works.

With each year that passed, it became more and more clear that I was the dumbest kid in Quest. These other students had a road map for their academic goals and eventual careers. They knew which college they wanted to go to, how to get a scholarship, what their major would be, and how they'd maintain a 4.0 GPA throughout.

During one roundtable discussion with the entire class, our teacher, Mrs. Hill, asked us to state which college we wanted to go to and why. Each student gave an impassioned argument for their school of choice. They'd be going to the University of Whatever because it ran in their family, because its charitable giving programs led the nation, or because they knew they'd excel in its football program while simultaneously earning a master's degree.

As the circle came around to me, I realized that I didn't know a single thing about any of these colleges. I had heard of the University of Kansas and Kansas State since they were local, and I had heard Harvard and Yale jokes on *The Simpsons*, but I knew zero details about any of them. When Mrs. Hill came around to me, I gave an answer that I genuinely meant.

"I want to go to DeVry."

Everyone in the class laughed.

"That's very funny, Dan," Mrs. Hill said. "What's your real choice of school?"

"Uh, DeVry?" I repeated.

The class realized that I was serious, and the laughter awkwardly subsided as Mrs. Hill moved on to the next student. I had no idea why my choice was met with unanimous laughter. All I knew was that I had seen commercials for DeVry on a regular basis, and it looked like the school had some kind of focus on technology. I wanted to work in the video game industry, so I figured that this was as good a choice as any.

To this day, I'm still not really sure what DeVry is and why that was so funny. At no point did I ever research any colleges whatsoever. I have to assume that DeVry is some kind of piddly online program or scam, and that's why it sounded like a joke in a class of kids with Ivy League aspirations. I also have zero idea as to what an Ivy League school is—I just know that the richest/smartest kids in my class always talked about going to one.

It was clear that my priorities were vastly different from everyone else's in Quest. I didn't take the laughter at my DeVry answer as a kick in the ass to look into colleges because I still didn't care (nor would I ever). It didn't interest me, and I had no intention of forcing myself to learn about colleges just because that's what everyone else was doing.

Moving into high school, the chasm between me and the other students only grew. Plenty of resources were available to us when it came to college prep. Representatives from universities visited Olathe East to talk to prospective students, campus tours were offered, and special classes were available that counted toward college credit. I always heard my classmates talking about this stuff, but I would immediately lose interest and tune out. I had zero plan for college and just assumed that everything would work out fine. College loans were a thing, right? I'd just go to the closest school, take out a ton of loans, and then get a job afterward and pay them off. I didn't see why the process warranted any further thought.

While everyone else was applying for schools and scholarships, I funneled all of my energy into learning more about professional wrestling. Later years would see me angling my independent study selections toward video production, but I spent a couple of years focused on the pro wrestling industry in Quest class.

"Studying" is perhaps too strong a word for what I did early on. It mostly consisted of me spending my Quest hour browsing sites with names like WrestleZone and Rajah's WWF News & Rumors. It didn't take long to realize that I had no real plan as to how I'd spend my time. We were encouraged to write papers or make presentations based on our independent study choice, but this was far from enforced.

Sitting around and reading wrestling websites started to feel like a waste of time if I didn't have some kind of goal. My early attempts at remedying this sense of aimlessness didn't help matters. I maintained a spiral notebook where I listed every single wrestling move I could identify. If I took a bathroom break during class and there was no one else in the hallway, I'd take a drink from the drinking fountain and try to spit it into the air like Triple H. Even more embarrassingly, I recorded a video with the intention of giving it to Vince McMahon—chairman and CEO of the WWE—when I grew up. In it, I spoke earnestly to the camera about how "even though I'm only fifteen years old, I already know so much about the wrestling industry." I proceeded to list a bunch of "insider" terms that were already well-known to any wrestling fan with an internet connection.

These were before the days when I could spend the time going down YouTube rabbit holes, so my options were limited. I'd realize a new avenue thanks to a great coincidence during a shift at the movie theater. My early years at AMC were filled with box office, usher, and concession shifts. I was bumped up to guest services a couple of years into my tenure. This was the front desk area, and I'd be the guy manning the station in case customers needed help with anything.

During these shifts, my only company would be whoever was tasked with tearing ticket stubs. This was frequently a girl from my high school named Gabby. We didn't have much in common, and I probably wouldn't have known even if we did because I was a teenager and she was a girl.

My buddy Chris would always come up to the desk when he had downtime during his usher shifts. One evening, we started chatting about whether our theater would be featuring *Beyond the Mat*, a wrestling documentary set for release later that year.

"You guys like pro wrestling?" Gabby asked.

She clearly hadn't overheard any previous conversation between Chris and me, because we were always talking about wrestling. We told her that yes, we loved wrestling.

"Cool," she said. "I don't watch it, but my grandpa used to be a big deal."

My head spun, wondering who he could possibly be. I assumed he had to be some low-rent nobody who talked up his days of being a famous wrestler like a former high school quarterback who can't stop talking about the glory days.

"Who is he?" I asked.

"Harley Race."

WHAT.

The Harley Race. The eight-time NWA World Heavyweight Champion. The man who went to war time after time with "The American Dream" Dusty Rhodes and "Nature Boy" Ric Flair. The man who spilled blood and sweat across the nation, earning a reputation as one of the most legitimate "tough guys" in the professional wrestling industry.

I couldn't believe it, but I had no reason to doubt her. Why would Gabby lie about this if she had no interest in wrestling? She told me that Harley was running his own small promotion out of Eldon, Missouri. It was a rural town of less than 5,000 people, and it was about two-and-a-half hours east of where we were currently standing.

"You should go to one of the shows!" she said. "I'll tell him you're coming and you can meet him if you want to."

If I wanted to? I had never met a professional wrestler in my life, and I had desperately wanted to pick the brain of one for years. Not only was I getting the opportunity to meet a wrestler, I'd be meeting a genuine legend who had worked in the business for over three decades. His fame came primarily from his time as an active competitor, but he also had years of experience as a manager and promoter. If I had my choice of picking anyone's brain about the business, it'd be hard to find someone more ideal than Harley Race.

I told Gabby that I'd be going to the very next show in Eldon. Since I refused to drive on the highway until my mid-20s, I made sure Chris was willing to drive. A couple of weeks later, we hopped in his car and made the drive through the deeply depressing area of the country that is rural Missouri.

We arrived in Eldon, and it was everything I could have hoped for. Harley greeted me at the community center with the firmest handshake I'd ever felt. He didn't have much time to talk before the show, but he assured me that we'd get a chance later. Chris and I sat in the bleachers during the show, and I kept pulling out my spiral notebook to jot down more questions that I wanted to ask Harley.

Once the main event concluded, I approached Harley and asked if he had some time to chat. He asked if I wanted to hop in the ring for a photo op with him first. We entered the ring, snapped a picture, and then sat down in the bleachers to talk at length about professional wrestling. Various fans stuck around after the show and would approach him for autographs and pictures, but they eventually filtered out until it was just Harley, Chris, me, and the crew members and wrestlers who were tearing down the ring.

For the better part of an hour, I asked Harley every question I could think of about professional wrestling. He was soft-spoken and somewhat intimidating, but he never seemed annoyed by the questions. I got the sense that even after all of those years, he still loved chatting about the business. When it was time to go, he gave me his phone number and told me to call if I ever had more questions.

Chris and I were ecstatic during our drive back to Kansas. We had just sat down with an icon who was more than generous with his time and knowledge. When I got back to school, I would have bragged to everyone about my amazing weekend if I had felt like anyone would have known about Harley's legacy. My classmates were familiar with Stone Cold Steve Austin, The Rock, and D-Generation X, but few of them had wrestling knowledge that predated the current "Attitude Era" boom period.

I was still thinking about my weekend when I arrived at my Quest hour after lunch. As I always did, I sat down at a computer station and started clicking around to wrestling news sites and message boards. After a couple of minutes, I realized something. I had been wanting to find a real focus for my independent study class, and now I had the phone number for an amazing resource.

I called Harley and told him that I wanted to do a more formal interview for a school project. He agreed, and told me to get some questions together and call him on Sunday. It seemed to take forever, but Sunday eventually rolled around and I was ready for the call. My stepfather's office phone had a speaker on it, so I placed it on the ground next to my boombox, which had a built-in microphone. I pressed record, called Harley, and once again picked his brain about a variety of wrestling topics. That week, I presented my Quest teacher with a transcription and analysis of my interview with Harley Race.

My teacher seemed impressed with my newfound focus and said she'd love to see more of it coming from me. I suddenly realized that asking "Can I speak to you for a school project?" would sound a lot better than "HEY I LIKE WRESTLING, CAN I TALK TO YOU?" if I wanted to continue to learn about the business from those within it.

With a legitimate reason to request interviews, I started scanning the internet for any wrestling-based appearances around the Kansas City area. Wrestling legend Mick Foley was supposedly retired from the business and focusing on his new career as a *New York Times* best-selling author. As a result, he was scheduled for a book signing during a car show downtown. Interviewing him would be a dream, but there were no obvious contact listings for him online. Instead, I contacted the convention center that would be hosting the car show. They put me in touch with the guy who handled press requests for the show, and in turn, he got me in touch with Foley's agent. I explained that I was a high school student who wanted to speak to Foley for a class project, and the agent told me that he'd ask Foley about it. A few days later, I was told that Foley had given the thumbs-up—I'd have a half-hour to speak with him after the book signing.

I was blown away by how easy this all was. By calling a few people and saying the right things, I was granted a half-hour chat with one of my favorite wrestlers. People waited in line for hours just to get a book signed by the guy, but I'd be getting a full sit-down interview just because I asked. I couldn't help but be reminded of the advice that my AMC manager had given me just a year or two earlier: "The squeaky wheel gets the grease."

When the day of the car show arrived, I stuck around the stage while Foley worked his way through the winding line of autograph seekers. I grabbed anyone who seemed to be there in an official capacity, telling them that I had an interview scheduled with Foley after the signing. After annoying several security guys who had no idea what I was talking about, I eventually found the agent that I had spoken with on the phone, and he confirmed that the interview was good to go.

My breathing became rapid and my heart almost beat through my chest when the signing ended. I needed to keep my cool while introducing myself to Foley and maintain calm for at least thirty minutes past that. As he stood up from behind the signing table and started walking toward me and his agent, I took a deep breath and tried my best to look like I wasn't nervous.

"Hey Mick," the agent said. "This is Dan. He's the student that's gonna interview you."

Foley shook my trembling hand and said "Nice to meet you." We headed to an administrative room in the convention center and sat down on the same style of metal folding chair that had slammed into his skull on hundreds of occasions. My nerves were at their peak as the interview began, but my anxiety quickly subsided as Foley proved tremendously easy to talk to. At one point, I congratulated him on the recent birth of his third child. He thanked me and said that he didn't want to talk about that much, because he preferred to keep his family life private. He must've had a change of heart between that interview and 2016, since he and his entire family later starred in a reality show.

Many years later, Foley made another transition from author to stand-up comedian. One of his shows in 2012 coincided with WWE's SummerSlam event in Los Angeles. I was downstairs at the Hollywood Improv before the show, and figured I should probably pee before Foley took the stage. Searching around the lower level of the club didn't yield any obvious restrooms, so I took the stairs up and entered a doorway. In that room was one person. It was Mick Foley, sitting on a couch and looking over his notes for the night.

"Oh!" I said. "I was trying to find the restroom, and I accidentally found Mick Foley."

He looked up and laughed. I could tell he was worried that I was a fan who was about to pester him before he went onstage. Before I excused myself, I had to say one thing.

"I know you're getting ready, so I won't bug you long. I just wanted to say that when I was 17 years old, you were nice enough to give me a half-hour of your time for a school project. That meant a lot to me and I just wanted to thank you."

"I did?" he asked. "Boy, I must have been a lot nicer back then. Now I'm just gonna yell at you to get the hell out of my green room!"

His mock anger turned to a smile as he waved goodbye and told me to enjoy the show.

THE DUMBEST KID IN GIFTED CLASS

My idea of utilizing the "school project" excuse instantly netted me an interview with one of the most famous wrestlers of all time. The ball kept rolling when I learned that Jerry "The King" Lawler would be signing autographs at a baseball card convention in Overland Park, Kansas. I used the same technique I did with Foley to secure a similar interview.

This one was huge for me on two levels. One was as a wrestling fan, and another was due to my fascination with Andy Kaufman. Lawler engaged in a brilliant feud with Kaufman that involved an infamous confrontation on *Late Night with David Letterman* in 1982. Not only was I able to ask Lawler a ton of questions about his wrestling history, I also heard firsthand about the process of planning an elaborate hoax with a comedy icon. I kept asking question after question long after my allotted thirty minutes were up, prompting his then-wife Stacy "The Kat" Carter (a former WWE performer) to yell at him for taking too long. He told her to be patient, she stormed off, and we kept the conversation going.

Like I did with Foley, I reminded Lawler of this years later. We were both at a bar in Dallas during WrestleMania weekend in 2016, and I approached him to say thanks for being so kind to the teenage version of me. When I showed him a picture of us from the interview on my phone, he grabbed it, showed it to his new fiancée, and said "Look—I wasn't as fat back then!"

Not every idea or opportunity I had yielded positive results. My family and I were eating at a Japanese steakhouse one evening when my ears perked up at the mention of professional wrestling. At the table next to ours was a large guy who was speaking to the rest of his table. I couldn't make out the whole conversation, but I picked up tidbits like "back when I was in the ring" and "Foley."

Halfway through dinner, I got up and approached the guy.

"I'm sorry, but were you saying that you used to be a wrestler?" I asked.

"I did! Got hurt and took a bunch of time off, but I'm looking to get back in there."

It didn't take long to realize that the rest of the table seemed relieved that I had taken the conversational burden off of them. This was one of those hibachi places where they'd seat you with strangers, and I got the feeling that he was boring them with his wrestling talk.

I didn't want to talk his ear off for the entire dinner, but I did get a few key pieces of information in the short time I spoke with him. He had been in a tag team with Mick Foley at some point, and he had a plan to get to the WWF. It involved sending a promo video to Vince McMahon, so I mentioned that I had experience with video production work. He gave me his number and said that we should set up a time to discuss some ideas.

That weekend, I met up with him at Borders. He brought pictures of himself and Foley in the ring, assuaging my fears about him being completely full of shit. That said, I've tried in recent years to track down information about this guy, and I haven't found any regular tag team partners of Foley's who fit this guy's description. My guess is that he was in one or two independent matches alongside Foley before he got hurt and Foley went on to bigger things.

I was willing to go along for the ride, even though I was already thinking that this guy's grand plans to get hired by the WWF seemed ambitious, based on his age and look. As I took notes and disingenuously nodded, he listed off cheesy character names and told me about all of the green-screen fire effects he wanted in his video. When I asked him if he had any kind of highlight reel of his signature moves so that we could demonstrate some of his in-ring ability, he said that he had nothing of the sort. He was dead-set on his vision, and my suggestions and ideas bounced right off him.

We had a green screen at my high school, so I received permission for him to come in over the weekend. I had arrived at 1:30 p.m. to prepare the studio for our planned 2 p.m. shoot, and soon realized that he might be flaking on me. Two o'clock passed, then another fifteen minutes, then another and another after that. I tried to call him several times from my teacher's phone, and was met each time by an answering machine. Eventually, I gave up on the idea and left.

Later that night, I received a call at home. It was the wrestler guy, breathlessly apologizing and explaining why he didn't show up. Earlier in the day, he had made a run to the gas station after picking up his son from a friend's place. For some unexplained reason, Wrestler Guy tasked his young son with filling up his car. This somehow ended with Son of Wrestler Guy screwing up and filling his arm cast with gasoline (?) and having to go to the emergency room.

He said we'd figure out another day to shoot the video, but I decided that the "opportunity" to be a part of a delusional guy's doomed attempt at wrestling stardom wasn't worth pursuing.

I now had experience meeting with former wrestlers who never made it (Wrestler Guy) and internationally known superstars (Harley, Lawler, and Foley). To learn more, I wanted to meet with wrestling personalities who fell somewhere in between.

Kansas City was a hotbed of wrestling in the territory days, but its local prevalence had fallen off almost completely before I was old enough to appreciate it. If independent wrestling had been around during my teenage years, I'd have been the obnoxious fan in the front row who acted like he knew everything about the business. After years of fruitlessly searching newspapers and the internet for signs of wrestling in the area, I eventually found a Midwest-based upstart in the early 2000s.

Its website looked like every wrestling promotion's website from that era (and some from this era, frankly). A lot of text was on fire, many buttons were spinning, the roster page was almost entirely inaccurate, and a counter at the bottom measured how many hundreds of people had visited the page. Most importantly, the contact information was an AOL e-mail address. This meant that I could potentially have a direct instant message conversation with whoever was answering their e-mail. I plugged the screen name into my AIM account, and they almost instantly appeared as online.

"Who is this?" the person on the other end of the window asked.

"My name is Dan Ryckert," I said under a screen name that was almost certainly along the lines of HomerJamesBond007316. "I'm a really big wrestling fan from the KC area, and I've been hoping to contact an independent promotion. I want to learn as much as I can about the industry. If possible, I'd like to interview some of your wrestlers for a school project. Your website says you have a show coming up in a couple of weeks. I'd be interested in doing it there if at all possible."

The man on the other end of the window introduced himself as Sam. He said that not only was he the owner and head creative force of this promotion, but he was also one of its most popular wrestlers—and the direct cousin of WWF legend Shawn Michaels. I probably would have been more skeptical of this claim if I'd been a little bit older. Sam's website made it clear that he idolized Michaels in numerous ways. He called himself "Kid Heartbreak"—Michaels was known as the "Heartbreak Kid"—and bragged about appearing in *Playgirl* just like Michaels. As our conversation progressed, he even passed along some supposedly exclusive insider info.

"My cousin Shawn called me yesterday," Sam said. "He's announcing a big return on Monday. This is just between us, OK?"

Michaels had been retired for years at this point, and a potential return had always been a hot topic of conversation on message boards. When Monday came around, Michaels was nowhere to be seen on *Raw*. Somehow, I still believed Sam's other claims.

We'd chat off and on in the days leading up to the event, and I was always surprised by Sam's willingness to talk wrestling with some random teenager. He agreed to let me interview the wrestlers, even telling me that I could spend the entire show backstage if I wanted. Boy, what a nice guy!

When I told my mother about this opportunity, she wanted me to go with someone she trusted. She worked at Macaroni Grill at the time, and a local cop would walk the waitresses to their cars after late shifts.

Cop Friend was my ride to the event. Once he realized it was at a town festival that featured food stands and other things to do besides watch professional wrestling, he promptly disappeared. He told me to run along backstage, and said we'd meet up after the wrestling was over.

This was an outdoor festival, so "backstage" translated to "over by those big trees." A small curtain was erected to provide some level of separation between the wrestlers and the couple of dozen festival attendees who actually sat down around the ring. A lot of tough-looking dudes that I didn't recognize were back there, and the only one who knew I was supposed to be there was Sam. Several wrestlers looked at me with obvious "who the fuck are you?" expressions. Eventually, I introduced myself to one of the guys and explained why I was there.

"Sam's not here yet," he said. "I'm Mark Stryder."

Kansas City may not have been a big wrestling town anymore, but Mark Stryder—not his real fake name—was one of the most experienced active wrestlers in the area, despite being in his late twenties. He had been trained by the legendary Dory Funk Jr., and had worked hundreds of matches by the time I met him.

Since Sam wasn't around and there was still time before the show, I asked Stryder if I could interview him for my class. He agreed, and we chatted for close to an hour. As with Foley and Harley, I was surprised by how soft-spoken and calm this guy was (Lawler was the exception, as his real-life personality didn't seem too far from his television persona). Stryder answered all my questions thoughtfully, without ever rolling his eyes at this wrestling-obsessed kid who had just wandered backstage.

At one point, I gestured to the bamboo rod sitting by Stryder's duffel bag. It was a kendo stick, a commonly used weapon in professional wrestling.

"How much do the kendo stick shots hurt?" I asked.

He grabbed it and asked if I wanted an example. I said sure, and he reconfirmed that I was all right with taking a quick hit. Nodding, I closed my eyes and told him to go for it. A stiff whack came down on top of my head, almost knocking me out of my chair. I'm sure that he put forth a small approximation of the force he'd have given in the ring, but it was an eye-opener nonetheless.

By fifteen minutes before showtime, the other wrestlers were loudly wondering where the hell Sam was. After all, he was supposed to be the "creative force" of the operation. Suddenly, he ran through the curtain and threw a duffel bag on the ground. Breathlessly, Sam started pointing around the "locker room"—an unremarkable grassy area—and telling the wrestlers who would be winning each match and how long the matches were scheduled to last. I didn't want to butt in, because the wrestlers were obviously frustrated and Sam seemed like he was in no mood for an actual conversation. Instead, I sat on a tree stump by the side of the curtain and watched the matches.

At no point did Sam seem to calm down. He was either arguing with a wrestler about a planned match result, talking on his cell phone, or putting on his gear for his main-event match (naturally, he booked himself in the main event). Before that match arrived, a scary spot happened in the ring. A wrestler named Icepick was supposed to take a German suplex, but he jumped with a bit too much force and landed on top of his head. He managed to finish the match, but he was clearly rattled when he came back through the curtain.

"Somebody get a bag of ice," Stryder said to no one in particular.

I glanced around to look for a cooler, finding nothing but duffel bags. No one else seemed to be on the case, so I sprinted to one of the concession stands at the festival and explained the situation. They gave me a plastic bag filled with ice, which I ran backstage to give to Stryder. Sam acknowledged me for the first time, giving a quick "thanks" before heading out for his match.

After the match, the mood was considerably lighter backstage, and I felt comfortable approaching Sam.

"Hey Sam, I'm Dan. I'm the kid from AOL that's putting together the school project."

"Oh right, cool," he said. "Did any of the guys help you out?"

I told him that Stryder had given me more than enough for a report and that I appreciated the opportunity to be backstage.

"No problem," Sam said. "Tell you what, let's keep in touch. I might have something in mind for you if you're interested."

He didn't elaborate, but I told him that I'd love to help out behind the scenes in some capacity. I had once leaned over a WWF barricade and repeatedly screamed "I'm going to work for you!" into a confused Vince McMahon's face. This seemed like a more reliable way to get some work in the wrestling industry.

Sam and I continued to chat on AIM, but the conversations became increasingly odd. He went on angry rants about their current ring announcer, whom he called "old" and a "dumb piece of shit." According to him, wrestling fans would prefer someone young as a ring announcer, not "some old guy in a cheap suit."

"Think you could pull off being a ring announcer?" he asked.

"Absolutely," I said. It was an opportunity to get involved, so I enthusiastically agreed even though the idea made me nervous.

"How bad do you want to be a part of this industry?"

"It's something I've wanted to be a part of for my entire life. It'd be a dream."

"Yeah, but how bad? What would you be willing to do if it meant you'd get a chance to get into wrestling?"

My teenage naiveté wasn't strong enough for me to ignore how creepy Sam's phrasing was. It sure sounded like the words of a child molester, even if I was 16 and probably off the radar of most child molesters.

"I'd be willing to work hard and improve at what I do," I responded.

It probably wasn't the answer he was looking for, but he continued with the ring announcer talk.

"All right. Tell you what, why don't you come to my apartment this weekend, and I'll show you some tape and give you some tips. We'll give you a shot at our next show."

I agreed, with a heaping of increased skepticism. This guy had come off as erratic and weird while he was backstage at the first show, and this AIM conversation struck me as more than a little odd. Going to this dude's apartment by myself wasn't in the cards.

I went to my father and requested that he join me. Under any normal circumstance, he'd have absolutely nothing to do with anything wrestling-adjacent. Once I explained the situation to him, however, I think his fatherly instincts of "don't let my son get raped by a shady wrestling promoter" kicked in. He agreed to accompany me, as did my friend Chris.

That Saturday, we followed our printed MapQuest directions to Sam's apartment in a shady neighborhood near Arrowhead Stadium. None of us were tough guys by any stretch of the imagination, but we figured that three of us would be enough to handle the situation in case Sam got weird.

I knocked on Sam's door five minutes before we had agreed to meet. Sounds of shuffling briefly came from inside the apartment. No one came to the door, so I knocked again. More shuffling, then more silence. Chris, my father, and I looked at each other, all wondering what the hell was going on.

One more knock seemed to do the trick, triggering even more random noises followed by the sound of a lock unlatching. Suddenly, the door was yanked open several inches before the chain lock caught it. A shirtless, wild-eyed Sam stared out from behind the opening.

"What do you want?" he asked.

"Hey Sam," I said.

"Hey what? What do you need?"

"You told me to be here today to talk about the ring announcer thing."

"God dammit. Hang on."

The door shut, and Sam disappeared for a minute before unlatching the door and opening it all the way. He was now wearing a shirt.

"You can't just do that," he said.

"Do what?"

"You can't just show up and surprise me like that."

I explained once again that I was simply arriving at our previously agreed-upon time, and that I didn't intend on surprising him at all. He eventually calmed down and invited the rest of us to take a seat. We sat down and glanced around at his posters of "funny sex positions," wizards, and mushrooms—all of which made his apartment look like a Spencer's Gifts.

Not only did Sam forget about our scheduled visit, but he also seemed to forget about what it was supposed to be about in the first place. Instead of talking about the ring announcer opportunity, he treated the meeting like he was trying to get us to invest in his wrestling promotion. Fifteen minutes into a rambling pitch, Sam grabbed a tape and threw it into his VCR.

"I wanna show you how much pull I've got in this business. Take a look at who came to one of our shows."

A shaky video appeared on his television showing a line-up of wrestlers selling t-shirts and eight-by-ten photographs. In the middle was a tall guy with a blond ponytail and sunglasses. I instantly recognized him as Billy Gunn, a WWF veteran who was currently on hiatus due to injury. Even though he had never been a bona fide main event star, I was impressed to see that Sam had brought such a recognizable name to one of his shows (more than 15 years later, I would become a manager on the independent circuit and interfere in one of Gunn's matches).

This was all well and good, but it had nothing to do with the reason I was there. I eventually interrupted Sam's rambling and asked about the ring announcer gig.

"Oh right," he said. "Yeah, you wanna do that at the next show?"

"Yes, I already said that. You said you wanted to discuss it and give me some tips this weekend."

"Don't worry about it, it's easy. Just show up a little early for the next show and we'll go over everything."

We obviously weren't going to get anything of substance from this guy while he was in whatever state he was currently in, so we thanked him for his time and got out of there. I eventually did announce a few shows for him, always accompanied by friends or family. These shows were largely uneventful, but the thrill of being involved in any capacity was great.

A couple of months into my time with Sam's promotion, my mother attempted to drive me to a show that was over an hour away, during a torrential downpour. It was one of the worst Midwestern storms I can remember, with water coming down in sheets on her windshield. Vehicles were pulled over all along the highway, and it was impossible to see more than a couple of feet in front of the car. Eventually, she had to throw in the towel.

"I know this means a lot to you," she said. "But this just isn't safe. I need to turn around."

If things were going great, I might have been more upset about this. A no-show was surely going to upset Sam, but his personality had made me uneasy from the start. Perhaps it was for the best that we turned around. I never attended or worked any of Sam's shows again.

My first foray into the world of independent wrestling had been less than ideal, so I set my sights back on the big leagues. I bought tickets to a taping of *WWF SmackDown* at Kemper Arena and was determined to somehow weasel my way behind the scenes.

I didn't think it was possible to sneak my way backstage using pure stealth, but maybe I'd be able to deceive a security guard or two and wind up behind the curtain. My brilliant plan involved printing up fake press passes. There were plenty of wrestling news sites out there, and I for some reason assumed they were always allowed special access behind the scenes. Now that I've worked in the media for twelve years, I realize how insane and poorly conceived this plan was.

"Rajah's WWF News & Rumors" was too wordy, so I imported a WrestleZone logo into my photo editing software. I included my name, some form of "editor" as my title, and printed the pass. One trip to Kinko's and a cheap lanyard later, I had myself a laminated press pass with my name printed clear as day on it. Surely I'd be strolling around backstage like I owned the place.

Chris attended the event with me and wanted no part of my plan. He wasn't about to try to sneak backstage, but he agreed to drive me to the arena early so I could get the lay of the land. The wrestlers wouldn't be arriving until late in the afternoon but I was there scouting the area by 10 a.m.

It seemed that there was one clear entrance point for WWF crew. Production trucks were being unloaded in a fenced-in parking lot, which was guarded by security tasked with keeping fans out. I had to assume that this was the lot that the wrestlers and creative team would be parking in as well.

I did another lap or two around the arena even though the guarded fence was surely the only access point. Like it or not, it was my only option and I'd have to give it my best. I'd have my badge proudly displayed and then walk right past the guy like I was supposed to be there. If he gave me any guff, I'd just flash the obviously genuine credentials at him, he'd apologize, then he'd usher me right to Vince McMahon's office.

I told Chris that I was going for it, and he left to grab McDonald's while I embarked on my harebrained scheme. In a rare display, I was wearing a polo shirt and slacks to look more professional. I put the lanyard and "press pass" over my head, making sure the text and logo were facing outward. With a deep breath, I rounded the corner leading to the security guard.

His eyes locked onto me the second I became visible, and they didn't move an inch. When I was about twenty feet from him, I looked at the guard, smiled, and gave a friendly nod. He responded by sticking his arm straight out in front of him in a "stop" gesture.

"I need to see your badge," he said.

"Oh, okay! Here you go," I said, as I flashed my homemade credentials.

"This isn't it. I need credentials from Kemper Arena or the World Wrestling Federation."

"Oh, I'm not with either of them. I'm a member of the press, from WrestleZone.com. I'll be reporting on tonight's show."

"Not from backstage you won't. Do you think media outlets print their own badges?"

I instantly realized how stupid the plan had been from the beginning.

"Well, uh, we always have in the past, and it hasn't been a problem. Give me a second—I'll call my editor-in-chief and we'll get this straightened out."

Defeated, I went back around the corner and tried to think of a new strategy. I didn't have a cell phone, so I couldn't even mimic a fake conversation. This lack of a cell phone also made my backup plan tricky. Plan B involved Matt Murphy, one of Harley Race's standout wrestlers from his promotion in Missouri. I had kept in contact with Matt ever since I met him at Harley's show, and he was scheduled to have an untelevised match before the *SmackDown* taping. Matt had mentioned that if he could figure out a way to get me backstage, he'd do his best. But with no phone and no sign of Matt, I gave up on getting backstage and joined a group of fans waiting on the public side of the fence.

As the show drew closer, some of the wrestlers approached our group to take photos and sign autographs. Earlier in the day, I pictured myself meeting Vince McMahon and having chats about the business with The Rock and Kurt Angle. Instead, I settled on receiving a perfume-drenched hug from Trish Stratus and getting Steve Blackman's autograph on an empty package of Corn Nuts.

I made one last attempt after the show to get backstage, explaining that my name was "Steven Hickenbottom" and that I was Shawn Michaels' cousin. Even with a new security guard at the post, it proved to be as ill-fated as my first effort.

Eventually, I would make my way backstage at a big WWE event. I don't think my methods of getting there would have made much sense even if I explained them in detail to the teenage version of myself:

Here's the deal, Dan. What you have to do is become a well-known gaming journalist, design a really hard Super Mario World *level, and then get on something called Twitter to challenge another gaming journalist to beat it. He won't be able to, and then you can get your WWE wrestler friend to take you backstage to make fun of him with a bunch of other wrestlers. Also, Goldust is gonna talk to him for a while about* Skyrim.

Now that I think about it, this barely made sense when it actually happened in 2016.

Cold Calls

I was seven years old when I went to Branson, Missouri with my father, his thirteenth wife, and my stepsister. It took me a while to remember how old I was, until help came in the form of Billy Ray Cyrus (as it often does). For most of the trip, "Achy Breaky Heart" was playing everywhere we went. My dad spent a good chunk of our time going off about how much he hated the recently released song. Wikipedia informed me that it came out in early 1992, placing me smack-dab in the middle of my seventh year.

Branson is a great city if you're either seven or seventy, with not a lot for anyone in between. Water parks and campy attractions like Silver Dollar City sit alongside elderly friendly activities like inoffensive comedy shows, tributes to the glory days of country music, and tons of slot machines. I loved Silver Dollar City, and I maintain that it's our country's greatest source of painfully rickety wooden roller coasters and weird wooden pistols that shoot rubber bands. Everything at Silver Dollar City seemed to be made of wood, except for those softball-sized chunks of caramel corn that always hurt my teeth.

We arrived at the hotel one evening after a long day at White Water, the main water park in town. Sunburnt and exhausted, we needed to get some food in our stomachs that didn't cost amusement park prices. My stepmom and stepsister broke off to go to a restaurant, while my father and I were dead-set on a McDonald's that we spotted down the street from the hotel.

It was fully dark when we started walking at eight or nine at night. I'm not sure if Branson even has a downtown, but if it did, we were definitely not there. There were only two other people to be seen as we walked up the hill to McDonald's. Their posture and slow walk made it clear that they were an elderly couple even though the darkness made it impossible to make out features from afar. We eventually passed them and exchanged quick hellos before continuing on our way.

For about 30 seconds, I could tell my dad was thinking about something. He seemed distracted and kept glancing behind him at the old folks, who were getting farther away. Out of nowhere, he did a 180 and started sprinting back toward our hotel.

"Keep up!" he yelled. "I'll explain later."

Later in the night, I'd learn what was going through his head during those 30 seconds. The sign below our hotel's logo read "WELCOME BOB AND DOLORES HOPE." When we passed the old couple, my dad felt like he'd seen the man before. Then he remembered the sign. We had just walked right by Bob and Dolores Hope.

I was seven, and zero seven-year-olds in 1992 knew who Bob Hope was. All I knew was that my father had passed a couple of old people, acted weird for a bit, and then sprinted back toward them faster than I'd ever seen him move. Not wanting to be by myself in a strange city at night, I did my best to keep up. To be fair, I doubt that any part of Branson could be that dangerous. Its most dangerous street gangs probably consist of a handful of polite Travis Tritt impersonators.

We reached the old couple and my dad struggled to catch his breath for an introduction.

"Excuse me, sir," my wheezing father said. "I couldn't help but notice the sign at the hotel and I had to ask if you're Bob Hope."

"Yes, I am," he said. "It's nice to meet you. Is this your son?"

"Yes, this is Danny. Danny, this man is Bob Hope. He's one of the greatest comedy legends of all time."

Without any context regarding his career and accomplishments, I could still tell that this guy was important based on my father's tone. I had never heard him sound so reverent. It made sense when I got older. My father and I are both lifelong fans of late-night television. Being born in 1984, two of my heroes from a young age were David Letterman and Conan O'Brien. My father loved them both and was old enough to have also watched many years of Johnny Carson hosting *The Tonight Show*. Hope's frequent "surprise" appearances on the show were legendary, and my dad was understandably starstruck in front of him.

Even if I couldn't fully appreciate meeting Hope at the time, the encounter stuck with me as I grew up and learned more about his legacy. It also kicked off a desire to meet my own heroes as I grew up.

I've been fortunate enough over the years to make this happen on numerous occasions. Either from being in the right place at the right time or through my job in the media, I've interviewed or met most of the people on my checklist. Conan O'Brien, Norm Macdonald, Louis CK, Ric Flair, and Vince McMahon were checked off over the years, with Letterman being the big exception. I don't know if anyone in the world has been responsible for making me laugh more than him, and I've never had the chance to meet him. Given his almost reclusive nature, I can't imagine a scenario in which that'll ever happen.

Writing about video games was always my first choice for a career path. That never changed, even when I started making comedic short films as I inched closer to college. I wanted to get as much advice as possible before I landed on a major. Should I go for a journalism degree to help with games writing, or should I go the film route and utilize the studio and other resources that the University of Kansas had? I decided that I didn't need any help writing about video games, so I'd major in film and write on my own time. Plus, the idea of watching a bunch of movies during class seemed like a solid deal to me.

I took an odd approach when it came to getting advice before I officially signed up for my major. I didn't want to ask guidance counselors or teachers about what I should do. I'd ask those who had actually landed positions that I hoped to someday get myself. If I was considering a career path related to video production, I certainly wanted it to be in the field of late-night comedy.

Late Night with Conan O'Brien was my first choice. O'Brien was young and I imagined he'd be around for a long time, so I wanted to get a hold of someone at his show to ask about how they got there. I'd have to think of a way to make this happen, since there wasn't any kind of contact information on the show's website.

As the credits rolled on Conan's show, I had a realization one night. These writers weren't big celebrities. Their names were in the credits and I doubted that they'd feel the need to keep their phone numbers unlisted. It's not like I had access to a New York City phone book, so I found an online version.

I recorded his show the next night and paused during the credits to read the writers' names so I could look them up.

Bigger names like Robert Smigel weren't listed in the directory, but most of the others were. I tried calling the numbers listed for Brian McCann, Jon Glaser, and Brian Stack to no avail. These numbers either led to error messages or people who were in no way late-night comedy writers.

One of the calls eventually went through. It was Andy Blitz, a writer who frequently appeared on the show. Most memorably (for me, at least), he played the "Chanting Sports Fan" character, who sat in the audience and performed chants that went on for way too long. Those bits always killed me and I was thrilled when he picked up the phone.

"Hi!" I said. "My name is Dan, and this is going to sound really weird. I just turned 18 and I'm about to go to college. I want to be a comedy writer, and I'm calling to see if you'd have any advice for me."

Andy seemed surprised at first about receiving a cold call from some kid. Eventually he became more relaxed and gave me advice for over an hour while occasionally strumming on a guitar. It seemed like I had caught him at the perfect time. His advice boiled down to persistence. *Keep writing, keep thinking up funny bits, keep shooting short videos. Some things won't work and some things won't get a reaction, but you have to power through that stuff and don't get discouraged.* This wasn't surprising advice to hear, but it was reassuring nevertheless to hear it from somebody who had made it.

Once I had gone through the Conan credits, I moved on to *The Daily Show*. One of my first calls was to Madeleine Smithberg, the co-creator of the program. She picked up just as she was sitting down to dinner. I apologized and told her that I'd let her go but she told me to call back in a half hour. I did, and she was just as gracious with her time and advice as Blitz had been. Once again, the biggest takeaway was the importance of persistence.

Years later, I was at a college house party with my friend Nikki Glaser. She went on to find great success as a stand-up comedian, hosting shows on MTV and Comedy Central. Back then, she was just starting her stand-up career and looking for advice on getting her name out there. I thought back to how nice the recipients of my cold calls had been.

"I'm telling you, you can just call them," I said. "None of them were offended that I called, and they had no problem giving me advice. Just look up info on comedians and writers that you'd want to get advice from, and cold-call them."

"That's insane," she said. "That sounds like something a crazy person would do."

She never took me up on my cold call recommendation, but things wound up working out for her without calling strangers at their homes like a goddamn weirdo.

Cold calls had worked for advice, so I wanted to expand on that idea. If people in the entertainment field were willing to talk to some random kid on the phone, maybe I should ask celebrities to make cameo appearances in my films.

I knew that nabbing a celebrity for a role would be a long shot. I was 18 and had zero industry experience, so any actual celebrity was unlikely to even acknowledge my request. But when it came down to it, all I needed was one "yes." I could send out 100 requests to various celebrities who were coming through the area, and it was worth it if a single one of them agreed to be in one of my projects.

COLD CALLS

Early in my freshman year of college, I was still excited about video production and was moving forward with it as a possible backup career path. As such, I worked on several scripts simultaneously. They were all dumb comedies with a variety of roles that could easily be filled and tweaked if I landed a cameo.

Each week, I'd keep an eye on websites that tracked concerts coming through Lawrence and the Midwest. If there was a musician or comedian that I liked, I'd do my best to find some channel to get a hold of them. Most of their websites had contact sections for press requests. I'd typically send an e-mail to that, hoping that the public relations person in charge of the account would pass me onto a tour manager or someone higher up.

Nine times out of ten, I wouldn't hear anything back. That tenth time was usually a flat-out denial. I kept going, though. The first celebrity who seemed like an actual possibility was Ted Nugent. This was before I had a full grasp on how insane he was. I was just excited at the prospect of getting the "Cat Scratch Fever" dude to do a bit.

Nugent's press people requested a script. I sent one that I never wound up making, and it revolved around a young Morgan Freeman trying to join The Allman Brothers Band. I was still at the age where I thought "random equals funny," so this seemed like a good idea at the time.

In the script, Morgan Freeman fails at securing a gig in the band despite following advice from the ghost of Duane Allman. His girlfriend breaks up with him, leaving him down in the dumps. A friend of Freeman's says he's got a connection with someone who can help him with his lady troubles, and sets him up with some life coaching from Ted Nugent.

I sent the script to Nugent's management and they moved it along to Ted. Word came back from his tour manager that Ted liked the script and wanted to chat with me about details before locking anything in. Before a concert that he co-headlined with ZZ Top, he was scheduled for a book signing at a Borders in Olathe. We were to meet there, go over the scene, and then shoot it after his set at Sandstone Amphitheater later that night.

When the book signing concluded, I approached the tour manager and introduced myself. He introduced me to Nugent, and we went to the employees' back room to discuss the script. It seemed like Nugent had skimmed it at best, but he was willing to do it as long as it wasn't a big time commitment. I explained that it would take 15 minutes at the most, and that the script was intentionally stupid and weird.

"I can do weird," he said. "Buzz my tour manager once I'm offstage, and we'll meet up and get it done."

This brief chat seemed to confirm that the cameo would be happening. I was thrilled. A genuine celebrity had agreed to be in one of my films. This would surely help in terms of getting exposure. An 18-year-old making a short film wasn't a news story, but maybe an 18-year-old making a short film with Ted Nugent was.

We hadn't shot anything else for the film yet, as its entire production hinged on the involvement of Nugent. If we couldn't get this scene in the can, I'd have to overhaul or trash the script and go in another direction.

I tapped my friend Brandon to play Morgan Freeman, so he'd be coming to the concert with my father and me. We arrived at Sandstone just as Kenny Wayne Shepherd was finishing his opening act. Nugent's tour manager had given me backstage media passes, but I wanted to get some shots of Brandon's character in the concert crowd before the backstage scene.

COLD CALLS

I managed to get my small MiniDV camera into the venue without security finding it. If anyone gave me trouble, I was confident that the media pass in my pocket would remedy the situation. Not long after we posted up on the lawn, Nugent took the stage. The Morgan Freeman character had only been told to meet up with "Ted," so we shot a scene in which Brandon walked into the concert crowd and realized that it was Ted Nugent that he'd be meeting with.

Brandon (as Morgan Freeman) walked through the crowd and looked at the stage as I panned around and shot from over his shoulder. My viewfinder had Nugent performing a solo on the right side of the frame and the back of Brandon's head on the left. As I monitored the shot from behind the camera, a security guard entered the frame. He was beelining toward me with his hand out.

"Put that fucking camera down," he yelled. "Put it down!"

I stopped recording and brought the camera down to my side. The security guard was furious as I tried my best to explain that I had permission to shoot there. When I produced the media passes, he told me that they didn't permit anyone to film from the amphitheater crowd. As he was explaining this, Nugent was onstage shooting a flaming crossbow into an effigy of Saddam Hussein.

"I need to watch you delete that footage," the security guard said. "Pull up the screen and delete the footage right now."

As soon as I did, the guard ordered us to leave the premises. I pleaded with him to contact Nugent's tour manager. He wasn't having any of it, saying that an act's manager couldn't override venue policy. Nothing I said was getting through to this dude and we were kicked out. I tried to call Nugent's tour manager several times to no avail. The cameo wasn't going to happen.

Nugent's cameo falling through was a disappointment, but I was still determined to nab a big star. For weeks, I sent out requests to PR people and tour managers, trying as hard as I could to garner even a shred of interest.

After sending out e-mails to every notable act that was coming through the area, I heard back from one of them. A tour manager for George Clinton and Parliament Funkadelic was up for chatting about the idea and asked for a script. I was working on one about a young Canadian hitman who moves to Kansas to try to corner the local assassin market. It would be easy enough to write in a mafia godfather character, and naturally, I'd have it played by the Godfather of Funk.

I finished the script, adding a scene where George Clinton orders the Canadian hitman to assassinate one of his organization's enemies. Not long after I sent it in, Clinton's manager responded enthusiastically. She had brought it up to Clinton, and he was all for it. She was setting up me, my actor, and my second cameraman with passes to a P-Funk show in East St. Louis, Illinois.

Since I was already going to be there with cameras, she had another request: footage of the current tour. I immediately agreed. She wanted one roaming cameraman onstage throughout the concert, one in the crowd, and one stationary wide shot from the back of the room. I wasn't about to pass up on the onstage role, so I took that and tasked my actor and cameraman with the other spots.

In the weeks leading up to the concert, the plan was for my friend Chris to drive us to St. Louis in his car and serve as one of the cameramen. The hitman role would be played by Tyler from my floor in Hashinger. He and I may not have been great friends, but he was a theater major with an acting background, so I picked him for the role.

Days before we were set to head out, Chris told me he wouldn't be able to go because of a school commitment, leaving us without a driver. Tyler didn't have a license and I was terrified at the prospect of driving for four hours on the highway. Merging on a highway was enough to give me a panic attack, let alone driving across the entirety of Missouri. At one point, I was actually researching ways to get across the state without getting on a highway. MapQuest told me that the drive would take four hours if I took I-70. I wasn't able to find any routes that would take me across the state exclusively on local roads.

Thankfully, my friend Nick stepped in and offered to drive. He also had video production experience, so I could trust him to get good shots from the crowd. A couple of days before the concert, we packed into Nick's car and made the drive. For those who haven't taken I-70 through Missouri, just picture one long, boring road with at least 6,000 billboards for fireworks, pornography, and Jesus every half-mile.

The day of the concert came and everything went much smoother than the Nugent situation. Clinton's manager greeted us at the venue a couple of hours before the show and gave us all-access passes. She told us that we were free to film anywhere in the building. We were to shoot concert footage during the show and then meet up with Clinton afterward and head to the Renaissance Hotel for the cameo shoot.

Scouting the club for shooting locations didn't take long. We set up a tripod in the back and stored the rest of our gear backstage, then just hung around the catering table until people started to filter in. Parliament Funkadelic seems to vary between having about 16 or 600 members at any given time. Based on how packed the backstage area became, I think they were closer to the latter at this point.

Despite most of them having no idea why we were there, everyone seemed enthusiastic when we said that Clinton would be doing a cameo in our short film. As I introduced myself to the band, I kept noticing a tall guy who looked tremendously familiar. I eventually had to ask somebody.

"Hey, where have I seen that guy before?" I asked a guy who introduced himself as "Poo Poo Man."

"Ever seen the Urkel show?" Poo Poo asked. "That's Darius, he was the older brother."

Holy crap. I had watched a ton of *Family Matters* growing up and was just informed that Eddie Winslow was backstage at this P-Funk concert for some wholly unexplained reason.

The band took the stage once the crowd had all funneled into the venue. They started jamming for a while with no sign of Clinton. I hadn't even seen a glimpse of him backstage despite being there for hours.

"Where's George?" I asked a man who was at least 50 years old and wearing nothing but a diaper.

"This must be your first time," he said. "George always gets 'relaxed' on the bus until he's ready to come out."

For almost two hours, Parliament jammed onstage as a revolving door of vocalists jumped on and offstage whenever they felt like it. George's niece took the stage, followed by Eddie Winslow. Diaper Guy danced around for a while. There was no real rhyme or reason to anything that was happening, but the crowd was loving it. It was fascinating to be backstage and see just how loosely the entire crew operated.

This was all treated like a warm-up to the main event. I wasn't expected to start filming until Clinton was ready to kick things off in a proper manner. Without warning, I heard clapping near the catering table as the back door opened and the sea of roadies and musicians parted. George Clinton was done with his fun on the bus and floated through the backstage area with a gigantic smile on his face.

I didn't have time to be starstruck. I grabbed my camera from the bag, ran up the stairs on the side of the stage, and hit record. Ducking down by the drums, I filmed Clinton as he walked up the stairs and emerged onstage to loud cheers.

For the rest of the concert, I did my best to film the band without drawing attention to myself. I hoped that the crowd was too busy staring at George Clinton, a guy in a diaper, and the gyrating dude with the giant prosthetic nose to notice the dorky white 18-year-old in a polo shirt. Parliament's drummer kept yelling at me to see if I wanted Heinekens from a plastic tub. Between songs, I occasionally snuck one or two while trying to stay incognito. People were doing drugs openly backstage, and I was still worried about somehow getting caught drinking a beer while underage.

When the show ended, the fans started heading out of the venue's front door while the band headed to the parking lot in the back. Crew members wasted no time tearing down the stage and hauling equipment to the buses. Before Clinton left, I wanted to make sure that he remembered we'd be shooting the scene back at the hotel.

His manager made sure I wouldn't have to worry about that. As the band dispersed, she was trying to secure a ride for Clinton. More equipment needed to be loaded onto the tour buses before they could head to the hotel, so other arrangements needed to be made for the man himself. After asking a couple of people if they had space in their car, the manager approached me, Tyler, and Nick.

"Hey, do you guys have room in your car?" she asked.

She was seriously asking three teenage strangers if we'd be willing to transport the Godfather of Funk to his hotel. There was only the three of us, so we agreed to act as his chauffeurs. Clinton was holding a Styrofoam container of fried chicken from catering and talking to a couple of the band members when she pulled him away.

"George, these guys are gonna give you a ride to the Renaissance," she explained. "They're the ones that are shooting the video with you."

He shook our hands, mumbled a bit, and walked with us to Nick's car. One of his backup singers was with him, so we did our best to squeeze in. Nick jumped in the driver's seat and Tyler took the passenger seat, while I crammed into the back with Clinton and his backup singer.

My brain was already reeling at how ridiculous this situation was when I heard a frantic knocking on the window to my left. I turned to see Eddie Winslow through the glass, about six inches from my face. When I rolled the window down, he asked if we had room for him in the car. I told Eddie Winslow that no, there was no room for him in my friend's car.

Making conversation in the backseat with Clinton was difficult. He was mumbling and easily distracted. Tyler asked Nick about the best way to get to the hotel, and Clinton perked up. Before we went to the hotel, he said he needed to meet up with someone behind a nearby convenience store. His backup singer led us there, and we remained parked as she talked to someone on the phone.

COLD CALLS

That someone walked up to Clinton's window and knocked on it. The Godfather of Funk rolled his window down, handed money to the mystery man, took something from him, and slipped it into his pocket. I was still processing the part where Eddie Winslow had been knocking on my window, and now I had definitely just watched George Clinton buy drugs from the seat next to me.

We got back on the road as the backup singer made another phone call. She was telling somebody that we were going to shoot a quick movie scene at the hotel. Not long into the conversation, she put her hand over the phone and relayed a question to me.

"Can the band be in it?" she asked.

"The band? They want to be in the scene?"

"Yeah. Poo Poo, Sir Nose, Kim, Darius, and Garry are on the way. They wanna be in it."

Darius was Eddie Winslow, which meant I'd be getting a wholly unexpected second cameo in the same scene. Adding more members of Parliament Funkadelic surely wasn't something that I was going to turn down, and they could easily be written in as henchmen of Clinton's mafia godfather character.

We arrived at the Renaissance Hotel at the same time as the car filled with other Parliament members. George walked behind us with his backup singer and the Parliament guys asked questions about what they'd be doing. I told them it was a dumb comedy, and they didn't have to worry. George was gonna play their boss and they'd flank him as he gave a young hitman his assignment.

I was worried about how lucid George would be, but he came to life almost instantly when we got to the room. When I handed him his script, he slid his sunglasses up and read every word several times before we started filming. He asked a couple of questions, I did some basic camera prep, and we got right into it.

Eddie Winslow wanted to be involved, so I added a quick bit where he greeted the young hitman at the door to the hotel room. From there, I just had to film a brief conversation between Tyler and Clinton about his assignment. Clinton handed Tyler a photograph, told him to "put some funk in [the target's] trunk," and sent him on his way.

Once the scene was done, we hung around for a bit and drank more of their seemingly endless Heineken stash. I was worried for a moment that this little afterparty was going to get druggy thanks to the transaction I had witnessed earlier, but it never did. A few beers later, the three of us thanked the entire band (and Eddie Winslow) profusely, and headed back to our own hotel.

After I finished shooting and editing the entire project back in Lawrence, I was thrilled to get the word out. I took great pride in having been able to make such a weird thing happen. It was ready to be released online, and I wanted it to get as much exposure as possible. I sent news tips to just about every local outlet I could think of and got a few bites. The *Kansas City Star* ran a large article with a photo, as did *The Kansan*, our campus newspaper. A George Clinton fan site—the prestigious *New Funk Times*—also ran a story and an interview.

While the *Kansas City Star* piece would certainly reach more people, I knew that those in my immediate vicinity would be more likely to see the *Kansan* article. Editions of *The Kansan* were all over campus every day, and it was actually read frequently in the days before smartphones. In my mind, I'd almost certainly be stopped a few times on the day the article ran.

"Hey, you're that guy from the paper!" is what they'd say. Most of them would be attractive women, I imagined, and this article would almost certainly give them the desire to have sexual intercourse with me.

On the morning the *Kansan* article was supposed to run, I rushed down to our dorm's first floor to confirm it. Sure enough, the top of page 5A read "Student Film to Star George Clinton." Below the headline was a photo of Clinton and me from the video shoot. It wasn't the cover of the paper, but surely the big picture would be enough to get people to recognize me.

Desperate to be recognized in public for the first time, I went to Mrs. E's cafeteria. This was the dining hall that served all of the dorms, and plenty of students read *The Kansan* there while they ate. Classes could never get me to wake up this early in the morning, but the chance of being recognized for my short film certainly did. I sat by myself at a table, slowly chipping away at a giant plate of sausage and bacon.

As I expected, several students were reading *The Kansan* at Mrs. E's that day. From over their shoulders, I could even tell that some of them were on the page with my article. I waited for someone to look in my direction and make the connection. My vain hope of being recognized was something I was able to live with, but I wasn't about to walk up to someone, point at the picture, and pull a "hey, that's me!" or anything so overt. After about an hour with no luck, I swallowed my pride and headed back to my dorm room.

I gave it one more shot later in the afternoon. Maybe by then more people would have read the article. Instead of Mrs. E's, I strolled around campus aimlessly. Once again, the chance of recognition had me doing something—visiting campus—that classes almost never did. It ended up being as ill-conceived as the cafeteria attempt.

I'd continue making short films and comedy sketches for a couple of years. As time went on, I became less concerned about being recognized and more interested in doing it just for fun. During the few times that I actually would attend classes, I learned to hate my fellow film students. They somehow seemed even more pretentious than the worst musicians, poets, and artists in Hashinger Hall.

All of their projects were drenched in contrived metaphors and everyone was convinced that they were going to become the next great filmmaker. I eventually started making all of my productions as lowbrow as possible, in some form of silent protest. One of my shorts featured a rapper whose colon and bowel function were destroyed by a raccoon that crawled into his ass during summer camp. As a result, he became plagued by a condition that constantly made him fart and pee his pants. I still have a robust folder of fart sound effects on my computer thanks to that one.

My fellow students turned me off to the very idea of pursuing film as a career. A handful of older classmates graduated and moved to Los Angeles, only to come back within a year with nothing but bad things to say about the city and the industry. Getting work in Hollywood seemed like the best-case scenario if this was going to be my chosen path, and that didn't sound all that great to me. I certainly didn't want to work in a field that had me working alongside the types of people that were in my classes.

Making sketches and short films kept me busy for a couple of years, but I eventually couldn't justify spending that much time on something that I didn't want to pursue. Video games were still my greatest passion, and it was time to dedicate 100 percent of my efforts to making inroads in that arena.

Game Shark

Turning 14 meant that I was finally eligible to work with one of my passions. I made that happen once by getting hired at AMC Theatres—twice if McDonald's counts as a passion—but I wouldn't be able to work around video games until I turned 16. That's when I'd be eligible for a job at FuncoLand, the used game retailer that eventually fell under the GameStop umbrella.

FuncoLand was my favorite place growing up. I'd spend hours there as a customer, excitedly asking questions about upcoming consoles and ogling new games that I didn't have the money to buy yet. Once I had mowed enough lawns and accumulated enough old games to trade in, I'd head to their location off 95th Street and grab whatever new game I was obsessing over. This usually involved trading in my old favorites for next to nothing, but that didn't matter as long as it was getting me closer to the newest thing that I wanted. I'll admit that it did sting a bit when I traded in my NES and many of my favorite games so that I could afford a Sega CD.

I was a kid with no real social life, but at FuncoLand, I felt like I belonged. The cashiers were willing to humor all of my questions, and they didn't mind changing out games in their demo kiosks so that I could try out the newest releases. FuncoLand is where my excitement for the Virtual Boy instantly evaporated once I played a few games. It's where my jaw dropped when I saw the killer whale demolish the dock in *Sonic Adventure* before the Dreamcast came out. It's where I had my first conversation with Seaman.

It's also where I discovered *Game Informer*, the magazine that would eventually give me my first full-time job in the games press.

"Mortal Monday" was the marketing term built around the console release of *Mortal Kombat*, and I was at FuncoLand with NES trade-ins in hand the moment the store opened. I impatiently waited for the cashier to ring up my copy of the game that I had spent so much time obsessing over at my uncle's gas station. Soon, I'd be able to play it in my own home on my Sega Genesis.

While the cashier processed my trade-ins, I noticed an issue of *Game Informer* strategically placed at the register. A giant image of the *Mortal Kombat* dragon logo was splashed across the cover and I instinctively lunged for it. As any FuncoLand cashier worth his salt would do, the guy ringing me up jumped into the pitch. He told me about the discount card that came with the magazine, which would save me money on any used game in the store. His pitch was unnecessary. I was sold as soon as I saw *Mortal Kombat* on the cover.

For weeks, I spent almost all of my time at home playing the game. Whenever I had to get in the car to go somewhere, I brought the issue of *Game Informer* along for the ride. The "Meet the Editors" section was fascinating to me. These were grown men, and they had found some way to make playing and writing about video games their full-time jobs. No matter what, I knew that I had to angle all my major life decisions toward making that a reality.

At nine years old, there wasn't much I could do besides continue to play games and subscribe to every gaming magazine I could get my hands on. Every time my mother went to the grocery store, I'd park myself in the magazine section with a spiral notebook and jot down codes for my favorite

Genesis and Super Nintendo games. When it was time to leave, I'd grab subscription cards for *Electronic Gaming Monthly*, *GamePro*, *Nintendo Power*, *Ultra Game Players*, *Next Generation*, *Official* [insert console name here] *Magazine*, *Incite*, and more. If I didn't get subscriptions for Christmas or my birthday, I'd do more chores and mow more lawns until I could afford them myself.

My family moved from Lenexa to Olathe in 1996. This was still close enough to go to my original FuncoLand location, but I was thrilled to learn that another would be opening close to my new house. Once I was 14, I started bugging the store about getting a job. Store policy said that they wouldn't hire anyone under 16. Within a week of my sixteenth birthday, I went into the store and asked for a job. They had seen plenty of me in those few years, and knew that I was more than enthusiastic about video games. I applied, interviewed, and got the job.

In the year 2000, I was a 16-year-old with jobs at a movie theater and a video game store. The former expected more from me in terms of actual work—even if I was good at avoiding it—but the latter was a cakewalk. It was a new location and foot traffic in the area was light. Six display stations were set up around the store, spanning numerous generations of video games. FuncoLand would eventually phase out older consoles, but when I started, we had everything from the NES to the Dreamcast. With so few customers entering the store, nothing was stopping me from grabbing games I had never played and working my way through them at one of our stations.

Most of my shifts were spent working alongside Tom, the assistant manager. If a Hollywood writer who didn't play games were to create a "Video Game Store Assistant

Manager" character, it would be Tom. He was in his mid-30s, severely balding, had never kissed a girl, and lived in his grandmother's basement. During every one of his breaks, he'd sit in the back with a spiral notebook, filling it with a comprehensive list of each *Final Fantasy* creature's stats and weaknesses.

I could have gotten away with anything while working with Tom, but for once I actually wanted to do my job. Whenever someone would enter the store, I'd put down whatever I was playing and enthusiastically answer their gaming-related questions. We had a few regular customers, and it was always rewarding to introduce them to new titles and then hear their reactions after they had played them for a bit.

Sometimes my efforts to steer customers toward games they might like didn't pan out. During one shift, a gigantic woman in a tobacco-stained Tweety Bird shirt came into the store with her son, who looked about twelve years old. They scanned the shelves for a few minutes before the mother approached me.

"My son likes that spy shit," she said. "You got any cheap PlayStation games where he can sneak up on bad guys?"

This couldn't have been any more of a lay-up recommendation for me. One of my favorite games was called *Metal Gear Solid*, and it was cheap since it had been out for a couple of years. I enthusiastically explained the game to both of them and her son seemed intrigued.

"How much is it?" she asked.

"It's $12.99."

She thought about it for a moment before taking another lap around the store. When she returned to the counter, she was holding a $9.99 game called *Spec Ops:*

Stealth Patrol. This was a bargain-basement action game, and didn't even deserve to be mentioned among the likes of *Metal Gear Solid*.

"How 'bout this one?" she asked while holding up the case.

"Eh, I can't really recommend that one. I guarantee that your son would have a lot more fun with *Metal Gear Solid*."

"But this one's ten dollars."

"I know, but I *promise you* that *Metal Gear Solid* is much more than three dollars better than *Spec Ops*."

She'd have none of it and bought *Spec Ops* despite my urging. I've often wondered if her desire to save three dollars came at the expense of her son's potential lifelong love of video games.

Tom didn't share my enthusiasm for talking to customers. He didn't seem to have enthusiasm for much of anything, actually. As far as I could tell, there were only two things in life that he had strong feelings about. One of them was pickles. Every day, he'd pay for my McDonald's if I agreed to pick up his lunch, too. It was the same order every day: a super-sized #2 value meal—two cheeseburgers, fries, and a Coke—with extra pickles. Having my car smell like pickles for years seemed like a small price to pay for a regular supply of free plain Quarter Pounders, however.

His other strong feelings related to women. Despite never venturing outside of the store or his grandmother's house, he couldn't fathom why he was having trouble meeting a girl. I was far from an expert on the matter, but I tried my best to explain to him that nothing was ever going to happen if he didn't at least leave the house. My suggestions bounced right off of him, and he opted instead to get angry whenever he saw an attractive girl walk by our storefront.

If Tom was devoid of personality, the next member of our team had way too much. He was close to my age and his name was Peter. Despite this being the name on his birth certificate, Peter insisted that everyone refer to him as "Cryo." This was his handle when he played *Halo* competitively, so he wrote it on a piece of tape and put it across his employee nametag. He'd answer the phone by introducing himself as Cryo, and refused to respond whenever one of us referred to him as Peter. This was annoying, but it was nothing compared to when his girlfriend, "DangerGrrrl," also started working at the store. It's always taken a lot to anger me, but hearing the words "Cryo" or "DangerGrrrl" during my shifts always triggered a Pavlovian response of pure rage.

If Tom was the stereotype of the basement-dwelling virgin who lived with his grandma, Cryo fit nicely into the stereotype of the "hardcore gamer" who swilled energy drinks and talked unironically about "pwning noobs." I felt sorry for Tom and had trouble relating to him, but at least I didn't actively hate him the way I hated Cryo.

As time went on, the makeup of the staff continued to decline. Our nearly absentee store manager left and was replaced by his polar opposite. Stepping into the role was Josh, a guy who gave a terrible first impression that only got worse as you got to know him. Nothing felt genuine about the guy, from his fake smile to his obviously forced friendliness.

Josh also came off like a pathological liar. No matter the topic of conversation, he always seemed to have a close personal connection to it. When the Xbox was released and it allowed you to rip music CDs to the console, I brought in a Lynyrd Skynyrd album to test out the feature. Immediately upon seeing me pull out the disc, Josh jumped in with his coincidental connection to the making of "Sweet Home Alabama."

"My cousin had a big impact on that song," he told me. "Right before the piano solo at the end of the song, you can hear Ronnie say 'My donuts, god damn.' That's because my cousin was a janitor at the studio they were recording in, and he had taken Ronnie's tray of donuts away before they started the 'Alabama' recording. That line wouldn't be in the song without my cousin."

Everything was like this with him. If you were playing a game, his best friend had designed the best level. When he saw a cool car in the parking lot, he'd talk about how many chicks he picked up when he had that same car in high school (despite repeating this same story about numerous different cars). Oh, you got a high score in a video game? He could double it easily.

His personality was insufferable and his managerial tendencies were just as annoying. Only two things in the world mattered to him: securing pre-orders for games and selling *Game Informer* subscriptions. Granted, this seemed to be the entire focus of GameStop—the new name of FuncoLand—as a company.

When it came to pushing pre-orders, Josh was prone to making wild claims that any gamer could see through. *Halo* had been the hottest game on Xbox ever since the console launched, so Josh always used it to trump up his pre-order pitch for other titles. For what felt like a year, I heard the same refrain every time a customer purchased anything.

"Hey, you've heard of *Halo*, right?" he'd ask the uninterested customer. "Well you're not gonna hear about it for much longer."

This is the point at which he'd pull out an issue of *Game Informer* and open to the *Brute Force* screenshots. These images typically featured the dumb lizard guy you could play as.

"Once *Brute Force* comes out next spring, *Halo*'s gonna be left in the dust," he'd say. "This is the game you bought an Xbox for!"

No matter how apathetic the customer acted toward the game, Josh wouldn't shut up about how they should pre-order it (whether or not they had an Xbox). Once his pitch succeeded or failed, he'd pivot straight into his attempt to get the customer to subscribe to *Game Informer*.

I never felt comfortable with canned sales pitches, even for a magazine that I had enjoyed since I was a child. GameStop owned the magazine, and they wanted us to push it hard onto every customer who came into the store. Back when the store was called FuncoLand, they'd even give us a two-dollar commission for every subscription we secured.

Selling *Game Informer* was clearly a big priority for the company. Advocating for the magazine didn't make me feel bad, especially considering that I had grown up wanting to write for it. It was the company's aggressive strategy that bugged me. Around this time, I started thinking about a way that I could pitch the magazine while simultaneously inching me closer to a job writing for it.

Every month, GameStop would send a VHS tape for us to loop on our in-store television. These tapes contained trailers for upcoming games, accompanied by constant prodding for customers to place pre-orders. One of the company's big focuses was covered, but there was never any mention of *Game Informer*. If the company cared so much about pushing subscriptions, why wouldn't they include a brief spot on the VHS tapes that they produced for their stores?

My video production experience was limited to high school video announcements, short comedy sketches, and a few weddings, but I felt like I could pull off a commercial for in-store use. Any *Game Informer* exposure on those VHS tapes would be better than nothing, even if I didn't have access to professional-grade cameras or other equipment.

I sure as hell wasn't going to pitch this idea to a doofus store manager like Josh. Instead, I looked up contact information for GameStop's corporate headquarters in Texas. Starting with the number for their front desk, I explained my idea to several people as they kept transferring me up the chain. Eventually, I got to a woman who was in a position to give the green light to marketing plans.

My idea for the ad wasn't revolutionary, but I thought it would be quick and effective enough for these purposes. It would be a parody of *Metal Gear Solid*, featuring a spy sneaking into *Game Informer*'s headquarters to obtain the new issue (I specifically included the headquarters so that I'd have a reason to travel to Minneapolis and meet the editorial team). After the spy was caught by editor-in-chief Andy McNamara and thrown out of the building, the commercial would cut to me in my GameStop uniform. I'd explain that there was "an easier way to get *Game Informer*," and then pitch the subscription offer.

I explained all of this to the woman on the other end of the line and said that I'd be happy to make the ad for free. All I'd ask of them was to cover my flight to Minneapolis and a hotel. I expected to hear a polite but immediate "no" in return. Surprisingly, she told me that she'd bring it up with others in her department and get back to me. In the meantime, she wanted me to e-mail her a script for the shoot.

It was nice to not be rejected outright, but at no point did I ever expect this to go through. I didn't even expect a call back. They were just being nice to this kid who was enthusiastic about his idea. There was no way they'd actually consider the offer.

I tossed together a quick script and sent it her way. A few days later, I received some big surprises. One was a call back. The second was that GameStop's marketing team had talked it over and given my idea the green light. This seemed insane, and then the woman hit me with a third surprise.

"There's only one issue," she said. "Legally, we can't have you do this for free; we have to pay you for your work. How much would you charge for a project like this?"

In no way had I prepared for that question. Just getting the go-ahead for the ad seemed impossible, and now they were asking me how much money I wanted to be paid (on top of travel expenses). I made my short films and comedy sketches for fun, and the only experience I had with making money for my videos came from a few weddings that I filmed. Those jobs had netted me about five or six hundred dollars apiece, so I figured that I should aim a little higher than that.

"Um, for a project like this, I'd charge $2,000. I'd also request another $500 so that I can bring a second cameraman and buy the spy outfit."

She didn't hesitate for a second, moving right along to booking dates for travel. I requested a week in late August, just before my sophomore year of college started. After she took down my information, she thanked me for reaching out and said that we'd be hearing from GameStop shortly.

Even if they were actually thinking about doing this, it surely couldn't be the end of the process. After all, they hadn't asked for a demo reel of my work or *any evidence whatsoever* that I wasn't completely full of shit. This was before YouTube existed, but they could have at least asked for me to mail in a VHS or DVD of some samples.

Nope. They apparently needed zero confirmation of my video production chops, because a FedEx package arrived at my place a week later. In it was flight and hotel information; an American Express card for cab and food expenses; and a check for $2,500. It was the biggest check I'd ever received, and I hadn't even done anything besides make a few phone calls. If I were a con man, this would have been the easiest score of all time. I was looking for more than money, however. This was inexplicably working out so far, and I was set on going to Minneapolis and doing my best to make an impression on the *Game Informer* staff.

In the weeks leading up to the trip, I visited military surplus stores around Kansas City and bought the components for the spy suit. One element of the video required a brief shoot with my grandfather at his home, so I got that out of the way. He was to play the spy's commander, who radios in to check on the status of the mission.

My grandpa had two lines. One was "Cobra, have you reached the infiltration point?" The other was "Good. Remember...that magazine is mission-critical." His full appearance in the video is eight seconds long, and it took over an hour to get the lines out of him. Playing a role for a video was an alien concept to him, much less one for a commercial that he didn't understand in the least. He'd get a few words into each line before bursting out laughing.

"What the hell are we doing here?" he'd ask. "This is crazy."

It really wasn't that crazy, and his bewilderment at the entire process was cracking me up. For the entire shoot, my grandmother held a lampshade at an angle to better illuminate my grandpa. She was laughing the entire time as well. After the first half hour, she grabbed a couple of poster boards and wrote his lines on them with a Sharpie.

They were great sports about it, and it was good to get some footage in the can before I headed to Minneapolis. I also shot the ending of the commercial, in which I pitched the *Game Informer* subscription from inside a GameStop store.

This entire time, I was expecting the floor to suddenly drop out of the operation. At some point, a marketing dude was bound to see the plan, say "what the hell is this?" and snuff it out. With each day that brought me closer to August, I started feeling more and more like it would actually happen. My buddy Kiu was available during the proposed travel week and could hold a backup camera, so I explained the ridiculous story to him and recruited him as my cameraman. He loved games like I did, so getting him to agree to hundreds of dollars and a visit to *Game Informer* wasn't a hard sell.

The day finally arrived and we took off for Minneapolis. Once we stepped off the plane and grabbed our camera bags from baggage claim, we both just stood there for a second.

"Why is this happening?" he asked.

"I have no idea," I said. "This really shouldn't have worked."

With a mix of bewilderment and excitement, we cabbed it to our downtown hotel and unpacked. GameStop set each of us up with our own suite, complete with kitchens. We dropped off luggage in our rooms and reconvened to discuss what we'd do next. Since we were 18 and 19, bars weren't an option. Instead, we decided to utilize our in-room kitchens.

There was a Target nearby, so we walked there and made full use of the $200 daily expense allowance on our corporate card. We went up and down the aisles, tossing junk in our carts like the kids who won Toys 'R' Us shopping sprees on Nickelodeon. Pizza Rolls, Hot Pockets, cheese-filled soft pretzels, ice cream, candy, popcorn, beef jerky, and plenty more weighed down our plastic bags as we walked back to the hotel.

We stayed up late and gorged on our bounty, keeping a revolving door of seemingly endless junk food cooking in the suite's oven. Kiu had brought his PlayStation, and we worked through several hours of *Final Fantasy VII* while talking about how excited we were to visit the *Game Informer* office the next day. Both of us had grown up reading the magazine, and we couldn't wait to meet the guys whose jobs we envied more than anything.

At around three o'clock in the morning, we decided we should probably hit the hay. Our shoot wouldn't be for a couple of days, so tomorrow was set to be an easy day of meeting the staff and discussing plans. Kiu retired to his room, and I did my best to catch some sleep, despite the toll that the night's culinary endeavors were taking on my stomach.

Our hotel was just over a block away from *Game Informer*. We got up and showered, then walked to the old Warehouse District building that housed the magazine. I have no idea what GameStop corporate told the *Game Informer* guys about our visit, because everyone seemed to be some shade of confused when we arrived.

We were greeted at the office by Andy McNamara, *Game Informer*'s longtime editor-in-chief. I had been reading his reviews and his letters from the editor for a decade. He was always featured first in the "meet the editors" section that I loved, and one of my first issues featured him on the cover wearing a backward baseball cap and dunking a basketball. I'd come to learn years later that this cover was routinely mocked by the staff.

"Nice to meet you," he said as he let us in. "I'm Andy. So what are we doing here? They told me that a video guy would be coming by for a commercial, but that's about all I know."

"I'm shooting an ad for *GI* that's gonna air in GameStop locations. It should be easy—I just need someone to play Solid Snake and try to sneak in to steal a magazine from the building."

Andy brought it up to the writers' room after introducing me to everyone. Most of them seemed to have zero interest, but an editor (and part-time pro wrestler) named Justin jumped at the opportunity. We spent a while going over the script, scouting locations around the office, and making sure that Justin would fit into the outfit that I had purchased.

This entire time, I was doing all I could to not geek out over everything around me. It was exactly what I had always pictured a video game magazine's office to be. One editor sat in the corner, cussing as he played through a terrible Aquaman game. Another was getting annoyed at a Game Boy Advance game that used actual solar panels, forcing him to regularly step outside of the office. Promotional items, action figures, and other toys were scattered across every desk. A giant stack of envelope art that readers had sent in towered over one work station. Most importantly, you couldn't look anywhere without seeing tons of video games, many of which hadn't been released yet. I was in heaven.

Justin was game for everything and the suit fit him fine. We'd need to shoot the following day, since the staff was trying to finish up some articles before the next issue's deadline. It was still early in the afternoon, so Kiu and I would have to find something to fill the time before we returned to the office the next day. We had saved round two of junk food and *Final Fantasy* for later in the night, so we decided to run around the city until then. The Twins were a couple of innings into a game against the Royals that day, so we bought tickets from a scalper outside the Metrodome and headed in. When the game let out, there was plenty of time left for whatever we wanted to do.

Minneapolis is a gorgeous town, so it's a shame that its best-known tourist attraction is the dreadful Mall of America. Not knowing any better, Kiu and I made it our destination. A cab dropped us off at this monstrous assortment of shops, and we wandered around for an hour. Even with so many options, we spent most of our time looking at games in one of the mall's several GameStop stores.

We did find one nongaming store that caught our eye. Halloween was still two months away, but a large costume store had already opened in a corner of the mall. After looking at a variety of costumes, I found one that I loved. It was a big, stupid shark outfit. When worn, it looked like the shark was staring straight up with its mouth agape. Something about it cracked me up and I had to have it.

GameStop suggested we spend our $200 daily allowance on food and cabs, but no one said we were *required* to use it for that. There was still plenty of junk food in our suite's refrigerator and we already had lunch with the *Game Informer* guys, so we had barely put a dent in the funds. The only rational thing to do was to use the GameStop corporate card to buy the shark suit.

Nothing at the mall was going to interest us more than the shark suit, so we bought it and then jumped in a cab back to the hotel. On the way there, I saw a familiar sight. Members of the Westboro Baptist Church were protesting on a sidewalk downtown, holding their usual assortment of bright "GOD HATES FAGS" signs. There was some kind of evangelical convention in town, which had made national news due to the presence and acceptance of an openly gay minister. Naturally, this showed up on Fred Phelps' "something gay is happening somewhere" radar, and he dragged his family of sociopaths up to Minneapolis. I was finally far away from their frequent protests in Kansas, and yet they had made the trip north with me.

Kiu and I looked out the window for a moment at the screaming church members, and I suddenly had an idea.

"Excuse me," I said to the driver. "We can just get out here."

I paid for the ride and we got out. Kiu could already tell what I had in mind as I grabbed the plastic bag from the costume store and ran behind a tree. When I emerged, I was wearing the full-body shark suit and sprinting straight toward the Westboro protesters.

They were used to counter-protesters standing across the street with signs promoting diversity and LGBT acceptance. The church members thrived on it, as they loved screaming hateful gospel verses at people promoting equality. They seemed significantly less prepared to deal with a man dressed as a shark frantically running circles around them. A couple of them seemed to think I was on their side. Most just seemed perplexed.

While I was doing this, the group of counter-protesters across the street were laughing. Some even started a "Shark! Shark! Shark!" chant. When I heard this, I gestured toward them with my shark fins like a pro wrestler pointing toward a crowd to rile them up. They cheered, and I sprinted over to their side and hugged everyone. I'm not sure if any of that meant anything or made any kind of statement, but I loved confusing the Westboro people as a shark, only to betray them and ally myself with the tolerant side of the street.

Later in the week, I'd wear the shark suit to *Game Informer* for some reason. This led to the staff asking if I'd be all right with a picture of it being included in the next issue. Each month, a "GI Spy" section showcased a handful of photos from the office and gaming industry events. I'd always enjoyed the section, and was thrilled at the offer. They took a picture of me in the suit, sitting at one of the editors' desks while playing the Aquaman game. It ran in the October 2003 issue, with *Jade Empire* on the cover, and marked my first appearance in the magazine that I'd get hired at almost six years later.

Getting hired was the end goal for all of this, so I made sure to spend plenty of time talking to all of the magazine's editors. These conversations weren't schmoozing or networking solely for that purpose, however. I was fascinated by what they did and couldn't hear enough of it. I wanted to confirm that this line of work was indeed what I wanted to do with my life, and everything that they told me only reinforced my feelings.

We wound up filming the two-minute spot without much issue. Justin had fun playing the spy and the lack of significant dialogue made it an easy shoot. *Game Informer*'s editors were incredibly kind to me during the visit, especially considering I was just some random kid who was bumming around the office.

Kiu and I left Minneapolis thinking that things couldn't have gone better. The shoot went well, the staff was great, and I was personally thrilled to learn that the job seemed to be everything I'd hoped for. This plan that seemed impossible had come together without a hitch.

To this day, I'm not sure if the commercial ever actually ran in-store. GameStop received the finished product from me and requested a couple of minor changes, which I was happy to make. I sent in the new edit, they thanked me, and that was the end of our correspondence. By the time it would have run, I was back in Lawrence for my sophomore year of college and no longer working at the store. I'd check the televisions whenever I went in to pick up a game, but never wound up seeing it.

It didn't matter. My feelings on the experiment didn't hinge in the slightest on whether my ad actually appeared on those televisions. I was more motivated than ever to direct my career path toward video games rather than film or television.

A little over a year later, I got hired to write video game reviews for a local newspaper. It wasn't a paying job, but it resulted in me getting every major video game for free throughout the rest of my time in Kansas. More importantly, it gave me a massive amount of experience.

With legitimate press credentials, I was now eligible to attend the annual E3 trade show in Los Angeles. This weeklong event summoned everybody around the gaming industry, from developers to publishers to the media. In 2006, I started paying my own way to the event each year in an effort to play the newest games, meet people from the industry, and pitch my work. It was thrilling to meet game designers like Ed Boon, the co-creator of *Mortal Kombat*. These were the people responsible for some of my fondest childhood memories. While I was by no means their peer, I was at least allowed in the same building as them.

Meeting these gaming industry personalities was a blast, but it was the *Game Informer* editors that I was really keeping an eye out for. They'd surely remember me thanks to the unique nature of my visit, and I wanted to let them know that I was absolutely gunning for a job with them. During one of the days on the show floor, I saw Andy McNamara and executive editor Andrew Reiner outside the convention center's cafeteria.

Despite my entire E3 plan being "FIND THESE GUYS AND BOTHER THEM UNTIL I GET A JOB," I didn't want to egregiously impose or take up too much of their time. They seemed to be killing time in between appointments, so I approached them.

"Andy and Reiner!" I said. "I don't know if you remember me, but I'm Dan Ryckert. I'm that kid that ran around your office in a shark suit a few years ago."

That costume wound up being a good purchase, as they didn't seem to have any trouble recalling "the shark suit kid." We briefly caught up, and I mentioned that I had been reviewing video games for a newspaper for over a year. In that time, I had written over a hundred reviews. I told them that my primary career goal was to write for *Game Informer*, and that I'd love to send some sample reviews along if they had any openings. They didn't, but Andy told me that I should keep bugging him about it in the future.

I used the same approach the following year with Andy, Reiner, and other *Game Informer* editors that I ran into.

"I've done 250 reviews now," I told them.

In 2008, I did it again.

"I've written over 400 reviews, and I'd love to send them your way."

During the time between E3s, I'd see occasional job openings at big video game sites like IGN and GameSpot. I'd always apply for them, even though I hadn't met anyone on staff like I had at *Game Informer*. Sometimes this led to interviews. On many occasions, I'd think that an interview went great only to hear that they had decided to go with someone else. This was always disappointing, but it never discouraged me from continuing on this path. After all, none of those places were *Game Informer*.

2009 would be the last year that I had to bug Andy. After the Nintendo press conference across from the Staples Center, I spotted the entire GI crew as they left. They stopped briefly in the courtyard as Andy and Reiner caught up with an industry friend. Not wanting to butt into the conversation, I sat on a ledge across the courtyard until I could tell that they were done. They said their goodbyes, and I sprang into action.

"Hi, Andy!" I said as I walked up and shook his hand. "I'm..."

"Yeah, I know," he cut me off. "The shark suit kid. How are you?"

We exchanged pleasantries and I went into my usual pitch. Over 600 reviews at this point, etc. I fully expected to hear his usual response about not having openings, but he surprised me.

"E-mail me in a month. We might have some motion on our end by then."

This was the first time I had heard anything at all about potential job opportunities at the magazine, and I was thrilled. I e-mailed him a month to the day after that statement, and he requested a résumé, sample reviews, and some time to talk on the phone.

Two months later, I was driving through Iowa on my way up to Minneapolis and my new job as an Associate Editor at *Game Informer*. I'd be writing for the magazine that I had read religiously from the age of nine. The road to my dream job wasn't paved by any one particular thing, but I always wonder what my life would look like today had I not made a long-shot call to GameStop's headquarters with a ridiculous offer at the age of 19.

I'm sure that I would have still applied for (and landed) the reviewing position at the Lawrence Journal-World and Lawrence.com. I'm sure that I would have written just as many reviews with just as much enthusiasm. Hell, I was a college student who was getting every video game and console for free. Of course I was gonna stick with that gig for as long as I could ride it out.

But without making that call when I was nineteen, I wonder if things would have been different. Would I still have been as confident with approaching Andy and the others at E3? Would I even have bit the financial bullet to fly out there every year if I didn't have specific people in mind that I felt that I could talk to? There's no way to know how things would have shaken out if I hadn't made that call. All I know is that I'm damn glad that I did.

Social Lubricant

Most college students are content with one year living in the dorms, but I couldn't shake the feeling that I had made a mistake when it came to my freshman choice of Hashinger Hall. I never quite fit in with the lifestyle there, even though I had a great time and it proved critically important to my social skills.

By "lifestyle," I really mean drugs. Pot, mushrooms, acid, and home remedies were rampant in Hashinger. Beer and whiskey were suiting me fine by this point, but drugs didn't jibe well with my neurotic mind. In my first semester at Hashinger, I smoked pot maybe a dozen or so times and tried mushrooms twice. This always seemed to end with me becoming uncomfortably high. I'd wind up sitting on a staircase with my head in my hands, or laying in a bed thinking that I'd doomed myself to a lifetime of feeling that way.

My classmates in Hashinger were so drug-focused that I felt like I needed a do-over. I always assumed that college was supposed to be far more drinky than druggy, so I started scouting other options for year two. Lewis Hall and Templin Hall were two possibilities, and I had experience with the former thanks to my summer orientation program. I ruled those out based on their reputation as the personality-deprived homes of business students. Hashinger was right out, as was Naismith, the private "rich kid" dorm.

That left McCollum Hall. It was the largest dorm on the hill and it attracted a wide range of students. Most foreign students landed at McCollum and the domestic tenants tended to come from all walks of life. It housed artsy kids, rich kids, potheads, and business students without being solely made up of any group. The variety sounded promising and I was ready for a second round of the dorms.

As I had seen at Hashinger, the first couple of weeks in a new dorm are a whirlwind of learning names. Some of them are forgotten immediately or attached to people who never leave their rooms. With others, you shake their hands and learn their names and can never predict the amount of hours, beers, and laughs you'll share with them going forward.

It was hard to get a read on these seventh-floor McCollum characters. With Hashinger, 80% of them fit into the same pothead template. They might have differed when it came to "dreadlocks or no dreadlocks" or "Flaming Lips or String Cheese Incident" preference, but it was largely a cut-and-paste situation. During my early days in McCollum, I had no way of guessing which floormate was capable of putting turds in Pringles cans and which ones I'd want to kick in the testicles until they vomited (in Hashinger, the correct answer for both was "pretty much all of them").

McCollum was a full reset of my college social life, for all intents and purposes. I kept in contact with a few folks from Hashinger, but this might as well have been a complete mulligan of my first year. One exception from even further back was Bryan, my classmate from Olathe East and coworker from the movie theater. He was now my roommate. Most of Bryan's behavior was unremarkable. He'd go to class, do his best to socialize, and play video games with others on the floor. The difficult part of living with him came whenever he'd be reminded of the existence of homosexuals and become inconsolably angry. Bryan was still years away from being the last person on the planet to realize that he was gay, so his confusing (and telling) outbursts were par for the course throughout the year.

SOCIAL LUBRICANT

Within a couple of days at McCollum, I felt like I made the right choice. The people around me felt like a cross-section of the country instead of varying shades of the same future burnout—a large percentage of my Hashinger floormates did not stick around for a second year of college. I found a sense of humor and self-awareness all over McCollum that I rarely saw during my freshman year.

In the early weeks, a good chunk of the seventh floor would scour the residential areas of Lawrence for anything resembling a raucous house party. We'd enter, give our five dollars for the keg cups (or in my case, find a cup on the ground and clean it out in the bathroom), and naturally begin to section off into our own little groups based on interests and personality. I quickly jelled with a handful of guys on our floor, and we formed a close friend circle.

Brad was an English guy who loved comedy, liquor, Schwarzenegger movies, hip-hop, and designing graffiti. I wasn't particularly knowledgeable about those last two, but we shared a love of the rest. Our senses of humor matched up well, and he became my primary actor when I created a sketch comedy show for local television later that year.

His cousin and roommate was Derek, who was born in England but grew up in Israel. Going anywhere with Derek was equal parts fascinating and infuriating. This was through no fault of his own, as girls would literally stop him on the street just to hear him speak. More often than not, these encounters would end with an exchange of phone numbers. I can't count the number of times I saw Brad sitting in the floor's lobby while he waited for Derek to conclude his lady business in their shared dorm room.

Going to parties with these two played out like a script. All three of us would get blindingly drunk and hope to get laid. My brilliant plan was to get drunk enough to not be nervous in the event that a girl randomly started talking to me. Weirdly enough, this plan never worked, and I'd end my sophomore year every bit the virgin I was when I started college. Brad would get drunk and actually talk to girls, which wasn't always successful but certainly worked better than my approach.

Derek's story was almost always the same. While Brad and I slammed beers and reminisced about our favorite action movies or late-night comedy bits, Derek would just talk. It didn't matter what he talked about, or if it was even remotely interesting. He could have stood stone-cold sober in the middle of the party and read the Declaration of Independence (or whatever the Israeli version of that is), and the most attractive girls at the party would immediately flock to him. On more than one occasion, I asked Brad about Derek's whereabouts and learned that he was "bonin' some chick in the laundry closet." I accidentally confirmed this once when I entered what I assumed was the bathroom, only to see a girl sitting on the dryer with her legs spread and Derek in front of her.

Another member of our social circle was Darren. In retrospect, he was the worst designated driver on the planet. Actually, that's not even fair to say. "Designated driver" implies sobriety, so I guess Darren was just our driver. He drove an old Cadillac and would frequently drive us to and from parties that were beyond walking distance. Every memory I have of being in Darren's car involves him blaring rap with a gigantic blunt in his mouth and a handle of Tanqueray (or a forty of Mickey's malt liquor) in his hand. We always got home fine, but the 32-year-old version of me looks back on that and wonders how the hell we thought his rides were really the best option for getting back to the dorm.

Darren loved drinking forties, and frequently joked about how he was fulfilling a stereotype by being a big black guy who loved malt liquor. On one occasion, he was eating fried chicken and drinking a forty of Mickey's while wearing a white tank top. He wanted to get a picture of it as a parody of the stereotype. We took a picture of Darren grinning from ear to ear, proudly posing with his drumstick and forty. Later, it would resurface in an unexpected place.

After he was eventually kicked out of school for poor grades, Darren continued to live near campus and use the rec center's basketball court. The only problem was that the rec center was reserved for students. Since his student ID was useless, he adopted a brazen approach: casually walking past the front desk and completely ignoring staff members' attempts to get him to check in.

This worked without a hitch for weeks until it came to a sudden stop one afternoon. I ran into Darren on my way into the gym and chatted with him as we approached the front desk. Just before we passed the turnstiles, he stopped in his tracks and collapsed to the floor laughing. I looked up at the corkboard above the front desk to see the infamous "fried chicken and a forty" picture plastered up like a wanted poster alongside the text "DO NOT LET THIS MAN INTO THE GYM. HE IS NOT A STUDENT." They had found Darren's Facebook account and used this profile picture as a point of reference. Once Darren gathered himself from off of the floor, he walked out the front door and used another basketball court going forward.

Brad, Derek, Darren, and I hung out constantly, with an assortment of other characters frequently in tow:

- **Lenis:** Not his real name, but no one ever said his real name once Lenis was coined. Brad mentioned at a house party early in the year that he wished this guy's name rhymed with something funny, and "Lenis" (pronounced like penis) was born. He embraced it and started to introduce himself as Lenis from then on out. In terms of personality, he was pretty quiet unless the topic of his father owning a bunch of Domino's Pizza franchises came up.

- **Matt:** Quiet when sober, loud as hell when he was drunk or arguing with his girlfriend (which was a frequent occurrence). He made more of an impact post-dorms than he did in McCollum, primarily during that time he broke into my apartment and tried to stab me.

- **Idiot Derek**: We had several Dereks on our floor, so each of them received their own nickname. There was British Derek, Sports Derek, and Idiot Derek. As his name suggested, the latter was a massive idiot. He smelled terrible and spent most of his nights trying to lure young women from Craigslist to his dorm room. This and his tendency to sleep in the nude almost drove his shy, Muslim roommate insane. On one occasion, we convinced Idiot Derek that sour apple candy in an eyedropper was LSD. He put two drops on his tongue and spent hours rolling around on the floor and claiming he could hear colors and see sound.

- **Kaci:** A fan of frequent drunken dares. When a bar crawl scavenger hunt called for her to shave her eyebrows, she did it without thinking twice and passed out not long afterwards. Her roommates drew angry cartoon eyebrows in permanent marker where the real ones used to be. Kaci woke up late for her public speaking class the next morning, rushing out the door without looking into a mirror. She gave an entire presentation while she had bold, inch-thick angry eyebrows on her face without realizing it.

- **Anthony:** The single angriest man I've ever met. He'd never return a "hello" or even a nod in the hallways. He always slammed his door, and he perpetually seemed half a second away from putting his fist through a wall. His demeanor suddenly made sense when a girl from our floor slept with him and immediately reported to everyone that she "didn't even know penises could be that small."

- **Ethan:** A staunchly conservative guy who would try to turn any house party conversation into a political debate. His love of George W. Bush contrasted with the mostly liberal makeup of the seventh floor and the university in general. Politics aside, he was about five years older than anyone else, and that meant he could buy beer.

- **Roy:** A tremendously rich kid from Chicago that instantly rubbed everyone the wrong way. He seemed desperate to fit in with our group, but his habit of incessantly talking about his wealth didn't do him any favors ("I live in the same neighborhood as Oprah" was a common refrain). Whenever anyone was telling a story, he'd interrupt it with his own version that he sold as bigger and better and cooler. As much as he liked to brag, he'd sometimes get too drunk and tip in the opposite direction. On one occasion, he collapsed on a couch in the dorm lobby after a house party and declared that no girl would ever want him because of his "mediocre penis." He'd eventually get kicked out of the dorms after he stole items from a floormate, but not before trying to save himself by throwing Brad and Darren under the bus. In a last-ditch effort to stay in McCollum, he told management that he could be an inside source for them. They didn't seem impressed at his revelation that Brad and Darren smoked pot in their rooms, and they carried out his eviction.

If my circle of friends from college seemed pretty dude-centric, it's because I was still a year or two away from being able to have a conversation with a girl without coming off like a stammering idiot. I was able to be funny and comfortable around girls who weren't available or whom I wasn't attracted to, but I clammed up in the presence of any girl I had an interest in. For some unfathomable reason, a girl on my floor named Nadia took a liking to me. She was an Indian pharmacy student who took her academic life super seriously, but frequently joined us for house party nights. After a few weeks of pretty obviously flirting with me, she and I wound up making out in my dorm room one night.

This led to us messing around off and on for years, and she had the patience of a saint for dealing with me during the most stubborn, pain-in-the-ass period of my life. Between the ages of about 21 and 23, I had virtually zero tolerance for opinions that differed from my own. My father has exhibited this attitude for his entire life and I found myself leaning into that aspect of my genetics hard during these years.

When Nadia and I would go to her room after a party, she'd frequently have top-forty hip-hop and pop music playing on her computer. We'd finish messing around and I'd immediately launch into a discussion about how the songs were soulless and terrible. Eventually, I brought over a USB stick with a playlist of music that I deemed acceptable. Her Ying Yang Twins and Chingy tracks may have annoyed me, but it's not like the Bob Dylan, Neil Young, and Creedence

Clearwater Revival soundtrack I provided was any more appropriate for drunken fooling-around sessions.

My guy friends were more entertained than infuriated by my obnoxious behavior in those days. They had a sense of humor about themselves, and I felt comfortable bringing back some of the rampant griefing that I had grown up doing. An early favorite bar of ours was called Charlie's East Side. It's closed now, most likely due to its very public reputation for serving underage college students.

The basement at Charlie's was a genuine dump. Graffiti covered every wall, the whole place smelled like urine, and its one pool table was off balance, beer-stained, and torn up. One element of its layout was particularly attractive to me, though. A huge *Golden Tee* arcade machine sat directly between the doors leading into the bathrooms. I call them doors, but they were really just tall sheets of plywood that were erected to keep people from seeing other people poop.

Every time we were there, I would eventually make use of the machine. Not to play it, mind you, since I don't think I've ever actually played *Golden Tee* despite seeing it in at least 95 percent of the bars in the Midwest. Instead, I'd wait for my friends to enter the "stall" and then immediately lower my shoulder into the side of the machine to scoot it in front of the door. This was usually followed by me running upstairs to order another beer or two. Between songs, I could hear the sounds of my friends banging on plywood in an attempt to escape the disgusting basement bathroom.

Another bar that served minors (although not as openly) was the polar opposite of Charlie's East Side. It was called It's Brothers, but everyone just called it Brothers because the actual name was stupid. Whereas Charlie's was filled with genuine grime and character, Brothers had the aesthetic and heart of a Chili's and the clientele of a dance club.

Nothing made me feel more out of place than the nights I got dragged to Brothers. The music drove me insane, with the bar playing "Get Low" and "Tipsy" seemingly on repeat every single night. Most of the patrons were identical, popped-collar frat boys and shrill sorority girls. They'd head to the dance floor and drunkenly grind on each other for hours, with the girls spilling drinks and the guys nearly getting into fights whenever they accidentally bumped shoulders.

Brad, Derek, and Darren would head to the dance floor once they had a few drinks in them. Derek would have six girls rubbing up on him by the time he finished ordering a beer in his accent. Brad and Darren would try to dance with girls to varying levels of success.

I took an odd amount of pride in not dancing. In those years I told myself that dancing served no purpose and was only for idiots with bad taste in music. I'd look for some corner of the bar where I could hole up and drink excessively in the hopes of some girl approaching me. To this day, I have no idea why girls weren't throwing themselves at the shaggy-haired guy drinking alone in the corner, wearing an old Lynyrd Skynyrd shirt and clearly hating being at this bar.

Drinking was my ticket to comfort in these situations and I viewed it as my only chance to meet a girl. I sure as hell didn't have the courage to approach a girl, but I assumed I'd be a little more relaxed and funny if I had ten or twelve beers in me.

Catching a bartender's attention to get these beers was an infuriating process during weekend nights. I'd always order two beers to minimize the amount of time I'd have to spend at the counter, but it was still an ordeal. Bartenders at

Brothers always tended to girls first, even if they had just waltzed up to the bar after I'd been standing there with cash in my hand for ten minutes.

On one night, I hatched a plan to make buying drinks a bit easier. In my pocket was a three-pack of stink bombs. A friend of mine had pulled a prank on me earlier in the week, so I got him back during the walk to the bar by sticking a stink bomb into the hood of his sweatshirt and breaking it open with a punch. He left his offensively stinky hoodie in the bushes outside Brothers, leaving me with two stink bombs still in my pocket.

I couldn't make the bartenders serve drinks or notice me any quicker, but I could sure as hell reduce the overall number of patrons lining up at the counter. Standing behind others at the bar, I slipped a stink bomb underneath my shoe and quietly shattered it. Within seconds, the stench wafted up to my nostrils. I knew it wouldn't take long for its effect to spread to the rest of the area.

In a growing circle, people around me started to scrunch their faces and glance at each other. A lot of "what *is* that?" and "did someone tear ass?" could be heard, and it intensified as the smell lingered for far longer than even the worst fart. Ninety seconds or so passed before a large chunk of the bar's customers determined that the smell wouldn't be going away anytime soon. There were plenty of other bars on Massachusetts Street, and they marched out of Brothers and on to less farty establishments. My friends stayed in the relative sanctuary of the dance floor across from the bar and I happily bought beers in a fraction of the time it usually took.

For all the times I've messed with people, I always considered myself to utilize a loosely defined moral code. As long as no one was actually hurt by my actions, I didn't feel bad. When my friends and I made a fake dating profile to lure a dozen or so dudes in matching blue shirts to a pizza parlor, "Heather" only invited the most aggressively douchey suitors. When I would sprint through giant lecture halls while wearing a shark suit, it was nothing worse than a temporary distraction.

Occasionally, I'd overstep my self-imposed boundaries, and morality would enter the equation. I was firmly opposed to stealing anything of value, but I would sometimes nab things that seemed silly or inconsequential. An IHOP rug welcomed visitors to my apartment for years.

During one early morning walk home from the bars, I made an error in judgment that I later felt terrible about. Lenis and I were scaling the 12th Street hill that led to his campus-adjacent apartment when we spotted something odd on a nearby porch. It was metallic and appeared vaguely human in shape, so we approached it to get a better look.

For some reason, this house had a robot-like figure made of old cans sitting in a chair on the front porch. This oddity fascinated us, and we immediately snagged it and took it to Lenis's apartment. Our new robot buddy sat silently as Lenis and I had a few more beers, watched *Commando* for about the 45th time that year, and called it a night. My place was only a few blocks away and I wanted the robot to be a new fixture in it. When it came time to leave, I heaved all four feet of cans and googly eyes over my shoulder and made the trip home.

I typically woke up no earlier than 2:00 p.m. in college, but Saturdays during football season were different. Living a couple of blocks from the stadium comes with the added benefit of fighter jets serving as your alarm clock once a week. As was tradition during this time of year, I shot up in bed terrified before I realized what the noise was. This was almost always accompanied by the hangover setting in shortly after the F-15-induced adrenaline wore off.

On this Saturday, I woke up to the jets, vomited for a bit, and then shuffled over to my oven to make my breakfast. At the time, that meal typically consisted of two Totino's Party Pizzas (Combination flavor). I'd place one upside down on top of the other to make a sandwich, which has proved to be a great idea to this day.

As my roughly 12,000-calorie breakfast was cooking, I plopped down on the couch to play some video games. The night before had been a particularly drunken one and I had almost forgotten about my new roommate until I saw him on the couch next to me. My robot buddy had sat upright all night, blankly staring ahead at the television.

I laughed to myself at first, recalling the silliness of the previous night. I stopped laughing when I noticed numerous spiders crawling out from the joints between his arm cans. After spraying the spiders on my couch with a bunch of Raid, I set the robot outside temporarily while I ate my pizza sandwich. Hypocritically, I was worried that somebody would walk by in the meantime and steal him.

When I went back outside after finishing my breakfast, I started to feel bad as I looked at the metal figure. This wasn't some IHOP rug or a glass from a bar that I had stolen. It was clearly some kind of art project. Someone had taken a decent amount of time in making this, and placed it on their front porch as a quirky decoration. I started to think that I should return him to his owners, regardless of whether he was filled with spiders.

It was a Saturday, so I knew that I'd be meeting up with friends later for another night at the bars. This usually involved pre-drinking at Lenis's place, so I'd have a chance to drop off the robot on his rightful owners' porch on the way.

Ideally, I'd get a chance to set him back in his chair without his owner recognizing me and kicking my ass.

If I was going to go to the trouble of returning the robot, I figured that I might as well bring him back in better condition than I had found him. Part of a metal hanger was attached to the top of the robot's head, so I held onto it and shook him around. As I expected, this caused a ton of spiders to scurry out. I shook harder so they'd fall off the exterior of the robot, and eventually dropped the whole thing with a girlish shriek once a couple of spiders crawled onto my hand. He didn't break apart or anything, so I brought the newly spider-free project back into my apartment until it was time to head to Lenis's place.

When the time came to head out, it would have been easier to toss the robot in the trunk of my car. However, I never went anywhere near my car when I was drinking. I opted to heave the robot over my shoulder and walk several blocks to Lenis's while looking like I had kidnapped a mechanical child from the future and returned to my time.

After walking about halfway there, I realized something: I had no idea which house I grabbed the robot from. We had been extremely drunk when we stole him, and it had been in the middle of the night. All I remembered was that it was from somewhere near Lenis's. I wasn't about to turn back around at this point, so I figured that I'd just patrol the block for a bit and hope that something triggered my memory.

It had to be somewhere near the corner of 12th Street and Ohio Street, so I focused on that area. Nothing was looking familiar and I was starting to feel a little nervous about being so conspicuous. I decided that the best course of action would be to leave the robot on Lenis's lawn in a very visible location. Ideally, the rightful owner would spot him before too long and take their robot child back home.

As soon as I decided on that course of action, I heard a voice ring out from the house to my right.

"*THERE IT IS!*"

I turned to see three guys who were roughly the same age as me. They had been drinking on a porch, and in that moment I instantly realized where I was: I was standing right in front of the house that I stole the robot from, holding him in clear view as his presumably drunken owners approached me.

I'm usually pretty good at reading people and situations. My gut instinct was that these dudes were mad and also seconds away from beating my ass. Some part of my brain subconsciously ran through possible scenarios and determined that running away wouldn't work. Instead, my brain assumed that the best thing to do was to stare at them, continue to hold the robot, and make some dumb "UHHH" noise. I didn't yet know what I was planning on saying, but trying to talk my way out of this was apparently the route I was heading down.

"Where the fuck did you get that?" one of them asked.

"Oh!" I said as possible answers spun around in my head. "Yeah? This is yours? Oh man, I'm glad to find you."

They stared at me, fully ready to be pissed at whatever my excuse was.

"So yeah, I'll be honest with you guys. Last night, my roommate and I were really drunk after the bars when we were walking home. He can be kind of an asshole when he's been drinking, and he stole this. I saw it this morning when I woke up, and it looks like it must have taken a lot of work, so I wanted to walk around and try to find its owner. He said it was around here, so I'm glad I was able to find you guys!"

Two of them looked like they weren't buying my story, but one of them seemed to come to some kind of realization while I was talking.

"Wait a minute," he said. "Aren't you that guy that makes the comedy show on channel six?"

Holy crap. I rarely got recognized around town for my sketch show. If there was ever an ideal time for it to happen, it was right now.

"Yeah!" I said. "That's me. You guys watch?"

All three of them smiled, and the tense situation immediately took a 180-degree turn.

"Holy shit, yeah!" the initial talker of the group said. "Dude, we always come back from the bars late at night and get stoned and laugh our asses off at that show."

Instead of kicking my ass or accusing me of stealing their robot, all three of them started thanking me profusely for being "so nice" by bringing it back.

"We've still got a ton left in the keg from earlier this week. Wanna come in?"

I agreed, handed the robot off to the guys, and headed into their house. We joked around for a couple of hours as I drank free beer, and then I thanked them for their hospitality and headed out to the bars.

Of all the people I annoyed in college, Brad got it the worst. It would range in severity, from a variety of minor pranks to more elaborate ordeals. Small things included dipping a sandwich in orange Fanta at the cafeteria and smashing it into his face, or waking him up by slamming an ice cream cone into his ear. He wasn't one for pulling his own pranks, so his retaliation was typically along the lines of a stiff punch to the arm.

Brad fancied himself quite the ladies' man, and would often brag about his conquests and unwillingness to contain himself to just one girl. He fully subscribed to the "love 'em and leave 'em" philosophy, and would always cut things off with girls when they started having feelings toward him. It's worth noting that he is now married with children and running a daycare center with one of his more frequent college partners.

After almost a full school year of hosting a revolving door of ladies in his room, Brad seemed to take a genuine liking to a girl named Monica. Considering how loudly opposed he had been to relationships or expressing feelings for girls, I knew I had to give him shit in some capacity.

One of our usual house party nights ended with Brad and Monica retreating to their dorm room. I wanted to grief him a bit, so I grabbed the phone book. For a couple of hours in the middle of the night, I called dozens of florists, wedding planners, limousine services, and other businesses to leave messages on Brad's behalf.

"Hello! My name is Brad and you can reach me at [phone number]. I'm getting married to the love of my life soon, and I'm going to need your best [assortment of flowers, catering package, fleet of limousines, massive assortment of heart balloons, etc.]. Money is no concern. Please give me a call tomorrow."

All through the next day (and bleeding into the next couple), Brad received calls with offers and congratulations from every Kansas business that was remotely associated with wedding preparation.

One of the harshest pranks I've ever pulled came after another long night at a house party. Roy and I were very drunk, and Brad was light years ahead of us. We got back to McCollum at about two or three in the morning, and I jumped into my top bunk to pass out. Brad apparently wasn't ready to call it a night, as he burst into my room in an attempt to rally me to continue drinking. He grabbed the supports of my bunk bed and rocked it back and forth, eventually pushing me in the face when that didn't work.

I resisted enough for him to leave the room, but I wasn't able to fall asleep afterward. It sounded like plenty of people were still up and hanging out in the lobby, so I threw on some pajama pants and joined them. By the time I got down there, Brad had grabbed a few floormates and retreated to his room to drink. He was in rare form as I entered the room, joking and laughing and passing drinks around while wearing a foam cowboy hat.

We drank more until the late night and copious amount of alcohol caught up to Brad. In the span of seconds, he went from giving people shit and preparing beer bongs to passing out face-first in his lower bunk. His cousin Derek was back in Europe for a week, presumably having sex with women on top of dryers overseas.

With Brad passed out hard—still wearing his cowboy hat—it was obviously time to fuck with him. Lenis went to town with a Sharpie, covering him in a cornucopia of penises. Roy grabbed a huge roll of duct tape, and we prepared to trap Brad in his bunk with it. Scooting the beds away from the wall gave us room to maneuver as we repeatedly passed the roll of tape over and under the bed, creating a silver cocoon that encased Brad.

Next, we put a cigar in his mouth and gathered all the laundry from his and Derek's hampers. We tossed it all on top of him until it piled all the way up to the underside of the top bunk. Then we took Derek's blankets and draped them down over our makeshift tomb to keep any light from getting in. None of this was annoying enough, so we grabbed chairs, couches, and loveseats from the lobby and surrounded the bed with them.

At this point, Brad was already going to have a really rough time when he woke up. He'd be hungover, unable to move, unable to see, and even once he wriggled free of the tape, he'd have to find a way to escape the furniture jail we had created around his bed. This was all a terrible idea in hindsight, but I'm glad that we at least taped him up on his side in case he vomited.

His room was already filled with obstacles, but Roy and I continued to brainstorm other things to add to this elaborate setup (everyone else had gone to bed).

"Ooh, I got an idea!" Roy said. "Let's throw a bunch of knives in his bed."

"What?" I asked. "Knives?"

"Yeah, it'll be hilarious!"

"Why is that hilarious?"

"He'll get all scraped up! Come on!"

I was game for setting Brad up to have a tremendously confusing morning, but throwing a bunch of knives into someone's bed seemed several steps too far. In lieu of Roy's idiotic plan, I offered a different idea. I turned on Brad's computer and downloaded the tremendously annoying "Yakety Sax" song from *The Benny Hill Show*. Before leaving the room, I made sure that the volume was loud and the "repeat" setting was on so that it would continue indefinitely.

When I got back to bed, I kept imagining what it would be like for Brad when he woke up. There was zero option that included him getting out of bed and on with his day without incident. He wasn't going to wriggle free of that tape in his sleep, the blankets wouldn't suddenly fall and let light in, and that damn song sure as hell wasn't going to stop playing. Whether it was at 4 a.m. or noon, Brad was destined to get hit with a wall of sheer bewilderment.

I woke up the next morning to my roommate Bryan laughing so hard he was almost in tears. He had been on his way to the floor's elevator when he heard yelling coming from Brad's room. We had left the door unlocked so that somebody would be able to get in and help him if he needed it, and he certainly needed it in that moment. Bryan entered the room to find Brad squirming around and mumbling a lot of four-letter words. With the help of some scissors and a lot of furniture reorganization, Bryan freed Brad.

"There's something I gotta show you," Bryan said before leading me to Brad's room.

Brad's whereabouts were unknown at this time, but he wasn't in his room. I was tip-toeing around the floor in an effort to avoid him, because I wouldn't have been surprised at all if he was in the mood to kick someone's ass.

Peering around the corner of the door frame, I glimpsed the scene of the crime. Brad's blankets and sheets had been completely removed from the bed. All that was left there were some crumpled-up balls of duct tape and an odd puddle of red liquid that sat dead-center on Brad's mattress.

"He told me that he had been laying there awake for almost an hour before I came in," Bryan said. "He didn't have any choice but to keep peeing."

We had anticipated a lot of confusion, but the seemingly obvious potential for hilarious and repeated bedwetting hadn't even occurred to me. His fitted sheet was responsible for giving the pee a red tint as the puddle lingered on his bed.

Talking to Brad about his morning was extremely tempting, even though I knew he'd be in some kind of mood. I just had to hear his beat-by-beat explanation of what it was like to wake up like that. Thinking that he had left the dorm at some point in the morning, I started walking back toward my room. Just as I was about to pass the door to the restroom, it opened and Brad shuffled out.

It was like a far less dramatic version of Sarah Connor seeing the T-800 round the corner in the hospital hallway in *Terminator 2*. Like her, I fell back directly on my ass. I laughed hysterically on the floor as a clearly disheveled and confused Brad stood before me, his face and arms still covered in penis drawings.

Part of me was bracing for him to kick me in the head or the crotch. Either would have been understandable. He went the opposite route, which involved acting like nothing weird had happened. Stepping over me, he casually walked back to his room and sat down at his desk.

Once I had caught my breath, I went into his room and asked him about his morning. His response was predictable. As it turns out, it's baffling to wake up immobilized, blind, and hearing only the repeated and frantic tune of "Yakety Sax." Adding to his confusion was the fact that Brad had zero recollection of getting back to the dorms the previous night.

"The last thing I remembered was being at the party," Brad said. "And then I woke up like that."

He was calmly explaining his morning to me, but I knew that retaliation would be coming sooner or later. I actually think both Roy and I got off easy, considering what Brad had gone through. While Roy was asleep, Brad grabbed an empty full-size trash can from the lobby and filled it more than halfway with water. He jimmied Roy's door open, hoisted the heavy trash can above his bed, and yelled "HEY ROY" before dumping gallons of water directly onto his face.

For over a week, Roy slept on a couch in the lobby as his mattress dried.

My punishment was even less severe, and I'd like to think that it was because I stopped Roy from throwing a bunch of damn knives into the bed. While I was asleep, Brad simply broke into my room and put superglue into my hair. For the second year in a row, I found myself in a dorm shower late at night while trying to rid my hair of glue. I didn't want to shave my head like I had to do with my chest, so I took some scissors and snipped off a few patches of hair.

Each year at the University of Kansas felt unique, but my sophomore year in McCollum was a turning point. I had never felt like I fit into any particular group in elementary school, junior high, high school, or even in that first year in Hashinger Hall. There were plenty of great moments throughout those years and a few close friends, but starting with McCollum, I finally felt like I had a real circle of friends. We were all drunken morons, but we hung out constantly and were always making each other laugh.

On November 25, 2015, I got a text from my father saying that McCollum Hall had been imploded by the university. I went to YouTube and pulled up clips of the demolition, and couldn't help but think of how pivotal that building had been to my social life. That seventh floor hosted so many funny moments, late-night editing sessions for my TV show, *Mario Kart: Double Dash* showdowns, hungover mornings in the bathroom, and a few awkward make-out sessions. There would be a lot more college left to go, but I don't think any one year had more of an impact on changing the course of the rest of my life.

Over the Edge

In early 1993, I was an eight-year-old who had never been exposed to professional wrestling. I was somewhat aware of Hulk Hogan and Andre the Giant through their status that transcended the wrestling industry and bled into pop culture, but I still had no idea what occurred inside the squared circle. A year later, I was combing through local TV listings on a weekly basis, desperate to figure out a way to watch even more wrestling than I already was. It became a driving fascination in my life, and Owen Hart was one of the main reasons for it.

When I first stumbled upon an episode of *Monday Night Raw* in 1993, it seemed to me that there were defined, unchangeable character alignments. Razor Ramon was the coolest guy in the history of the world, "oozing machismo" and beating his opponents while still being affable enough to high-five fans on the way to the ring. Shawn Michaels was the opposite: a cocky, flamboyant showboat with nothing but disdain for the fans. Good people don't suddenly turn evil (or vice versa) in real life, and I had no reason to expect that this alternate dimension of pro wrestling would be any different.

At this time, I saw Owen Hart as a good dude for all intents and purposes. Nothing about him seemed malevolent to me, even as he grew increasingly jealous of his older brother, Bret Hart, throughout 1993. Bret was one of the biggest stars in the World Wrestling Federation and a former world champion. Owen frequently made remarks that made it seem like he was tired of playing second fiddle. I thought Owen had a tendency to be a bit of a crybaby when he lost, and his clear jealousy of Bret was off-putting, but he was still firmly in the "good guy" column of my brain.

My view of Owen took a sharp turn in January 1994 after the Hart brothers lost a tag team title opportunity against the villainous Quebecers (the "bad guy" Canadian tag team) at the annual Royal Rumble event. Bret's leg gave out during the match, and he attempted to finish it regardless. Ultimately, the referee stopped the match as a result of the leg injury and rewarded the Quebecers with the win.

I was saddened enough by Bret and Owen losing, but the post-match events kicked my wrestling fascination into a higher gear than ever before. With Bret writhing on the mat, Owen berated him instead of helping him. He screamed "why didn't you just tag me?!?!" about 800 times before Bret finally made it back to his feet on his own. As soon as Bret was fully standing, Owen pivoted around to Bret's injured leg and kicked it out from underneath him. He left his brother on the mat as he exited the ring and screamed into the camera about Bret's selfishness.

Wrestlers had made me hate them before, but this was different. In my mind, bad-guy wrestlers were born evil and stayed that way. Now, I had watched a wrestler whom I used to cheer for do something so heinous that I wanted nothing more than to see him get his comeuppance. My positive feelings about Owen were dead and gone, and Bret deserved revenge.

This was the first alignment change I remember seeing, and it blew me away. In wrestling lingo, it's known as a "heel turn," and it's been a part of the act since the industry started. Bret's leg wasn't really hurt, Owen wasn't really a bad guy, and the ending to the match was planned well before it started. I didn't know any of this at the time, and none of it mattered to me. I would have hated a traitorous character in an action movie just as much, so it had nothing to do with whether it was predetermined or real.

Prior to Owen's heel turn, I had an inkling that something like it was possible. When I started watching *Monday Night Raw*, Razor Ramon and Doink the Clown were dyed-in-the-wool good guys. Once I got hooked on the product, I started renting old pay-per-views from our local video store and was often confused by what I saw. WrestleMania IX took place just a few months before I started watching wrestling, but when I rented it, I saw Razor and Doink acting like complete assholes. Razor was cocky and didn't high-five the fans, while Doink was bringing in fake clown doubles to help him cheat during his match. What the hell had happened in the months between WrestleMania IX and the nice versions of Razor and Doink that I had been cheering for on *Raw*?

As soon as Owen swept Bret's leg, it all came into focus for me. Wrestling characters aren't permanently fixed into position. They can change from pure good to pure evil overnight, or morph into different characters entirely. That witch doctor can turn into an MMA fighter before settling down as a cartoon pimp within the matter of a few years. If wrestling fascinated me before, Owen's kick helped turn it into a full-on obsession.

Owen's turn culminated with a win over his brother Bret at WrestleMania X and a loss to him later that year at SummerSlam. After this feud, Owen remained a fixture on WWF television for years, even after Bret infamously left the company with plenty of real-life animosity in 1997. Owen's storylines were rarely the focal point of the week's drama, but he was always entertaining on the microphone, gifted in the ring, and beloved by the other wrestlers backstage. In an industry with no shortage of troubled and contentious performers, Owen was one of the true good guys in real life.

Between my introduction to wrestling in 1993 and my first live event in 1999, the industry saw sweeping changes. The white-bread good guys who advocated for working hard and staying true to yourself were replaced by antiheroes—namely, the beer-swilling, foul-mouthed Stone Cold Steve Austin and the perennially gesturing-towards-their-penises D-Generation X stable.

With edgy personalities now in vogue, Owen's character was changed into a parody of a more innocent time. His initial run with the company in the late '80s saw him performing as the Blue Blazer, a masked superhero. For this parody character a decade later, the WWF put him back under the mask and had him lecture the crowd about saying their prayers, drinking their milk, and eating their vitamins (a frequent refrain of Hulk Hogan's).

During this period, my fascination with the industry only intensified. I was now in high school, and at one point I even considered dropping out and moving to San Antonio to attend the Shawn Michaels Wrestling Academy. I've always told myself that I stopped considering becoming a pro wrestler because my physique wouldn't allow for it, but that didn't stop Daniel Bryan. He was a scrawny kid who was three inches shorter than me, and he joined the academy and went on to win the WWE World Heavyweight Championship in a WrestleMania main event. With that excuse officially null and void, I guess I was just a coward who didn't want to fall on his back hundreds of times a month for a living.

Becoming a wrestler might not have been in the cards, but that wasn't going to stop me from obsessively following the industry. I still hadn't been to a live wrestling event and I wanted to see the action in person more than anything.

Those years of waiting seemed destined to pay off when the WWF announced that it would be holding its Over the Edge pay-per-view at Kemper Arena in Kansas City. I was finally going to get to see wrestling live, and it wasn't an untelevised house show, it wasn't a random *Monday Night Raw*—it was a pay-per-view.

It wasn't just any pay-per-view, either. This was at the height of the "Attitude Era" boom period for wrestling, and the show would serve as the payoff for a couple of feuds that I was hugely invested in. Triple H and The Rock were two of the company's biggest stars, and they'd be settling a long-standing grudge right there in my hometown. Even more exciting was the prospect of the main event, which saw Stone Cold Steve Austin defending his world championship against The Undertaker. A week earlier, Austin had crucified The Undertaker on his own cross-like logo and raised it above the ring while giving him his trademark double middle fingers. It was a great time to be a fan, especially if you happened to be 14 years old.

The opportunity to finally see wrestling live was in front of me; now I just had to figure out how to make it happen. I had a few friends who were good for chipping in five dollars or so when I ordered pay-per-views from my house, but asking them to commit to $80-100 for decent seats was a harder sell. Plus, my mom would be waiting tables at Macaroni Grill that night and my father sure as hell wouldn't consider doing anything that would help support my interest in professional wrestling. In my adult life, he's even sincerely offered to pay me $10,000 if I promised to stop watching it.

With no friends willing to pay the ticket price, and my parents either unavailable or unwilling to give me a ride, I was fully ready to save up and pay for a ticket and a taxi myself. I started working at McDonald's not long after I became eligible for employment after turning 14. Making $5.15 an hour didn't help my savings account grow very rapidly, but I was more than willing to save up for a good seat and a ride to Kemper Arena.

Before I had to save up, luck fell in my favor. One of my mother's coworkers at Macaroni Grill was an eccentric dude named Cherick. He was in his mid-20s, and his pale skin, ponytail, and sinister facial hair made it look like he had just stepped out of a Transylvanian castle. It seemed as though this was a look that he was intentionally pursuing, as evidenced by the tattoo of two bleeding fang marks on the left side of his neck.

More important than his look was the fact that he had two eighth-row tickets to Over the Edge coming to him thanks to 101.1 The Fox, a local classic rock station. My mother overheard him talking about winning the radio contest, and quickly let him know that her son was a massive fan, in case one of those tickets was in danger of going unused. He checked around the restaurant, but no one seemed interested in going to this professional wrestling event with a pasta-serving vampire man.

Cherick was an odd duck for sure, but my mother was confident that he'd be a safe chauffeur for the event. Plans were made, and on May 23, he pulled up to my house in an old red Honda Accord. I opened the passenger door and was almost knocked onto my ass by the wave of cigarette stench that washed over me. At this point, I couldn't care less about what he looked like or what his car smelled like. But at this point, my enthusiasm wouldn't have been dampened one bit even if he looked like Rasputin and drove a hearse filled with rotting meat and old diapers.

Being a wrestling fan helps to bridge any gap between age and lifestyle, which was helpful considering that I don't know what else a 14-year-old who never left the house and an undead Juggalo/future vaping enthusiast would talk about. Anything related to real life was happily left out of the conversation, as we focused on topics like whether the WWF would ever figure out something to do with Steve Blackman (they wouldn't) or whether Triple H would ever make it to the main event level (boy, would he).

We maintained our purely wrestling-focused chat until Cherick needed to run into a gas station to grab more cigarettes. There, the tenor of the conversation immediately swung hard in the other direction.

"Alright, Dan," he said as we pulled into the gas station parking lot. "I need you to listen, because your mom is gonna kill me if anything happens to you while you're with me."

"Uh, okay."

I wasn't aware of any impending danger, and we weren't in a particularly bad part of town, so I had zero idea where he was going with this.

"I'm gonna run in there, and I won't be gone more than five minutes. If anyone—and I mean *anyone*—comes up to this car while I'm in there, just open the glove compartment."

After I assured him that I understood what he was talking about, he left the car and I immediately opened the glove compartment to figure out what the hell he was talking about. As I should have guessed, it was a handgun. It was presumably loaded and I wasn't sure if the safety was on, but I wasn't about to find out. I'd never handled anything with more stopping power than a BB gun before, so I wasn't confident in my potential effectiveness if a would-be kidnapper or car thief decided to make his move during that five-minute window. Also, I didn't want to get my fingerprints on a handgun that had almost certainly been involved in several attempted murders of Van Helsing.

In a shocking turn of events, Cherick was able to successfully buy a pack of cigarettes without a swarm of criminals descending upon his Honda Accord like it was the Hope Diamond. I shut the glove compartment before he returned to the car, and we got back on the road to Kemper Arena. Before we even pulled into the parking lot, I was amazed by what I saw. For several blocks leading up to the event, the sidewalks were filled with people wearing Steve Austin shirts and holding signs. This was 1999, so it's a good bet that most of these signs were along the lines of "I'M CARTMAN'S FATHER" or "CHRIS IS GAY."

The sight of these people amazed me because it was the first tangible evidence I had that wrestling fans existed. This should have been obvious enough from the television ratings, the active message boards on the internet, and the sellout crowds on every *Monday Night Raw*, but I had never really *seen* them before. Outside of a couple of friends at school who were on-and-off fans, I had no one to talk to on Tuesday mornings when I breathlessly wanted to spew some nonsense like "HEY, DID YOU HEAR THAT HEEL PROMO HUNTER CUT LAST NIGHT? I CAN'T TELL IF HE WAS BREAKING KAYFABE, BUT HE WAS DEFINITELY SHOOTING!" Here, I felt like I could have said that to any one of the almost 17,000 people in attendance and fallen into a long rabbit hole of a conversation.

Once we parked and worked our way through the sea of fans, I gave the usher my ticket and stepped through the curtain that separated the concession area from the interior of the arena. After six years of obsessing over this product through my TV screen, it was surreal to see everything with my own eyes. The matches hadn't even started yet, and I was staring at the ring, the entryway, and the TitanTron like they were Abraham Lincoln's hat at the Smithsonian Institute.

An episode of MTV's *Sunday Night Heat* program was filmed prior to Over the Edge, and I was watching these throwaway matches from my eighth-row seat like they had the historical significance of Hulk Hogan versus Andre the Giant. Sure, I was watching Grandmaster Sexay versus Meat, but I was watching *live wrestling.* I was in attendance for a "wrestling match" featuring Mideon versus Vince McMahon, but I was in the presence of *Vince McMahon.* Any of my snarky message board opinions about the product went out the window in that moment. Being there in person took me back to being nine years old, watching Bret and Owen work through their sibling rivalry.

Owen was scheduled to perform during the third match of the pay-per-view as his comedic Blue Blazer persona, taking on The Godfather (the witch-doctor-turned-pimp) for his Intercontinental Title. It was far from a major storyline at the time, and paled in comparison to Owen's legendary feud with his brother, but I was still excited at the prospect of seeing the man who first taught me about how effective a wrestling bad guy could be.

Prior to the match, a taped interview began playing on the gigantic TitanTron that hung above the entrance ramp. An interviewer was asking the Blue Blazer about his upcoming match with The Godfather. Owen said The Godfather represented all the poor values that he was fighting against in the World Wrestling Federation, and assured fans that he'd come out victorious.

From where I was sitting, the TitanTron was located to my left. During the middle of this Blue Blazer interview, I heard a few gasps and saw something moving above the ring to my right. I snapped my head to the right in time to see a blue figure plummeting toward the ground. It was Owen Hart, and his body crashed into a turnbuckle after falling from a height of almost 80 feet.

His chest hit the turnbuckle first, causing his body to snap backward and collapse on the mat. For a brief moment, it looked like he was attempting to get up. His head rose slightly, and he tried to get his elbow underneath him for support. That didn't last long—his arm and neck went limp within a second or two, and he slumped to the mat, motionless.

Immediately, Jerry "The King" Lawler jumped out from behind the announce table and slid into the ring. As he cradled Owen's head in his hands, Lawler's panicked face made it clear that something terrible had happened. With no response from Owen, Lawler threw his arms up in the air and made an "X" with his forearms. This gesture is frequently used by wrestling performers to signal that a legitimate injury has occurred.

All of this happened within the span of ten or fifteen seconds, and the crowd didn't know how to react. Many had missed the fall, as their attention had been on the TitanTron at the time. I could hear dozens of people asking those around them to explain what had happened, and most of the responses were along the lines of "they threw a mannequin off the roof" or "a fake Blue Blazer fell." When some expressed concern that it was a real accident, others would say "Nah, it's a fake wrestling thing."

I may have only been 14, but I had seen enough wrestling by this point to spot the signs that something had gone terribly wrong. Lawler's "X" and clear panic were evidence enough, and the fact that a video interview had been playing on the TitanTron at the time of the fall cemented it for me. This event was being broadcast live to a pay-per-view audience of millions. I knew that the WWF wouldn't pull a stunt in the ring while the live audience was looking at the screen and the television audience was seeing the interview segment.

A tragedy was surely playing out in front of me, but you wouldn't have known from my reaction. I had gone from the high of my first wrestling event to the low of watching a childhood hero plummet to what very well might be his death. I was lost in the confusion of everything. I wasn't distraught or crying, because I had no idea what exactly had happened, and many of those in attendance seemed to be feeling the same way.

Owen had done this stunt before. If everything had gone correctly, he would have been lowered to the ring in overdramatic fashion as his entrance music played. Once he was low enough, he'd flail around and make a fool of himself as he tried to get out of the harness, then fall flat on his face once he flipped the release switch. That was surely the plan.

What could have happened up there? Owen was well-known as a happy family man who loved to make his fellow wrestlers laugh on the road, so the odds of this being a suicide seemed highly unlikely. All I could imagine is that something went awry as he was preparing to descend into the ring. Based on the gradual turn of the audience's mood, it seemed like the "it's a mannequin" people were starting to change their tune. This wasn't being treated with the theatrics of a pro wrestling storyline, and nothing about the urgency on the faces of the EMTs and ringside attendees seemed fake.

Cherick seemed to be in a state similar to mine, and we weren't saying a whole lot to each other. At no point was any information conveyed to the live audience. No updates appeared on the TitanTron screen, and no WWF or Kemper Arena employee said anything over the PA system. Owen had been lying in the ring for what felt like ten minutes, and the EMTs were now performing chest compressions.

I glanced to the right of the ring and saw longtime commentator Jim Ross speaking directly to a camera, and realized that he must have been giving some sort of update on the television broadcast. If this had occurred ten years later, I'd have been texting friends or checking Twitter to see what had happened, but I didn't have those options in 1999.

Later, I'd learn that Ross had indeed been speaking to the home audience, informing them that an accident had occurred and that it was "not a part of the entertainment here tonight. This is as real as real can be here." He went on to speculate about a harness breaking or experiencing some kind of malfunction, and his uncharacteristically rambling speech made it clear that he was just as baffled as everyone else.

Camera shots had been trained on the crowd during this time, and the TitanTron screen eventually cut to a prepared video package advertising an upcoming tag team match that pitted Val Venis and Nicole Bass against Jeff Jarrett and his girlfriend Debra. Owen Hart had often teamed up with Jarrett, and the interview that aired after the video package was nothing short of surreal.

With Owen still lying in the ring, the promo ended and the TitanTron cut to a live interview—shown to both the home and arena audiences—with a visibly distraught Jarrett and Debra. The script called for the villainous Jarrett to play up his role of Debra's jealous boyfriend, with the fate of their real-life friend still undetermined at this point.

In the interview, Jarrett paces around a bit until the announcer asks him about his upcoming match. Before launching into his character, Jarrett takes his sunglasses off, looks directly at the camera, and says "Owen Hart, I'm prayin' for ya, buddy." Immediately afterward, the script calls for him to ramble about how a porn star wrestling character named Val Venis is jealous of Debra's "puppies" (late '90s wrestling speak for breasts). Seconds after saying "These are my puppies, and they always have been," Jarrett drops the act and says "Owen, you're in our prayers," before walking out of the frame. Debra chokes out an "Owen, we love you" as she fights back tears.

Wrestling is an industry that's always joyously blended the worlds of fantasy and reality, but this was so far beyond anything I'd ever seen. Jeff Jarrett transitioned from giving his prayers to a dying friend to talking about how Val Venis needs to stay away from Debra's boobs, then back to Owen again in less than a minute. It was an awful position to be in, and the rest of the night would be filled with performers whose thoughts clearly lay elsewhere.

Eventually, the paramedics put Owen onto a stretcher and wheeled him up the entrance ramp. The crowd cheered as if it had seen a hero quarterback give a thumbs-up as he was taken off the field, but we had still received no word on what had happened or how Owen was doing. The event picked back up from there, which gave me hope that he might be all right. With Owen presumably on the way to the hospital, the show continued with no allusions to the accident outside of an "I'm praying for you, buddy" during an interview with the Road Dogg.

When the announcement eventually came, it was once again reserved for the television audience. With Jerry Lawler sitting silently next to him, Jim Ross delivered the news:

Ladies and gentlemen, earlier tonight here in Kansas City, tragedy befell the World Wrestling Federation and all of us. Owen Hart was set to make an entrance from the ceiling, and he fell from the ceiling. I have the unfortunate responsibility to let everyone know that Owen Hart has died. Owen Hart has tragically died from that accident here tonight.

Trying to snap back into a mindset that would allow me to enjoy the rest of the show was difficult, if not impossible. Even without any kind of actual information to go on, I feared the worst based on what I had seen. I can recall most of the early parts of the show vividly, but everything after Owen's fall is hazy despite the high-profile nature of the matches. Triple H versus The Rock is a legendary feud, and I witnessed one of their pay-per-view matches live without any real memory of it. Steve Austin and The Undertaker are two of my favorite wrestlers of all time, and sometimes I forget that I saw the WWF Heavyweight Championship change hands between them. Wrestling had mattered so much to me for so long, but the matches and storylines from that night were pushed far into the back of my mind.

As The Undertaker celebrated his victory, the crowd started to shuffle out. Some people in the audience had received phone calls from friends at home and were relaying news that I prayed wasn't true. In the hours after something terrible happens, rumors and speculation often prove to be wildly inaccurate. Hopefully, that would be the case with Owen.

Cherick and I got back into his Honda Accord. He turned the radio on, and the first thing I heard was the definitive statement that I had dreaded. Kansas City radio personalities were discussing "the incident at Kemper Arena" in which professional wrestler Owen Hart had fallen to his death. Neither Cherick nor I were prepared to hear that, and we rode the rest of the way home in silence. When he dropped me off, I went straight to bed without talking to anyone.

I went downstairs the next morning to eat breakfast, and saw a picture of EMTs attending to Owen plastered across the front page of the *Kansas City Star* with the headline "Pro Wrestler Suffers Fatal Fall." Barely anyone at school had wanted to talk about wrestling with me before. Now I was being bombarded with questions about what I saw. I've told the story many times since then, but it was hard to get much out besides a "yeah, it was messed up" when the incident was that fresh.

For about two weeks afterward, I had trouble falling asleep and sleeping through the night. At one point, I approached my father to let him know that I was really struggling with what happened at Kemper. His advice was to "look at the bright side. There's one less idiot in the world."

Professional wrestling has a long history of tragic stories. Drug addiction, suicides, and even murders have claimed the lives of many wrestlers at young ages. Owen's death was the one that hit me the hardest, and not just because I was there to see it live. He was one of the true "good guys" in the wrestling industry, even when his onscreen character was utterly despicable.

Being in attendance at Over the Edge in 1999 was memorable for all the wrong reasons, but the next night brought me as many smiles as it did tears.

Monday Night Raw was turned into a special "Raw is Owen" episode, with every wrestler and referee wearing black "OH" armbands. The night was filled with tributes to Owen in the form of classic clips of him and interviews with mourning colleagues. During many of these teary monologues, the interview subject couldn't help but laugh as they recalled some funny Owen moment or practical joke he had pulled. He was clearly beloved by his peers and it wasn't part of any script. Owen Hart left behind a legacy as a great wrestler, an honest husband and father, and most importantly, a genuinely good person in an industry where that can be rare.

I wish that the circumstances of me seeing Owen in person for the first time were wildly different, but I'll never forget the impact he had on my life.

Force of Nature

A number of poor decisions I've made or dumb situations I've put myself in could have conceivably ended my life, but there was only one instance when I honestly thought that it might happen. It would have been at the hands of one of my good friends, a guy named Matt who lived on my floor in McCollum during my sophomore year of college. Nowadays, Matt is still a good friend and seems to be doing great. He had to drop out of college early, but he managed to find a good corporate job in Kansas City and climb the ranks. His college girlfriend was a train wreck, and most nights involved drunken screaming matches between them, but he's moved on to get married to a girl who seems perfect for him. He's produced approximately 45 children since college, and they bring him great joy, if Facebook is any indication. Matt has mellowed out substantially in recent years, seemingly finding a really good place for himself.

In college, Matt was a different story. He'd be mellow while sober, and we'd frequently hang out and play Xbox or chat about classic rock. A couple of nights a week, we'd be stereotypical college dudes and have people over to his place for games of beer pong before heading out to a party or bar.

Most of these nights were typical college fare. We'd drink heavily at his apartment before the bars to save money, and then we'd go out to bars featuring specials so we'd save money there, too. Occasionally, our ample pre-gaming at his apartment would lead to especially rough nights later on. We ran out of Milwaukee's Best during one beer pong session, and substituted it with a ton of cheap whiskey from a plastic bottle. As we were walking *to* the bar that night, he spotted a police car at a red light and decided that it would be a good idea to jump on top of it. Despite the car being stationary, Matt slid right off of it and fractured his ankle on the street upon landing. I watched him sit injured on the ground, somehow talking the cops out of giving him anything stronger than a stern warning. His foot didn't get off so easy, as he left it untreated and limped around on it for the better part of a year.

Another night started with us inventing a drinking game, something we did frequently. This one was WarioWare Shots, which involved taking shots at various points during a darts minigame in a Wii title called *WarioWare: Smooth Moves*. When we arrived at Fatso's later that night, Matt must have set a campus record for the shortest amount of time before getting kicked out of a bar. We waited in line, provided our IDs, and were ushered in the front door. It was a snowy winter night in Kansas, and Matt instantly tripped over a space heater and fell flat on his face. We were immediately told to get out the same way we came in.

On these nights, it was easy to pinpoint the moment that Matt transitioned from silly drunk to "not actually here on any sort of mental level" drunk. He'd still be walking and talking and performing all of the bodily functions needed to stay alive, until his eyes would glaze over and his cheeks would turn bright red. My friends and I did our best to keep him from drinking further during these periods, but he was very much the "shut up, you pussies. I'm fine! Let's keep drinking!" guy who refused to slow down under any circumstances.

The night he nearly killed me almost certainly started with one of our dumb drinking games. It could have been Lizardman Shots, which involved taking a shot every time someone beats you with the Lizardman character in Soul Calibur. Maybe it was the checkers shots game, which my mother got me for Christmas and replaced checkers pieces with a couple dozen shot glasses. There's a chance it was the weird clock game we came up with, which had something to do with an alarm clock that shot a little propeller into the air. You had to flip a coin or something while the propeller was airborne, and take a shot or give out a shot based on god knows what before it hit the ground. I don't know, we were drunk.

Whatever caused it, Matt was beyond drunk by the time last call was approaching. We were there with his roommate Patrick and our friend Lauren. While we were all enjoyably inebriated by the end, we were lucid enough to realize that Matt should not be drinking any more. We walked back to our apartment building—Matt and Patrick lived directly above me—draped Matt's arms over our shoulders, and dropped him on his couch. We told him that he should chug a bunch of water and go to sleep, and then Lauren and I left.

She and I were good friends, and we'd had a long conversation about old Nickelodeon game shows earlier in the night. After leaving Matt and Patrick's apartment, we felt like having a couple more drinks and continuing the nostalgia train at my place. Luckily for us, the Nickelodeon Games and Sports channel that aired old game shows 24/7 was in the middle of a programming block that included *Legends of the Hidden Temple* and *GUTS*, two of our favorites.

Halfway through some kid's seemingly 20-minute long attempt to assemble the Shrine of the Silver Monkey, we heard a commotion coming from upstairs. Matt's girlfriend wasn't staying over that night, so it couldn't have been another drunken argument. We turned the TV down to hear better, and it sounded like a bunch of stomping and mumbling.

About 30 seconds later, we heard Matt's front door open and quickly slam shut. Loud stomps made their way down the wooden stairs outside, and Lauren and I prepared for a nearly incoherent visitor. Sure enough, the banging on my front door came from Matt. I opened the door to see him standing there with two six-packs of Milwaukee's Best, which would have been enough to put Lauren and me on his level if we had partaken in them.

"Let's drink, pussies!" Matt yelled as he stepped inside my apartment.

Within two steps, Matt fell face-forward onto the table in front of my couch, nearly breaking it in a display that would've made Chris Farley proud. He stumbled off the table in the direction of my newly purchased HDTV, and I immediately grabbed him and moved him away from the electronics. Matt would be fine. The expensive TV that I bought on a college budget might not be, if he stuck around.

Twelve shaken-up beers sat on the carpet, and Lauren and I had no intention of letting Matt get into any of them.

"Alright, buddy," I said. "Let's get you back upstairs."

Despite his protests, Lauren and I escorted Matt back up to the couch in his living room and laid him down again. We went back to my place and got about five minutes into *GUTS* before we heard more shuffling from upstairs. It was the same loud stomping, now accompanied by a confusingly angry voice. Matt had been silly-drunk that night, not emotional and combative—the angry nights were reserved for when his girlfriend was around. We didn't hear Patrick responding at all, so we assumed that he was asleep and Matt was just yelling at nothing in particular.

We didn't want to put up with another drunken display, especially since this time sounded significantly more hostile than the last. I got up from the couch and slid the deadbolt shut, hoping that Matt wouldn't even attempt to come in again. But sure enough, he stomped down the stairs again and pounded his fist on the door.

"Open the fucking door!" he yelled. "Why the fuck are you gonna shut me out? I know you're in there!"

I had dealt with a drunken Matt many times before, but I had never seen him like this. He only got angry with his girlfriend, and even then, it was never anything more than stupid drunken arguments. This time, he was blindingly drunk and suddenly seemed mad at me. Him falling through my TV was my original concern, but now I felt like he was out of his mind enough to try to start a fight for reasons unbeknownst to me.

"What is he so pissed about all of a sudden?" Lauren whispered to me as Matt banged on the door.

"I have no idea," I said. "He seemed happy the last time he came down here."

We never figured out what made the switch flip in his brain that night. Lauren and I had always been nothing more than platonic friends, so jealousy over me hanging out with her didn't make sense. Besides, Matt had a girlfriend. Could it be that he was really *that* mad that we didn't want to keep drinking with him? I'm as confused now as I was ten years ago when he was banging on my door.

Whatever the reason was, it was hard to ignore the incredibly angry, likely blacked-out man just beyond a door that sat five feet from us. I muted the TV as Lauren and I sat silently, hoping that he'd tire himself out and eventually make his way back upstairs. Half of our hopes came true, as he headed back to his apartment after a couple of minutes of futile yelling and knocking. We weren't lucky enough for him to tire himself out, however. Rather, we heard him slam his own door so hard that it shattered the wood around the deadbolt.

Holy shit, Lauren mouthed to me.

Before I had a chance to respond, I heard Matt's voice booming from above my ceiling.

"Patrick, get me a FUCKING KNIFE."

This was the moment that put Lauren and me beyond "wow, Matt's real drunk!" mode and into "we're gonna have to call the police tonight, aren't we?"

Patrick was the most responsible, sane person I knew in college, so we weren't concerned about him becoming an accomplice to the world's most confusing double murder. If anything, he'd wrangle Matt's drunken rage and help him pass out somewhere. That was assuming that all the commotion of the last fifteen minutes or so had woken him up. It hadn't.

Sobering up is easy to do when you hear someone rummaging through drawers in an effort to find a suitable knife to presumably stab you with. When we heard Matt coming down the stairs again, his state was no longer an odd curiosity. It was now a reason for immediate concern, and we needed to act. Still on the couch, I grabbed my cell phone and dialed 911.

"911, what's your emergency?"

"My friend Matt is really drunk and we think he has a knife. I don't know why, but he seems to be really angry at me and my friend Lauren."

The operator asked for my address, and in the middle of giving it to them, I heard a slow sawing noise coming from the front door. It didn't take long to realize that Matt was trying to make the slowest *The Shining* entrance ever by using his knife to cut around the doorknob.

"Okay, he definitely has a knife," I said. "He's trying to saw through the front door right now."

At this point, Lauren was visibly starting to panic. I motioned for her to run into the bathroom and lock the door as I continued relaying my address and providing details to the operator. Matt was larger than me and had actually been in fights, so I ran into the bedroom and grabbed a baseball bat in case he made his way inside. Under normal circumstances, I rarely want to beat my friends with a bat or send them to jail. This was different, however, and I wouldn't have felt guilty using force in that moment.

Officers were on their way, so all I needed to do was hope that Matt couldn't find a way into the apartment. His genius sawing plan didn't seem to be bearing any fruit, as I heard him start walking around to the side of the apartment. Just then, I realized that I didn't know how or if my windows locked. Considering that he was making his way toward them, I wasn't about to get close to them. I did the bravest thing I could muster in that moment, which was running into the bathroom and locking myself in with Lauren.

Terrified to make a noise, we stood in there and listened for any indication of Matt's status. As drunk as he was, I half hoped to hear him fall into some leaves and start snoring. Instead, I heard metal scraping against the edge of a window. With no idea of the window's locking mechanism, I could only assume he was trying to work his way inside. The amount of time that he spent messing with it was promising, as every second that passed meant another second the cops had to reach us.

After a couple of minutes of him messing with the window, I heard something that made it clear he had found his way inside. I was one of those idiots in college who displayed all of his empty whiskey bottles around his apartment like lame trophies. I'm not sure what the thought process was. Maybe I'd bring a girl home and she'd look around at all the seven-dollar liters of Old Crow and think "I wasn't sure about this guy before, but he has clearly ingested a large amount of terrible alcohol. I should probably have sexual intercourse with him."

Those empty whiskey bottles served as a low-rent alarm system, clearly marking the moment that Matt had breached the window. With no sounds of sirens approaching, I had to prepare for the possibility of having to actually deal with him myself. I clutched the baseball bat with full knowledge of my lack of strength, ability to fight, or threshold for pain. If he actually found his way into the bathroom that Lauren and I were huddled in, I'd probably be better off trying to spray shampoo into his eyes.

After the whiskey bottles hit the floor, we heard some grunts as Matt tried to heave himself over the window's ledge and into the apartment. Once we heard what sounded like a full-sized adult man landing on a carpeted floor, we assumed that it wouldn't be long before he kicked in the bathroom door. My apartment at the time was about 450 square feet and featured a living room/kitchen area, my bedroom, and the bathroom. Matt may have been drunker than I've ever seen him, but surely he'd be able to whittle down our location using process of elimination.

Instead of the ranting and raving and knocking and stabbing that we expected once he found his way in, his entrance was met with damn near silence. We assumed that he had stood back up after landing on the carpet, but if he was moving around, he was being stealthy about it. Lauren and I were expecting him to bust through the only closed door in the apartment and confront us at any second, but it never happened. The eerie quiet lasted for less than a minute before we heard the good kind of knocking on the front door.

"Police! Open up!"

I sure as hell wasn't going to exit the bathroom until I knew that Matt was in handcuffs or a cop car, so it's hard to know exactly how things went down once the cops arrived. There was some brief commotion, and I could hear Matt saying a lot of things like "I didn't do anything! I just wanted to come down and drink with my friends!" I wasn't entirely sure if the cops came through the window or if they managed to get Matt to let them in the apartment, but they were standing inside by the time I felt safe enough to come out.

They asked Lauren and me if we were all right. We said yes and relayed the events of the night the best we could. We explained that Matt had gone from zero to 100 in about five minutes, if zero was "hey, let's drink and watch old game shows together" and 100 was "I am going to stab both of you until you are dead." No matter how many times the cops tried to ask about why Matt would do that, we had no logical answer. It was the biggest and quickest 180 I've ever seen someone do, and it seemed to be entirely random.

Before the police left, they showed us the knife that Matt had broken in with. It was somewhere between a butter knife and a full-on murder knife, like something you'd cut a hard roll or a steak with. I guess there's a term for that, right? Steak knife? He had a steak knife, and it was bent almost 90 degrees near the top where he'd used it to get the window open. It wasn't the big *Psycho* knife that I envisioned as he was attempting to get inside, but it definitely could have murdered me if Matt had wanted it bad enough.

More cop cars arrived in the parking lot, and Lauren and I stepped out front to see what was going on. Matt was handcuffed and being led into the back of one of the cars, and his distraught mother had apparently arrived at some point. When she saw us, she started yelling.

"What have you done to my boy?" she cried several times.

I'm not sure if I responded out loud, but I remember at least thinking, *your boy broke in with a knife and wanted to stab us.*

After Matt got into the car, all of the cops and Matt's mother took off. Lauren and I were left standing out front by ourselves, and Patrick had woken up amid the commotion. He was standing on his porch directly above us, and Lauren and I went up for a chat.

Patrick told us that he remembered waking up briefly as Matt was asking for a knife, but that he dismissed it as him just being dumb and drunk. Lauren and I explained to Patrick that while we weren't mad at him, he should probably take notice if his hard-drinking roommate is stomping around and searching feverishly for a stabbing implement. Patrick apologized profusely, and there were never any hard feelings between the three of us.

It was around four in the morning by now. I had zero idea of what would come next as far as Matt's status. Do they keep people in jail for days after something like this? Is there a trial? Do they ask me if I want to press charges? I'd seen all the dramatic parts of situations like this—the knife attacks, the courtroom theatrics—on TV and in documentaries, but no one sat me down with a simple "all right, here's what happens next" breakdown. The cops were gone, and Matt was gone for an indeterminate amount of time. All I knew is that I hoped I wouldn't be there when he got back.

Lauren called her parents and got a ride back home. I locked the doors and windows—hey, there was a lock on those after all!—before attempting to sleep. Adrenaline kept me up for a while as I laid down, but the booze and exhaustion helped me eventually drift off.

When I woke up at around 10am, I wanted to discuss the night's events with Patrick in the light of day. I texted him to make sure Matt hadn't returned while I was asleep and spent hours pacing around the building with a bigger knife. Patrick gave me the all-clear, and I walked into his apartment and sat down in the living room.

It didn't take more than ten minutes of "wow, last night was fucked up!" conversation before we heard a car pulling up in the parking lot. Paranoid about Matt's return, I ran to the window and peered out. Sure enough, there was a cop car below us. The back door opened, and Matt stepped out. We never saw the officer who was behind the wheel, as he drove away down the alley as soon as Matt shut the door. Leaving a presumably still-drunk Matt at my building and taking off felt comparable to squeezing a bull through my front door, poking him in the ass with a hot branding iron, and saying "Have fun with this!"

Not expecting to encounter Matt this soon, I had to quickly consider my options. Ideally, I'd leave the area for several hours to give him a chance to sober up and settle down a bit before we talked. This was impossible because I was on the second floor, with only one staircase that led up or down. Considering the circumstances, I figured that my best option would be to calmly sit in his apartment—accompanied by Patrick and his sanity—and attempt to have an adult conversation about the incident when Matt came through his now-broken door. I expected him to be drunk-ish and belligerent, but maybe I was wrong. Maybe spending a few hours in a holding cell would have given him some time to reflect on his actions and feel sorry for them. He'd probably enter the apartment with his head hanging low, offering a hungover "I'm sorry, man," and things would go right back to the status quo.

BANG BANG BANG BANG BANG

"RYCKERT! OPEN THE FUCKING DOOR!"

Maybe I had been too optimistic.

Matt was downstairs, loudly banging on my front door and windows. It was far too early for this déjà vu. The tone in his voice as he continued to yell made it clear that this was the worst-case scenario. He sounded just as enthusiastic about murdering me as he had in the middle of the night, only now he was way more pissed since I had called the cops on him. It was a great situation.

In that moment, my brain went into self-preservation mode and ditched every option except for one: hide under a bed and call the damn cops again.

"Keep him occupied for a bit," I told Patrick as I sprinted into his empty bedroom.

My beer gut kept me from comfortably sliding under the bed, and I made a quick mental note to add "hiding under things more easily to avoid getting murdered" to my list of reasons that I should lose some weight. Once I had shuffled myself underneath the bed far enough to keep any appendages from sticking out, I called 911 for the second time in about six hours.

"911, what's your emergency?"

"You just dropped off my friend after he tried to stab me, and I'm pretty sure that he still wants to kill me. Can you pick him back up?"

With cops on their way, I silently and uncomfortably remained under the bed while Matt entered the apartment screaming about how badly he was going to fuck me up. Patrick did a great job of stalling and saying that he didn't know where I was, so Matt went back downstairs, assuming I was still in my apartment. From upstairs, I heard him fruitlessly banging on my front door until a car pulled up. The knocking stopped, and I hoped that the same cop who had just dropped Matt off was the one tasked with picking him right back up again.

Matt was shuffled off to jail again, and I figured that I should probably take advantage of this brief window in which he was temporarily unable to kill me. I thanked Patrick for keeping Matt busy, then hopped in my car and drove to the safe haven of Lauren's family home. She had explained the events of the night to her mother and father, and they told me that I could stay as long as I wanted.

Even though I had managed to get some sleep earlier, I was still exhausted from all the stress. A slight hangover didn't help matters, so I took a couple of ibuprofen and collapsed on Lauren's living room couch. For the next few hours, two gigantic black labs were constantly licking at my face or jumping on the couch as I attempted to rest. Under normal conditions, this would have been super annoying. In the moment, however, anything that didn't include the possibility of multiple stab wounds felt like a step up.

Staying at Lauren's place forever wasn't an option, so I went back home later that night. Patrick let me know that Matt was upstairs in his apartment and not happy, but that he seemed to be a few levels removed from "murderous rage" by now. I didn't fear for my immediate death anymore, and figured that I'd wait for Matt to make the first move toward reestablishing contact and discussing the situation.

That never happened. For about a week or so, I had zero contact with him. I hoped that he'd attempt to mend fences soon, as we were both set to attend a quickly approaching birthday party for a mutual friend. Talking to him about the incident during the party didn't seem ideal, but things were clearly heading in that direction.

At the party, Matt avoided making eye contact with me for at least five or six drinks. He seemed to be in a cheery mood after that, so I approached him and we started chatting about our usual assortment of topics. With the conversation staying friendly, it seemed like a good time to clear the air.

"So are we cool?" I asked.

"What do you mean?"

"You know, after the whole thing last week."

"I don't know, man. I didn't do anything wrong, and you sent me to jail for it."

This conversation clearly wouldn't bear any fruit, and things didn't get any better when his girlfriend approached us and took his side. I tried to calmly talk to her about what had happened, but she had clearly bought into Matt's confusing "I tried to go downstairs to hang out with them and he called the cops on me" story. No matter how many times I attempted to explain how that version of the story made absolutely no sense, they weren't budging.

We obviously disagreed on what happened that night, but we almost immediately got back to our normal drinking routine together. I knew that any conversation about the knife incident wouldn't go anywhere, and he certainly didn't seem to have any interest in discussing it further. He still lived directly above me and we'd had a good relationship for years prior, so I wasn't going to let one fluke night involving a knife almost sliding between my ribs get in the way of a good friendship.

One of our regular haunts was Louise's, a no-frills bar that spoke strongly to my college self with an unpretentious crowd and 32-ounce schooners of beer for $1.75. Many of my other friends wanted to go to Brothers or Quinton's or any of the other bars on the main drag of Massachusetts Street that catered to the frat/sorority crowd. I hated every second of being at those bars, so I always pushed for the place with the $1.75 schooners and classic rock.

My love of these schooners led to an awkward moment with my landlord, who also happened to own Louise's. At the time, my apartment was filled with dumb things that I had stolen from various bars. My IHOP rug greeted people when they came in and my bathroom wall was covered with numerous crappy plastic clocks, all set to different world cities like a NORAD control center.

Something about those schooner glasses was super appealing to me. They seemed far too large for their price, and the curved glass made me feel like I was drinking my Milwaukee's Best Light out of a medieval goblet. I wanted to utilize them outside of the setting of one bar, so I started swiping them from Louise's whenever I was there with a group that included a girl with a large enough purse. In the hustle of people leaving, I'd have the girl tuck away a schooner so that I could add it to my collection.

After a few months, my apartment was riddled with these easily identifiable schooners (to my knowledge, no other bar in the city used them). One hungover Saturday morning, I was roused from my sleep by someone banging on the door. I shuffled across the living room in my pajamas to answer it, and was greeted by my landlord. He needed to talk to me about the electricity meter or new plans for the parking lot or some other thing that I wasn't particularly concerned about in my current state.

Halfway through explaining whatever it was to me, he glanced over my shoulder and scanned the room a bit. A slight nod later, he cut his talk short and headed to the next unit of the building. A few days later, I found a package with my name on it sitting in front of my door. I opened it up to find a shirt from Louise's, along with a note that read "I get the feeling that you're a regular. Enjoy the shirt." I started wearing the shirt frequently, and stopped swiping my landlord's schooners at last call.

Things between Matt and me were friendly but slightly uneasy around this point. We were back to our bar routine, although I'd typically stick to talking to Patrick or Lauren while Matt stayed around his girlfriend. The dam seemed to break during one Saturday night at Louise's in which the subject of *Star Wars* came up after many schooners. This was 2006, so the prequels had already disappointed everyone and we were still years from any news about the new episodes to come.

Enthusiastic *Star Wars* banter went on among our crew throughout the night, with the usual talking points of the prequels sucking, Jar Jar being terrible, debates on whether *Episode III* was actually any good, etc. When our discussions got to the original trilogy, our drunken enthusiasm hit a fever pitch. None of us had watched *Episodes IV, V,* and *VI* in years, and our conversation turned into a ton of "Man, remember how cool it was when Luke was getting trained on Dagobah? Oh, and Lando was cool as hell! Man, *Empire* was great. So was the end of *Jedi*."

We reminisced about the movies long enough for me to offer a proposal: let's all go back to my apartment after last call, drink for the rest of the night, and watch the entire original trilogy back-to-back-to-back. Matt seemed on board at first, but his girlfriend went into one of her trademark drunken fits of drama, and he had to tend to that for the rest of the night. Patrick was always smart enough to call it quits and drink some water after last call, so he wasn't chomping at the bit at the concept of drinking for seven more hours.

"Fine," I said. "I'll do it myself, and it's going to be great."

Last call came, and we settled up our bills. I got home and switched into my pajamas the second I walked in the door. Tonight was all about pure comfort, watching good movies, and getting blindingly drunk. I was on a brief Guinness kick and had my fridge stocked with materials for making Black and Tans. Before popping in *A New Hope*, I prepared one using that weird spoon trick that I never fully understood, and settled in for a long night of nostalgia and lightsaber fights.

As I expected, watching *A New Hope* after a long night of drinking was great. I was about three Black and Tans deep by the end of it—on top of the numerous schooners I had ingested at the bar—and I made another as I popped in *The Empire Strikes Back* and watched the Battle of Hoth. I was drunk as all hell, but the nostalgia and booze made for a tremendously fun night. Every little scene and piece of dialogue was the best thing in the world to me, and I couldn't wait to toss *Return of the Jedi* into my PlayStation 3 next.

I did just that, and kept up with my pacing of three or four Black and Tans per movie. Considering that I had been slamming giant schooners all night before this cavalcade of Black and Tans, I had probably drunk enough beers to fill one of those helicopters that dump water onto forest fires. Despite my loopy mental state, I loved everything from the Sarlacc Pit to the build toward the climactic ending.

In the midst of my mental haze, I thought about how great it was to have hung out with Matt that night without any worries of a drunken force of nature bounding down the steps and lunging through my window with knife in hand.

There was still some uneasiness, but chatting with him at the bars and sharing *Star Wars* memories made me think that we were on the right track to being good again.

Hurricane Matt may have been tamed at this point, but I couldn't have predicted the other, much more literal storm that was about to make itself known. Near the end of *Return of the Jedi*, I started hearing loud crashes and what sounded like explosions coming from all around me. My surround sound system was far too cheap to be presenting the audio of the assault on the second Death Star with the booming clarity that I was hearing.

I was so close to the end of this three-film marathon, but I had to pause and figure out what the hell was going on. Sure enough, the booming continued and actually intensified once I stopped the movie. I shuffled to the front door to see if I could tell what was causing the noises. It was far too loud to be trash trucks, as it sounded more like full-sized trees crashing down into the road.

Upon opening the door, the first thing I noticed was an angry-looking sky that was a shade of dark orange. Intense wind hit my face and leaves blew into my apartment. The real warning sign that something was up came when I looked across the alleyway to see dozens of shingles being ripped straight off of the roof of a neighboring house. I've had plenty of times in my life in which I've felt my brain has just shut off entirely, but never more than in this moment. I was standing in my pajamas after drinking for close to a dozen hours, and the apocalypse seemed to be knocking on my front door. A power line crashed to the ground halfway down the block, which snapped me out of my stupor. *I should probably get inside.*

FORCE OF NATURE

Years of living in Kansas had taught me that when a tornado is coming, you get down into the basement as fast as possible. My ground-floor apartment had nothing of the sort, so my first instinct was to lie in bed and put a couple of pillows over my head and groin. I didn't know if this thing was gonna make the building collapse on itself, but if it did, I didn't want to get concussed and I didn't want debris landing on my balls.

Everything passed before too long, and I found out the next day that it had been a microburst that had wreaked havoc on the town. Local weathermen explained this as something like a giant bucket of water in the sky that gets dumped out all at once, causing intense winds to rush out in every direction. Power was out almost citywide, trees were down across campus, roofs had been torn off of buildings for blocks, and class was cancelled for a week due to the massive damage done to the area. During all of these nights, many houses around town hosted keg parties that were surrounded by downed trees and lit by campfires.

My microburst experience was a thoroughly confusing and potentially dangerous night that I couldn't have anticipated, but I'll take that force of nature over one that can wield a knife any day of the week.

Phoning it In

Whatever gene is responsible for creating a great salesman is nowhere to be found in my body. If it's something that I'm passionate about, I have no issues gushing about its virtues to anyone who will listen. If it's a product or service that I don't have strong feelings about, I find it impossible to put on a believable enough act to get someone to buy in. Luckily, only a few occasions have required me to even try.

When I first left for college, I effectively quit my job at GameStop. They kept me in the system so that I could come back in the summers to help out, but I was no longer on the weekly schedule. Even though I took out a large amount of student loans to help pay for tuition, I was really bothered by the idea of not having a job. Ever since McDonald's hired me at the age of 14, I had been employed. I didn't intend on stopping once I got to college.

Most job openings in Lawrence weren't up my alley in any fashion. School-related positions were less than ideal, considering that I didn't know anything about the university. Working at a bar wasn't an option since I was still a few years shy of 21. I hoped to avoid another retail job, but it seemed inevitable at my age. After applying to a handful of places, I got hired for seasonal work at a Best Buy in Olathe. Since I lived in Lawrence, this meant that I could look forward to a 40-minute drive to work before every shift. A job's a job, even if I wasn't thrilled about driving that far for a low-paying position.

Best Buy would hire extra staff members for the holidays, then place them in different departments based on the store's current need. When they asked me for my first choice, there was no question: I wanted to work in Media.

This department was all about movies, music, and most importantly, video games. As a film student who spent almost all of his free time playing video games, this was a no-brainer. I left Best Buy management with no doubts about my preferred assignment.

They put me in Digital Imaging. I had never owned or even used a digital camera at this point in my life. My job would be to push expensive cameras on customers, then push harder when it came to accessories and extended service plans. First, I should probably learn what a megapixel was, and what the hell a CompactFlash card did.

By all of the company's standards, I was a *terrible* Digital Imaging employee. I'd like to think that the customers appreciated me, however. When parents would ask me what the best camera would be for taking pictures of their kids' life events and birthday parties, I'd never try to upsell them.

"Look, you're not going to be printing up big posters of this stuff, are you?" I'd ask. "Then you don't need this $800 camera. The $200 Kodak will be more than enough. Also, you can find a case for cheaper online, and the service plan is a rip-off."

Weirdly enough, my numbers weren't hitting the marks that my supervisors were looking for. After a few weeks of me convincing customers not to spend money at their store, Best Buy decided to move me to a different department. This time around, my job would involve selling HDTVs in the Home Theater department. Never mind the fact that my primary television was still an old 19-inch CRT that I had gotten for free from a FuncoLand display.

Once again, Best Buy had thrown me into a department that I knew nothing about. In terms of training, all I was told was that the 56-inch Samsung DLP was the best television our location offered. I'd pace the wall of screens during my shift, and sure enough, that one did appear to have the best image. Selling customers on this television wouldn't make me feel like a turd because it was actually the one that I'd personally want the most.

Unfortunately, I knew zero details about why or how it was the best. When I asked my supervisor for some bullet points to share with customers, he wasn't afraid to get technical.

"DLP means there's a shitload of tiny mirrors in there. They bounce the light around and it makes the image look good."

Works for me! No matter what questions my customers asked me, my answer always had something to do with mirrors.

"How about this one?" they'd ask. "It's $300 cheaper."

"Nah, no mirrors in there."

"We just need something for basic cable. We don't have the HD package."

"I bet the mirrors will probably make SD stuff look better, too."

Throughout my life, I've been in countless situations where I've had zero idea of what the hell I was talking about. Working at Best Buy ranks up there in terms of the most clueless I've been. Meanwhile, the doofs who worked in Media were telling customers about the "insider info" that they were supposedly getting from within the gaming industry. This usually involved tips from "confirmed sources" about how PlayStation was buying *Halo* or how Nintendo was days away from announcing its closure. They had the one position in which I could be really helpful, and they somehow knew less about video games than I did about cameras and HDTVs.

During most of these jobs in my younger days, I'd count the minutes leading up to my lunch break. At McDonald's, I'd get two trays' worth of free Quarter Pounders (plain) and McFlurries, and watch wrestling in the back room. At AMC, I'd sneak into movies and chip away at them one half hour at a time. At GameStop, I'd read the newest issue of *Game Informer* as I ate plain Quarter Pounders and McFlurries that I had to actually pay for.

Usually, break rooms served as sanctuaries built for slacking off and occasionally complaining about work. At Best Buy, it was completely different. Their break room that consisted of some tables, a bunch of chairs, and one television was unremarkable. The reason that it felt like a really lame *Twilight Zone* episode was because of the employees. "How's your accessory attach rate today?" they'd ask around the lunch table. "I'm at 70 percent."

"Ah, damn!" another would respond. "I'm only at 60, but I'm killing it with the service plans!"

Wait a minute, I'd think. *Surely these guys don't actually care about this bullshit, do they?*

They did. They cared deeply, and not on an "I gotta pretend to care about this shit so I can get a raise" level. Something about the sales game and hitting percentages got these guys so excited that they'd talk exclusively about it during their lunch breaks. I'm sure that this trait wound up making them a lot of money in their adult careers, but it came off as painfully soulless.

During one lunch break, it seemed like I'd share the room with an actual human being. As I ate my plain Quarter Pounder and watched the Game Show Network, a guy from

Car Audio named Rob entered the room and sat across the table from me.

"What's up, man?" he asked.

"Not too much, how's your day?"

"Good, good. Getting tired out there on the floor, though!"

Oh, wow! A genuine human thought! It may not have been the most exciting conversation topic in the world, but at least it wasn't about boring-ass attach rates.

"How about you?" he asked. "You ever get tired out there?"

"Well yeah, on occasion. Being on your feet for that long can wear you down a bit."

"I hear ya, man. Do you ever use anything to give you a little more energy to get through the day?"

Hang on, was this guy about to offer me cocaine? I was starting to wonder if this friendly conversation was heading somewhere else.

"Uh, I don't know," I said. "I drink a lot of Mountain Dew?"

"Nah, man. That stuff is no good. Tell you what, come out here with me for a second. I've got something for you."

Okay, now I was curious. I surely wasn't about to do drugs if that's what he was offering, but I had to see where this was going.

Rob walked me out to his car and popped the trunk. He lifted its cartoonishly large spoiler to reveal four cardboard boxes, each filled with some brand of energy drink that I didn't recognize.

"This one's on me," he said as he handed me a blue can. "Drink one on your break and you'll be killing it for the rest of the shift! That Mountain Dew crap is filled with sugar, but this fuels you with healthy energy like taurine, guarana..."

I zoned out for the rest of his pitch, but I remember the part where he tried to get me to sign up for a subscription supply at $50 a month. For a brief moment, I thought I had found the one person in the store who was capable of a genuine conversation. Three minutes later, he was shilling products to me from the trunk of a car.

This run at Best Buy was mercifully short thanks to its seasonal nature, giving me a chance to head back to Lawrence and look for more fulfilling work after the holidays were over. I thought my search had come to an end when I saw someone in a full-sized chicken costume enthusiastically dancing on the side of Iowa Street. From my initial distance, I couldn't tell what it was supposed to be advertising. I just knew that I wanted to be that chicken.

I pulled into the parking lot and saw that the chicken was holding a sign for Bigg's BBQ. Surely that same chicken wasn't working around the clock. If he needed some backup, I was confident that I was the guy to pull it off.

"Is there a manager available?" I asked the hostess as I walked into the restaurant.

"There is! Can I tell him what this is concerning?"

"Yes. I'd like to apply to be the chicken."

She summoned the manager, who sat down at a booth with me for an interview that was exactly as long and rigorous as you'd expect it to be. It took about three minutes and consisted of him telling me that I'd be starting on Monday, making a little over six dollars an hour. We shook hands, and I spent the weekend getting excited about how stupid my new job was going to be.

By Sunday night, I had a realization. I had no idea how to dance and the entire job description was "dance while you're wearing this chicken suit." I probably should have thought about that when I accepted the job. If they wanted me to run a Bigg's BBQ sign through a lecture hall, I'd have no issues with that. Walking around as the chicken while clucking and pointing at the restaurant would work, too. But dancing? Nope.

I dealt with this realization in the most responsible manner I knew: on Monday, I no-showed and never thought about it again.

It was time to start considering other positions that I was completely unqualified for. My friend Scott painted campus buildings for a living and encouraged me to join him. I had never held a paintbrush in my life, but I figured that it couldn't be that hard to dip a roller in a tray and then run it along a wall for a while.

The interview process was about as involved as the chicken suit thing, so I got accepted ASAP and was told to start the next day. A couple of vans drove around town at six in the morning and picked up all the painters, and then they'd drop us off at a girls' dorm in need of remodeling.

Every room in the dorm had to be painted, so teams of two or three would tackle one room at a time. For the first day I told myself that I was enjoying it. Scott brought a boombox, and we'd listen to Patton Oswalt and David Cross comedy albums as we sloppily rolled paint on the walls. At the end of the eight-hour day, I went home happy with my first day of genuine manual labor.

When the alarm clock went off at 5:15 a.m. on day two, I was less enthused. My habit of sleeping in until two in the afternoon was in jeopardy, and my body was immediately rejecting the new schedule. I forced myself to get up and hop into the van as time seemed to move at quarter speed. Several times during the shift, I disappeared into rooms that were already painted and laid down for a while on the bunk beds.

Day three was the final straw for my lazy brain and body. I tossed paint on the walls for a few hours, then laid down on the bed. My eyes felt heavy, and I felt an immediate desire to stop doing anything associated with this job. I got off the bed, left the dorm, and walked home without telling anyone. I never went back.

I wasn't cut out to be a dancing chicken or a painter, so I really needed to find something that would stick. While I was at the cafeteria one day, a job listing in the campus newspaper caught my eye. It was for the Kansas University Endowment Association. They needed students to call alumni and ask for donations. The pay and hours were great by college standards. It sounded sales-y, but maybe the "I go to school here, and you used to! Let's talk about it" dynamic would make the process feel a bit more human.

KUEA knew that they'd have a lot of applicants, so they had interested parties meet at the office on a Saturday for a day of interviews and mock phone calls. At the end, they separated the 30 or so applicants into two different rooms. One group was told to sign up for their shifts, and the other was nicely told to go home. I was in the former group, so I signed up for my first of hundreds of shifts that would stretch on for four years.

Calling alumni was awkward at first, because we were encouraged to make small talk that none of the alumni seemed interested in having. You'd occasionally find an architecture or engineering alum who had specific questions about an old professor or building. I was always woefully unprepared for those—we were given fact sheets related to our day's calling pool, but I never actually read any of them.

If you were lucky, you'd get a call or two a week that was at least entertaining in some way. One Valentine's Day involved talking to a recent divorcee as she sipped wine in the bathtub. She ranted about the pratfalls of love and marriage, and would repeatedly remind me of her "sipping wine in the bathtub" status.

The most memorable call I ever made was to Brain. At least, that's one of the names he gave me when he picked up the phone.

"This is Brain, also known as Thomas Jefferson, 8-4-3-4-5-6-5..."

He kept enthusiastically naming numbers until I cut him off and went into my spiel. At no point during the conversation did he seem to understand what I was calling about, but boy, did Brain love to talk about an endless variety of things. When I asked what he was doing for a living, he alternated between stories about being an FBI agent and installing light bulbs for two dollars an hour. He said that Robert Plant from Led Zeppelin was the inventor of Kool-Aid and personally coined the term "space-time continuum." According to Brain, he also worked out of a laboratory in his home in which he subjected people to his music and then broadcast the process on closed-circuit television.

It was a rambling call that lasted almost half an hour. I was fascinated the entire time. There were clearly a number of screws loose in Brain's brain, but he seemed enthusiastic and happy. When the call finally ended, I jotted his number down on a note and put it in my pocket.

That weekend, I was drinking with some friends and told them all about Brain. I still had his number in my pocket, and I was drunk enough to bring up the possibility of calling him on speakerphone. None of us wanted to use our own phones, so we wound up calling him using a website meant for deaf people. This relay service let you call a number and type what you wanted to say, and a middleman would do the talking to the other party. Then, they'd type the response back to the website user.

We typed in the number and pressed "connect," then waited for Brain's response on the screen. It was late at night, and we weren't confident that he'd pick up. Then, we saw "relay operator typing..." appear on the screen.

You've reached John Adams, George Washington, Mr. Brain 3-4-2-8-6-4-3-2-1-5...

The relay operator continued typing numbers for a while until they gave up and entered "NUMBERS CONTINUE." We had him on the line. When we asked what he was up to, he said that he was having a party and that we should come over.

Oh, man.

This happily insane man who claims he performs scientific experiments on people in his home laboratory just told us that we should come to his party. This would be ill-advised under any circumstances, but we were drunken college students and this seemed way too good to pass up.

We may have been idiots, but even in our state we realized that this was potentially a bad idea. Eventually, we decided that if we had enough people coming with us, there probably wasn't much we had to worry about. Ten drunk college students should be able to take a 50-year-old crazy person if things went bad, even if he had a couple of crazy friends with him. Nothing about my original call or our late-night correspondence indicated any maliciousness, however.

It was a hard sell to most of our friends who were still awake, but we managed to find a few enthusiastic buddies. On the way to the address that Brain gave, we argued in the car about who would be tasked with knocking on the door and doing the initial talking. It probably should have been me, considering I was the initial contact and ringleader of this whole thing, but I was way too scared about an insane man bursting through the door and stabbing me to death.

My friend Mike agreed to serve as the front line for the Brain Party Brigade. When we arrived in the parking lot, he led the way while a few others refused to go into the apartment building until they received a text confirming that we weren't going to be murdered. Several of us stayed a few steps behind Mike as we carried beer down the long hallway leading to Brain's unit number.

As we drew closer, I started wondering why we weren't hearing any music or conversation coming from anywhere in the hallway. Wasn't he having a party? Our conversation happened over an internet relay service, so it's not like we were able to hear Brain's voice as he invited us to his rockin' get-together. Considering that he sounded absolutely insane when I talked to him, I'm not even sure what I expected a party hosted by him to look like.

Sure enough, there was nothing but silence as Mike walked straight up to the door. There was no shuffling coming from within, not even the sounds of a television. We had come this far, though, so we weren't about to leave before we figured out what Brain's party consisted of. Mike gave us a nod, then took a breath and knocked on the door.

It opened almost immediately.

"Abraham Lincoln here!" Brain said with a smile. "Andrew Jackson, Grover Cleveland, Franklin Pierce!"

As I had estimated based on his graduation year, Brain looked to be in his early- to mid-50s. He was wearing light blue pajama pants, black socks, and no shirt. His gray hair was receding and he had some light stubble, but he didn't look particularly disheveled. If he had been wearing a shirt, he wouldn't have looked very odd at all.

"Brain!" Mike exclaimed. "What's up, man?"

"Ready for a party! 3-4-1-2!"

He seemed thrilled to see us, and we were relieved that he appeared thoroughly unthreatening. I sent the go-ahead text to the rest of the group waiting outside. They headed in and joined us in Brain's apartment.

It was hard to get any real read on Brain based on the look of his place. The Albert Einstein calendar on his wall was from 1972. Black-and-white portraits of families from the 1800s hung on the wall. A bundle of at least 15 lighters was held together with rubber bands. One corner of the apartment featured almost a dozen basketballs, many of them with names written on them in Sharpie (we assumed that he was stealing stray balls from his apartment complex's basketball court). In the bathroom was a bottle of Pert shampoo that must have been at least thirty years old, based on the logo and accumulated grime.

It was a collection of odds and ends, but it certainly didn't feel like some serial killer's lair. The laboratory he bragged about didn't exist and he was in a great mood. Once we were all inside, he offered everyone Kool-Aid. Even though Brain didn't seem threatening, none of us were about to drink anything that he prepared.

We cracked open a few beers and found seats around his living room. Without any warning, Brain picked up a harmonica and began playing a manic tune that seemed to make sense only to him. He shuffled back and forth as horrible metallic squeals came from the instrument. We applauded and complimented him as if he were Bob Dylan.

Once the musical portion of the evening concluded, Brain floated between stories, jokes, and crazy claims about his professions. On top of being an FBI agent and a lightbulb installer, he was also a minister, a studio musician, a landscaper, and a Lawrence police officer. At one point, he leaned on his ministerial background to perform a wedding ceremony for Mike and his friend Carrie, who were in no way dating. Afterward, he explained the history of the internet to us. Did you know that the term "dot com" came about because all of us on earth are just part of one big commune? Also, on the Fourth of July, he prefers to make love instead of shooting off fireworks.

We spent about 90 minutes at Brain's place that first night. I was happy that none of my friends seemed to be making fun of him at all. Sure, the fact that he had a few screws loose was what drove us there in the first place, but he genuinely seemed thrilled to have company to talk to. When we left, he gifted his Einstein calendar to one of my friends and a basketball to another.

For a couple of years, we'd give Brain a call every few months after leaving the bars. If he answered, he'd always invite us over to tell us stories and play harmonica. We veterans of the Brain trips would always try to recruit a friend or two to experience him for the first time. This continued until one day when the calls stopped going through. We never did find out what happened to him, and I look back on those visits as tremendously odd but sincerely enjoyable. It seemed to be a great time for him as well.

Visiting crazy people wasn't a required part of my job at KUEA, as our actual jobs were supposed to follow a by-the-book protocol. We were assigned a calling pool at the beginning of each shift. Once we received our assignments, we were to flip to the appropriate school's fact sheet in our binder for potential topics for conversation. It was easy to estimate how many donations you'd get each night based on the pool you were assigned. Business and engineering alumni were easy fodder for higher contributions, while social welfare and theater majors would frequently respond to donation requests with laughter.

Even when you were in the more coveted calling pools, you could tell within 30 seconds whether you'd be adding anything to your night's donation tally. That's why I hated the script we were supposed to follow. It was called the Ask Ladder, and it required every caller to start with a request for $1,000. This level was called the "Dean's Club," and we were supposed to move down to lower tiers—$500, $250, and $100—if the person refused.

Asking for donations wasn't the part that bothered me. That's what we had signed up for when we applied, after all. It was the fact that we were supposed to pester these alumni by going through the entire Ask Ladder (complete with different script points for each tier) even if they directly told us that they wouldn't be donating this year. I hated that I was expected to plead at least three more times after an initial denial, putting them in the awkward position of considering hanging up on me. Plenty did, and I never blamed them.

I stuck to the script for the first month or two that I worked at KUEA. It never stopped bothering me. Eventually, I shortened the process and simply asked each person if there was a donation level they'd be comfortable contributing at. That led to shorter calls, and far fewer angry people.

Managers would occasionally monitor our calls to make sure we were sticking to the Ask Ladder, and I'd always get pulled into the office when they heard one of mine. No matter how much I tried to explain my reasoning, they weren't having it. I was warned numerous times about my call style, and these warnings didn't stop until about a year into my employment there.

PHONING IT IN

That happened because most of the old managers left KUEA or got promoted to another department. Luckily, several of my good friends stepped into these management roles. One of these friends was Shawn. We had been hired at the same time, and usually sat next to each other during our shifts.

Shawn started out as a saxophone performance major, and then took a hard right after a couple of years and became a med student. He's now a successful doctor in Kansas City. We worked together during my most egregious years of slacking off—both academically and professionally—and I was always amazed when I asked to see his weekly class schedule. While I was sleeping until 2 p.m. and going months without entering a classroom, he was running between wall-to-wall classes every day before starting his shifts at KUEA. His work ethic amazed me. My complete apathy toward school amazed him.

Even though he took academics super seriously, he had an appreciation for dumb humor. Whenever I saw him get up to use the bathroom, I'd take note of how long he was gone. If more than a minute and a half passed, I knew he'd be in the middle of taking a shit instead of peeing. As soon as I deduced that, I'd get up, walk into the bathroom, and turn off the lights, leaving him in total darkness. This was before everyone had cell phone flashlights to aid in situations such as these, so the idea of him having to shit (and somehow wipe) in the dark always made me laugh.

This was so funny to me that I started expanding it to pretty much every guy I worked with. If somebody was sitting on the pot at work, it was a surefire bet that I'd pop in and flip the switch. It never got old to me, and I probably did it hundreds of times.

On one occasion, I went in to use the urinal and noticed that somebody was in the stall. Despite not knowing who was in there, I did my usual thing by turning the lights off. I walked back into the call center and looked around to see who was missing from their desk. It surprised me to see that all 24 seats were occupied. All the managers were also present. Who could have been in the stall? Our shifts were in the evenings, and nobody else was supposed to be in the building except for us call center kids.

I sat back down and wondered whom I had left in the dark. Fifteen minutes later, the door leading to the bathroom hallway swung open violently. Standing there was a middle-aged man I only recognized from his picture on the wall. It was the head of the entire Endowment Association.

Standing next to him was a young boy who couldn't have been older than ten or eleven. He was sheepishly looking at the floor.

"Who in here thought that it'd be a funny joke to turn the lights out on my son as he was in the bathroom?" the man boomed.

I immediately averted my eyes, sulked down, and pretended to be in the middle of a call. Out of the corner of my eye, I could see Shawn struggling not to laugh. Several other people in the room were looking at me, the obvious culprit.

The man loudly asked several more times before realizing that he wasn't getting anywhere with this group. He left with his son, the incident was never brought up again, and on the next day I resumed turning the lights off whenever anyone was pooping.

Once my friends ascended to managerial positions, I gave myself permission to *really* slack off at work.

PHONING IT IN

Simultaneously, I also raised more money than any caller in the history of the organization. This was largely thanks to my quick approach to calls. While others were following the script and bantering with alumni for the recommended eight minutes before asking for money, I got right down to it.

Our monitors displayed a record of what each alumnus had donated in the past, so I used that as a reference. If someone had given $250 every year since 1992, it was as easy as saying "Hi, this is Dan from the Kansas University Endowment Association. How are you? That's great. I see that you've been a loyal donor to our programs for quite some time. Would you like to contribute again this year?"

They'd tell me to put them down for the same amount, and I'd thank them before moving on to the next call. If I saw that an alum had never once given us money, I'd "accidentally" hang up before the call started, and move on until I found a regular. My stats went way up, and upper management responded by putting me in the most lucrative calling pools as a result. These were often donors who gave thousands of dollars every year, and were more than happy to check that box again and get off the phone as soon as possible. Upper management loved my numbers and the student managers were my friends. They weren't about to tell their bosses that I got those numbers by going as far off-script as possible. By the time I quit, I had raised several hundred thousand dollars for the university. To this day, I have a large collection of certificates that KUEA gave me whenever I broke another record.

My time at KUEA overlapped with my time reviewing video games for a local newspaper and website. I got cocky enough to try to do both at the same time. Since I actually gave a shit about my games writing, I wanted that to receive 100 percent of my attention while I was on the clock at KUEA.

It would have been nearly impossible to do that while I was on the phone with alumni, so I came up with the perfect workaround.

At the time, the biggest portable console in the world was the Nintendo DS. Each week, I received a handful of games for the system. I was determined to review every game that came in, but there were only so many hours in a day (even considering that I was skipping virtually all of my classes). Writing reviews while I was on the clock at KUEA would be tricky to pull off. If I could find a way to do that, it would be much easier to get through all of the games I needed to cover.

My bosses didn't have a problem with me playing games if I wasn't actively on a call. Once an alumnus picked up, however, the DS had to be closed and out of my hands. This was enforced by a feature of the calling software at each station. If we were currently on a call, the background of the monitor would be bright green. If we were dialing, it would be yellow. If no activity was happening at all, it would be white.

Several student managers were present during each shift, and their primary role was to walk around the office and make sure that everyone's screen was either green or yellow. A white screen wasn't a big deal if someone was taking a quick break or going to the bathroom, but managers would eventually tell us to start dialing again.

Playing my DS games in tiny bursts between alumni picking up wasn't ideal, so I devised a way to play constantly. I'd dial an alumnus at the beginning of my shift, making my screen turn yellow. Before they picked up, I'd hit the Print Screen button on my keyboard and then hang up the phone. From there, all I had to do was paste the yellow screengrab into MS Paint, fullscreen the image, and play DS games for the duration of my shift. I'd typically call a few of the gimme donors just to ensure that I raised some amount of money, but it was all games all the time outside of that.

I was able to ride this out for way longer than I expected. My manager friends knew about it and thought it was funny, so upper management never got wise to what was happening. Eventually, my slacking started to catch up with me. When it came time for employee reviews, upper management would monitor calls without us knowing about it.

Angela was my primary manager, and she was mortified when she monitored a few of my calls. She noticed my extremely brief back-and-forth with alumni. Over the last few months, she also got irked with the amount of screwing around I did at the office—after all, that bathroom trick never got old to me. After being called into her office on numerous occasions, I started wondering if I was on borrowed time at KUEA.

Things came to a head in an unexpected way after a party at Shawn's house. Everyone had too much to drink, and Shawn passed out in the living room. Naturally, the Sharpies came out. People at the party took turns writing and drawing things on him, including me. My contribution was the phrase "SHAWN EATS POOP" on his back, next to a bad drawing of Shawn eating poop. I also drew a bunch of ejaculating penises on his calves.

It was another standard weekend night and everyone went home afterward to pass out. Shawn's alarm went off early the next morning, and he scrambled to get to his second job at a Chipotle. Unfortunately, he noticed most of the penises on his legs and scrubbed them off during a quick shower. *Fortunately*, he missed one—and wore shorts to work.

Shawn filled bowls with chopped chicken for several hours before a coworker pointed out the erect penis on his calf. He informed me of this later that night during our KUEA shift, and it became the funniest thing in the world to me. A faint outline of a penis could still be seen after his hasty attempt at cleaning it in a Chipotle bathroom.

I spent the first hour of my shift playing my DS while occasionally chuckling to myself about that weiner on Shawn's calf. Suddenly, he approached me with a look on his face that struck me as genuinely serious.

"Hey man," he said. "Can you come into the office for a second?"

His tone was totally different from the "aw, ya got me!" tenor of our previous conversation. We both sat down in the manager's office, and he let out a heavy sigh.

"So I'm probably not supposed to tell you this," he began. "But I went to print something just now and saw this sitting in the tray. Angela's not gonna be in until tomorrow, so I just thought I'd show you so you don't get blindsided."

Shawn handed me a piece of paper on KUEA letterhead, and my face sank as I read it. It was signed by Angela and addressed to her superiors, with the subject line *RE: Termination of Student Development Associate Dan Ryckert.*

It made mention of "several grievances that have been recorded and documented," and went on to point out my general negative impact on the office:

We have repeatedly bent our expectations of student callers in order to save Mr. Ryckert's position, largely due to his relationships with callers and student managers, but now I believe that we have reached the point with Dan where his continued employment would be a detriment to our program as his influence on callers and other students is beginning to create difficulty for our student managers and myself.

This all seemed fair to me. For quite some time, I had wondered how far I could push things before somebody finally came down on me. Apparently that time was now. It wasn't until the next paragraph that I became confused. In it, Angela claimed that she had received a returned pledge card from an angry alumnus. He claimed that he had spoken to me on the phone and declined to pledge, but I had put him down for the money anyway.

Slacking off? Sure. Putting up a fake screen so that I could play video games during my shift? Absolutely. But falsifying pledges? Even I wasn't dumb enough to pull something like that. The first part of the letter made perfect sense to me, but I was baffled by the falsification accusation.

I expressed this to Shawn, and he produced Exhibit B. It was the returned pledge card. On it, the alumnus had written "I did not make this pledge. I told the young man that I would <u>not</u> give this year."

Well, hell. I wasn't sure how that had happened, but I knew that the hammer was finally about to come down. In the last paragraph of her letter, Angela explicitly called for me to be fired.

"I'm sorry, man," Shawn said as he took the paper and pledge card back from me. "I just thought you should know."

None of this was unexpected. KUEA was totally in the right to want to fire me, even aside from the "falsification" issue. I was surprised by how I felt upon hearing the news. It wasn't anger at this justified decision; it was sadness over leaving this place where I had met so many friends. Those early years in the dorms helped me come out of my shell, but my social circle in later years of college consisted largely of my KUEA colleagues.

"Thanks, man," I told Shawn. "I appreciate it. Let's make sure that we all still hang out even though I won't work here anymore. I'm really gonna miss all you guys."

Shawn nodded and bit his lower lip, which I initially read as sadness. Considering how the rest of this panned out, I know now that he was holding back laughter.

I thanked him again and left the office, planning on leaving that day and never coming back to hear the official word from Angela. Between their calls, I walked up to my coworkers' stations to say goodbye.

"So I just found out that I'm getting fired," I said to Kyle, Theresa, Sam, Mike, Tori, Jeremy, and 17 other friends. No one was surprised, but most of them seemed sad to hear the news. Handshakes and hugs were exchanged, and then I'd move on to the next station.

Even the coworkers whom I had griefed the most seemed a bit sad. "You were a pain in the ass, but it'll definitely be more boring without you around" was a common refrain.

After talking to everyone, I went to my desk and placed my DS and spiral notebook in my backpack. I put on my jacket and walked toward the door, giving one last wave to the room that I had spent so much time in during the last few years.

"Hey Dan!" Shawn yelled before I left. "We wanted to tell you one more thing before you left."

He was standing near the front of the room next to the wall that served as our projection screen. With the room's attention, he pressed a button on the remote control to power up the projector. It took a few seconds for the gigantic Sharpie penis to fade into view on the wall. Next to it were a few words.

YOU'RE NOT FIRED. FUCK YOU, DAN.

I was so used to being the guy who fucked with people. I had no suspicions of the situation being a joke on me. Everyone in the call center started laughing as I looked at Shawn and realized it was all fake. He had typed up the incredibly realistic Angela e-mail and falsified the "falsified" pledge card. I fell for it hook, line, and sinker, and felt like the biggest moron for believing it all. Shawn had gotten me back good, and I gave him credit for pulling it off so flawlessly.

I dejectedly sat back down, and started playing my games and pretending to call people again.

Weeks later, Angela would threaten to actually fire me for all the reasons she should have, and I quit before she had the chance to pull the trigger.

Three Strikes

An awful lot happened in the ten years after I graduated from Olathe East High School in 2002. I started—and miraculously completed—college, developed severe anxiety disorders, lost my virginity, advised my father against at least two dozen marriages, earned the ire and legal attention of baseball legend George Brett, and moved to Minnesota to start my dream job at *Game Informer*. I had changed from the socially awkward high schooler wearing wrestling shirts to a confident 28-year-old who had worked his way into a career that drew a lot of envy (while still wearing wrestling shirts on occasion). When it was time to drive back down to Kansas for my ten-year high school reunion, I relished the idea of being the guy with the coolest job there.

From the moment that a Facebook group for our graduating class announced the reunion, I imagined how the whole thing would go down. Those jerks who had always punched me in the arm would tell me all about their boring jobs at car lots or in cubicle farms, and I'd tell them that I had spent the last two weeks reviewing *Borderlands 2* at work. I was sure that almost all of them would be making way more money than me, but it was a safe bet that I was having a lot more fun.

Gloating opportunities weren't the only reason that I wanted to go to my reunion. Even if I had never been a social butterfly at Olathe East, I did have a few friends whom I'd mostly lost contact with. Bragging about my job could only take me so far. At a certain point, it'd be nice to reconnect with the handful of folks like me who had avoided parties in favor of video games and pro wrestling.

I might have decided to stay in Minneapolis for the weekend if I had done even an iota of research into the reunion plans. Two red flags were in play. One was the location. We'd all be meeting up in the heart of Kansas City's Power & Light District, which was basically a shared courtyard area that was surrounded by bars. It was constructed shortly before I moved out of town and it wasted no time in establishing itself as the place where douchebags went to drink.

I'd be able to look past the annoying surroundings if I had good friends there to catch up with. Unfortunately, I neglected to touch base with any of them or even take a look at the confirmed guest list beforehand. If I had, I'd have noticed that none of my close high school friends—primarily Chris, Kiu, Bryan, and Afshin—were attending.

I was driving down from Minneapolis to "catch up" with a bunch of people I never even talked to back when I went to school with them. These weren't bad people by any means. They were just people with wholly different interests than mine, and an extra ten years probably hadn't done much to change that status.

When the day of the reunion arrived, I knew that I'd be drinking a lot. My father drove me down to the Power & Light District a bit early so that I could get a head start on the rest of my former classmates. I scanned the courtyard in an effort to find the least insufferable place where I could have a few beers. The dueling piano bar was immediately eliminated as a possibility, as was Angel's Rock Bar—a borderline strip club featuring scantily clad women swinging from the ceiling as Poison and Mötley Crüe tracks blared.

I wasn't familiar with every bar's reputation, so I assumed that the country-themed place in the courtyard would be all right. It was called PBR Big Sky, which I assumed stood for Pabst Blue Ribbon. With a modest exterior and name based on a cheap beer, how bad could it be?

I later learned that "PBR," in this case, stood for Professional Bull Riders. Naturally, this bar featured a mechanical bull. In my experience, a mechanical bull—despite how undeniably fun they are to ride—often served as a potent magnet for the types of people who annoyed me. Sure enough, this bar was filled to the brim with people I'd have nothing in common with. There were a lot of cowboy hats and boots, and the soundtrack consisted of songs about sexy tractors, red Solo cups, saving horses by riding cowboys, and honky-tonk badonkadonks.

Most of the commotion was centered around the bull. I just wanted to have a few drinks, so I sat myself at the bar and ordered a tall beer and a shot of whiskey. That turned into another tall beer and shot of whiskey. Eventually, I remembered that I hadn't driven all the way from Minnesota to drink by myself while listening to what sounded like Larry the Cable Guy's Spotify playlist. I paid up and headed over to the bar hosting the reunion.

Oh, right, I thought as soon as I walked in. Sure enough, I was instantly reminded of how much I didn't fit in at Olathe East. This was a nice place, and everyone was wearing appropriate clothes for the occasion. All the guys had on slacks and nice shirts or suits, and I had shown up half-drunk in jeans and a Lynyrd Skynyrd t-shirt.

I wasn't feeling dread or derision. It was just an immediate mental confirmation of what I had already expected. I saw a bunch of people who had never strayed from their old cliques in high school, and they seemed to be sticking to the script even ten years later. Most of them had never left Kansas City, so I imagined there was less "catching up" going on and more of the same old weekend routine. I

Kansas City area for the last few years, so I
ut of the loop than I had been back in high

the people there whom I had never wanted to talk to in high school were two people I very much did want to talk to. Amanda and Jessica were my two biggest crushes throughout junior high and high school, and I had completely blown my chances with each of them back then. Okay, maybe that's inaccurate because it implies that I ever had chances to begin with. I never really had any indication that either of them had been interested in me, but I certainly did myself no favors with the fumbling ways in which I expressed how I felt about them.

This tradition dated back to fifth grade with the first girl I ever felt bold enough to express interest in. Her name was Audrey, she was gorgeous, and she was the most popular girl in class. I was fresh off of leaving Holy Trinity halfway through the year. Being in public school for the first time might have made me overestimate how much of a fresh start this would be for me. I had never been able to talk to girls back in Catholic school, so I'm not sure why I thought things would be different now. It's not like I'd magically become some smooth operator just because I didn't have to wear a uniform or go to church during class anymore.

Simply talking to Audrey and getting to know her was a ridiculous concept. She was a popular and pretty girl; I was the weird new kid. Considering that this dynamic made me too scared to even talk to her, I have no idea why I thought it would be a good idea to express romantic interest right out of the gate. Also, I was 11 years old and I had no idea what "romantic interest" would lead to even if things went well.

THREE STRIKES

After months of thinking about telling her that I liked her, I felt like it was time to act. Zero percent of me was ready to say a single word to her. Instead, I did the only logical thing I could think of: I went to a gas station, bought a Butterfinger, wrote "from Danny Ryckert" on a note in my best cursive, and taped it to the candy bar. I put it in my backpack and prepared to make my big move the next day.

My heart was racing throughout the morning. At lunchtime, I was ready to set the plan into motion. The bell rang and our teacher assembled the class together to walk to the cafeteria. Once we were walking out of the room, I pretended I forgot my lunch card and needed to run back to get it. With no one else in the room, I took the Butterfinger out of my backpack and moved it to Audrey's cubby. She was bound to find it right after lunch. That's when we'd move into art class and she'd need to get her supplies from her cubby. Surely she'd find the Butterfinger, turn to face me, smile, and then we'd be kissing and dating forever and ever or something.

Lunch at this school already made me nervous thanks to my "new kid" status amid a bunch of kids who had known each other for years. Today put things on another level. My worries of not fitting in with the other kids were wholly replaced by the Butterfinger-spurred scenarios that were playing out in my mind.

I was staring directly at my watch when the lunch bell rang again, signaling for us to head back to our classrooms. Every second felt like a minute as we walked back. Audrey was fifteen feet behind me and only a couple of minutes away from finding out that I liked her.

I didn't really have a follow-up plan in place in case things went well; I hadn't thought that far ahead. Would she come up and talk to me right there in class? I hoped not, as that would bring too much attention to me. Ideally, she'd see the Butterfinger and then play it cool until recess or after school. Then, she'd approach me and tell me that she was happy that I liked her. She'd ask if I wanted to be her boyfriend or something, and then...kiss me? I don't know, I had no idea how any of this was supposed to work.

I wouldn't have to worry about any of that. I grabbed my art supplies, sat down, and watched out of the corner of my eye as she walked to her cubby. She pulled the Butterfinger out, looked at it for a minute, and then glanced over at me. I immediately put my head down. When I looked up again, she was sitting at her desk and laughing with several girls around her. She had placed the Butterfinger back into my cubby.

Audrey and I never spoke about the gesture (or anything at any point, actually). On the other hand, the boys in my class were *very* interested in talking about it. I was told in no uncertain terms at recess that "she's the hottest girl in class. You're just the new kid!" They mocked me for weeks, and my fear of expressing interest in a girl only intensified.

With one complete failure under my belt, I'm surprised that I worked up the nerve to give it another shot with a new crush a couple of years later. It didn't involve a candy bar, but my new approach may have been even worse.

I met Amanda in sixth grade and immediately had a crush on her. Unlike with Audrey, I actually did talk to Amanda on occasion. During a project in social studies class, we were split into groups of three and asked to perform brief educational scenes. All I remember about our scene is that I played a Lithuanian man who lived in a trash can.

Amanda and I were working with a girl named Kim. As we prepared our scene, I managed to make them laugh with some of the lines I came up with. It was the first time that I can remember talking and joking comfortably with a girl. It felt great.

Things went well enough for me to think that I had a shot with Amanda. My only problem was that I had no idea how to ask her out. Directly asking a girl if she wanted to do something outside of school seemed like an impossible task. My mother encouraged me to simply give Amanda a call and ask her to a movie. This seemed reasonable and I told myself that I could handle it.

But if I asked Amanda to a movie and she said no, I didn't think I could deal with seeing her in class afterward. Being in the same room as Audrey had been tremendously awkward for months after my Butterfinger-based wooing attempt failed. I couldn't go through that again with Amanda.

To avoid that, I told myself that I'd ask Amanda to a movie as soon as the school year was over. That way, if she said no, there would be a three-month buffer before I had to see her again. Plus, I wouldn't have to worry about my classmates giving me truckloads of shit. The week after school let out happened to coincide with a movie that I really wanted to see. *Mission: Impossible* was hitting theaters and I was going to ask Amanda to see it with me.

That was the plan. Time after time, I'd dial the first six digits of her home phone number as it was listed in the school directory. My finger would hover over the seventh number before I'd get too nervous and hang up. This was proving to be much harder than I expected.

I came up with a different plan. She lived near me in an adjacent Olathe neighborhood. What better way to ask a girl out than to just ride my bike around aimlessly in the hopes that she'd spot me, be interested in me, and ask me out herself? It was a bulletproof approach. A couple of times a week, I'd ride around the neighborhood in the hopes that I'd hear her voice call out my name. I didn't ever even see her, let alone get asked out by her.

Calling Amanda at any point during the summer would have cleared up the question of whether she had any interest in me. Instead, I chose to do nothing for three months. August eventually came, and it was time to go back to school. It would be my first year in junior high, and I was sure that Amanda and I would share at least one of our seven classes.

We didn't. California Trail Junior High split each grade into two pools of students who never shared classes. I was placed on the black team and she was on the gold team. This ensured that we'd never see each other during the year, outside of occasionally passing each other in the hallway. I hadn't been able to ask her out in sixth grade, when I shared a room with her seven hours a day. What hope did I have now? Her identical twin sister was on the same team as me, but I didn't have any of that critical "Lithuanian trash can dweller" experience with her.

I had the patience to do nothing about the situation for an entire summer, but I couldn't imagine going another school year without figuring out whether I had a chance with Amanda. I decided to lean on my friend Jared. He shared a science class with her and maybe he'd be able to help me out.

Jared was not the brightest guy. He'd eventually become a massive stoner, but in the seventh grade he was pretty slow without any outside influence. In the days before he got really into weed and the Insane Clown Posse, we'd do things like hang out and play *SimAnt* or watch *Die Hard* on VHS. Whenever a movie came out that I wanted to see, he was usually game for it. On one occasion, I wanted to see *Sgt. Bilko* with Steve Martin. Jared was unsure, so I circled Siskel

& Ebert's "Two Thumbs Up!" review in the *Kansas City Star* ad for the movie and faxed it to him. I didn't have a whole lot to do in the mid-'90s.

Entrusting Jared to help me find out whether Amanda liked me was a poor idea from the start. I may not have been smooth or confident, but I was at least smarter and more lucid than he was. Walking up to Amanda in the hallway myself and saying "Hey, would you like to see a movie sometime?" would have given me way more of a chance if I'd just had the balls to do it.

Instead, I tasked Jared with asking her during their shared science class. I didn't even want him to directly say my name. Not wanting her to pick up on who had asked him to do this, I told Jared to ask her if she liked anyone in our grade. If there's anything girls love, it's random classmates they barely know asking them to list every boy they might have interest in. This was bound to work.

The conversation between Jared and Amanda was set to happen during the third hour of the day. They were in their science class while I was in geometry. Waiting to meet Jared in the hallway after that hour felt just like waiting for Audrey to find the Butterfinger. After months and months of having a crush, I was hopefully about to find out if there was any interest in return.

When the bell rang and signaled the end of third hour, I sprinted to my locker. Jared and I had agreed to meet there, but he apparently didn't have the same sense of urgency as I did. I stood by my locker for a couple of minutes and saw no sign of him. California Trail allowed us five minutes between classes, making every passing second feel like sand falling through an hourglass.

Three minutes into the passing period, I spotted Jared approaching from the other end of the hallway. It had to be him because no one else in school frequently wore a Blink-182 shirt with a skanking rabbit on it. Jared had a wallet chain, and so did the skanking rabbit on his shirt. It was a hell of a look (I'm one to talk, considering that I was probably wearing my NWO WolfPac "Bad Has Arrived, and It's Here to Stay" shirt).

He was taking his time walking down the hall as I jumped up and down and waved my arm frantically. When he finally spotted me, his wallet chain jingled back and forth slightly more as he upgraded from slothlike speed to a sleepy saunter.

"What'd she say?" I blurted out as he approached my locker.

"Uhh...she said...."

Jared's usually slow cadence might as well have been coming out of his mouth in slow motion.

"She said she doesn't have a crush on anyone," he said. "But then I asked her if she likes Dan Ryckert."

"What?! You said my name?"

"Yeah. I said 'Do you like Dan Ryckert?' She said that she hasn't really thought about you like that."

Before I had much of a chance to be disappointed, Jared continued.

"So then I said 'He really, really likes you.' She said that she didn't know that at all because you never said anything like that to her."

My disappointment turned into frustration. I had wanted Jared to remain vague when discussing this, and he had mentioned my name within two sentences. But things got even worse.

"So then I said 'Yeah, he said that he likes you so much that he'd give away his PlayStation if he had a chance to go out with you.'"

Oh good. Not only was this completely untrue, it painted me as even more of a huge nerd than I already was. Suffice it to say, that was the end of my hopes of dating Amanda.

Sixteen years later, Amanda and her husband were at the Power & Light District for our high school reunion. My ill-fated attempt to see if she liked me had been in seventh grade. I can't recall a single instance that we talked throughout the rest of our time in school. With it being such ancient history by this point, I figured it would be funny to tell her about how much of a dumbass I used to be. Her husband was with her, so I imagined that it wouldn't come off as me hitting on her this many years later.

I drunkenly ran down every dumb thought and plan that had gone through my head back then. Both she and her husband seemed really amused at how I clearly recognized that I had been a total idiot. Not wanting to spend too much time dwelling on a 16-year-old crush, I said it was good to see her again and that it was nice to meet her husband.

I grabbed more drinks and scanned the room to see who else I could talk to. A few minor acquaintances from Quest and my movie theater days said hello and made brief conversation before moving on. It didn't seem like anyone I was remotely close with was at this reunion.

Mere minutes after ending my conversation with Amanda, I spotted another girl I used to have a major crush on: Jessica. We met during high school, and I was instantly interested in her. We shared an English class with many of the rowdiest guys at school, and she seemed just as annoyed by them as I was. These guys were loud as hell and constantly bragging about how drunk they had gotten over the weekend.

I wouldn't start drinking myself for another year or so, but in high school, I looked down on classmates who partied regularly. Most of this was assuredly out of jealousy that they were confident enough to go out and socialize, but I convinced myself that it was because they were getting drunk.

Every time these guys started loudly recalling their wild weekends, I could almost hear Jessica rolling her eyes. She was really cute, but it was her personality and intelligence that drew me to her the most. Unlike with the sixth grade "she's cute!" crush I had on Amanda, I felt like Jessica and I would have a lot in common and plenty to talk about.

Naturally, I dealt with this by almost never talking to her. As a result of my shyness, I have extremely surface-level memories of these girls. Without ever having real conversations with them, all that I can recall are details like "Amanda was cute! Jessica was smart!" At no point did I know anything about them. Even back then, I wouldn't have been able to name one song they liked or a single interest that they had. I wanted to know these things, though. If I could have just worked up the nerve to have a conversation with them, I felt like I'd have an infinite well of curiosity about them and their lives.

I spent months hoping that Jessica would start a discussion with me out of nowhere. After all, it was just a matter of time before this attractive and intelligent girl approached me based on my keen sense of fashion. On any given day, I could be wearing my Kurt Angle "It's True! It's True!" shirt; my Tazz "The Mood is About to Change" shirt; or my favorite, the Triple H "Game Over? You're Damn Right I'm Over" shirt.

Allow me a moment to explain that last one. Being "over" in wrestling parlance means that you are capable of

~~garnering a reaction from the audience. Triple H started
referring to himself as "The Game" during a promo in the late
'90s ("You guys talk about being students of the game. I *am*
the fucking game!"). The front of the shirt features the
common video game phrase "Game Over," while the back is
essentially saying "Oh, you're saying the game is over? Well
yes, I am The Game, and I am over, because I am successful
at my job as a professional wrestling heel because people boo
me."~~

Jessica never approached me. When November came
around, I was convinced that my luck was about to change.
In addition to English, we shared a class called Conspiracy
Theories in Modern History. Believe it or not, our teacher was
very into the Kennedy assassination. He offered an annual
field trip to a convention in Dallas that commemorated the
event.

The trip sounded interesting enough on its own, but
my primary concern was whether Jessica would be going.
When I found out she was, I knew that I had my in. We'd be
driving down to Dallas in two large vans. If I could make sure
that I was sitting next to her during the more than eight-hour
drive, we'd almost certainly be able to have several long
conversations and get to know each other. Once she realized
that we had a ton in common, it would make it so much easier
for me to ask her out after we got back to Olathe.

On the morning we left for Dallas, all the students
were supposed to meet our teacher at Waffle House. We'd eat
an early-morning breakfast and then load into the vans for
the long drive. All I had to do was be aware of which van
Jessica was heading toward after breakfast and make sure that
I got in right after her.

Everyone ate their eggs and sausage while I scarfed
down my plain cheeseburger and fries—lunch/dinner food is

always better than breakfast food, no matter what time of day it is. It was time to spring into action as soon as I saw our teacher pay the bill. We needed to load our bags into the van we'd be riding in, so I made sure to throw mine into the same vehicle as Jessica's.

Once our bags were in the van, there was just one more critical step to ensure eight hours of fantastic conversation. All I had to do was remain somewhat close to Jessica as we walked the seven- or eight-foot stretch that separated the back of the van from the side door. I'd hop in right after her, secure my spot, and it would be smooth sailing from there until Dallas.

Jessica stepped into the van before me. Just before I raised my leg to hop in, the biggest goober on the trip jumped in ahead of me. He took the middle seat, Jessica was against the far window, and I was stuck on the right. There would be no way for me to talk to her without automatically involving the goob in everything. My plan was ruined.

The goob was Chad. He was a golf fanatic, and he was also one of the most obnoxious human beings I had ever met. Chad's brain housed the complete opposite of all of my anxious and insecure thoughts. He was a potent mix of being completely insufferable while simultaneously being the most unduly confident person on the planet.

The situation couldn't have been worse. Not only was I unable to talk to Jessica, I had to overhear Chad brag about his golfing prowess for the entire drive. He'd go over every detail of his favorite clubs, tees, balls, and courses. Oh, and he was super rich as well, of course. He let her know all about his financial situation during a couple of conversational detours about the cars his parents had bought him.

Jessica seemed wholly uninterested throughout it all. Chad didn't pick up on that, and kept bragging at a mile a minute. Once in a while, he'd make a bad joke and look over at me to see if I was laughing. I couldn't even muster a courtesy chuckle for this guy. All I could think about was all of the great conversations Jessica and I could have been having at that very moment.

All hope was not lost yet, as we still had a whole trip to go. Our time in Dallas didn't quite lead to long talks between Jessica and me, but we did hang out a little. With at least *some* conversations under our belt, I felt like I'd actually be able to ask her out once we got back to Kansas.

We returned from the Dallas trip just before Christmas break. My old "if she says no, I won't have to see her for a while" mindset came into play again. I snuffed out this train of thought and told myself it was time to actually grow some balls and ask her. *A Beautiful Mind* was about to come out, and it seemed like an appropriately intellectual-but-not-too-pretentious movie to ask her to see with me.

My attempts to woo girls with Butterfinger bars and friends who wore wallet chains had failed. It was time to actually ask a girl out for the first time in my life.

I got to our history class before she did and my plan was to ask her as soon as she sat down. Our assigned seats had been next to each other all semester long, but even that hadn't been enough to spur a conversation prior to the field trip. I took a deep breath as she entered the room and sat down.

"Have you heard anything about that *Beautiful Mind* movie?" I asked.

"Not a whole lot. It looks pretty good based on the commercials I've seen."

Here it was! Now was my chance!

"Would you want to go see it on Saturday?" I asked.

"Saturday? Actually, yeah...I think I'm free. Let's check it out!"

Holy crap. It happened. Not only had I directly asked a girl out, but she had said yes. I was over the moon. For the rest of the day, I couldn't help but gush to my friends whenever I saw them.

"I've got a date with Jessica on Saturday!" I'd say as soon as I saw them.

They all knew how big this was for me. All year, I hadn't shut up about how much I liked her.

Jessica and I didn't have cell phones, so we exchanged our home numbers and planned on chatting about details as Saturday drew closer.

I didn't have to wait long to hear from her. On the evening after I asked her out, she called me at home.

"Hey Dan," she said. I immediately noticed something odd about her tone.

"Oh, hey! How's it going?"

"It's going all right. Hey, I just wanted to clear something up about Saturday. Bryan told me that you were hoping this would be more than a 'just friends' thing. Is that true?"

My stomach tied into knots. I took a second to gather myself, and responded with something that was not my smoothest moment.

"Oh! Oh, okay. Huh, I didn't know he had mentioned that. Well, yeah. Yeah, I think you're pretty great. You're really cool and I'd like to get to know you more but if you don't feel that same way I'd be fine with it not being a 'more than friends' thing and we can just be friends but it's true that I was thinking it would be more like a date but if not that's all right too so we can do whatever you'd like on Saturday or whenever."

"Gotcha," she said. "Yeah, so I just wanted to clear that up. I'm not looking for it to be anything more than friendly. Do you still want to see the movie?"

"Uh, sure! Of course! The movie is at five, so do you want me to pick you up around four?"

"No. I'll drive myself and just meet you there."

Great!

Well, that was that. I was crushed, and now I was locked into a supremely awkward situation for 135 minutes (plus trailers). I called Bryan and asked him what the hell he had been thinking, but he didn't have much of an answer. It didn't matter at this point.

I showed up at the theater on Saturday fifteen minutes before Jessica, and got two tickets. When she arrived, I pulled them out of my pocket and tried to give one to her.

"Return that," she said. "I'll buy my own."

Great!

The rest of the not-date went exactly as I expected after a start like that. We barely talked as we headed toward our theater, and we then spent the entire run time of the trailers and film in complete silence. When it let out, we exchanged some brief reactions about the movie and then a couple of awkward goodbyes.

We barely spoke for the rest of high school. There were no hard feelings whatsoever; it was just painfully awkward.

The GameStop location that I worked at was directly next to a Dimples Golf store. At least once a week, that goob Chad would walk past our storefront, and I'd instantly be transported back to how angry I was in that van to Dallas. Chad sucks.

I relayed all of this to Jessica at the high school reunion. As with Amanda, this was in no way an attempt to hit on her. I just thought it would be funny to give her some insight into how dumb I was back in high school. Like Amanda, she seemed entertained to hear my take on everything in hindsight. We chatted for a bit longer, then said goodbye in a manner far less awkward than the one in the AMC parking lot over ten years prior.

The reunion had been going on for a while at this point, and it didn't seem like there was going to be a sudden influx of people I wanted to catch up with. I must have been drinking really fast during those conversations with Amanda and Jessica because I suddenly realized how drunk I was. A high school reunion seemed like an appropriate place to get super drunk, so I kept ordering more drinks and having brief conversations with former classmates.

Soon, I was on the verge of total sloppiness. I caught myself before falling down half a flight of stairs, which let me know that it was probably time to text my dad. When he told me that he was en route, I had time for another couple of drinks as he drove from Shawnee to Kansas City.

By the time he arrived at the bar, I was in a rough way. A "rough way" for me never meant that I was angry or getting into trouble. Even at my drunkest, I'd just get goofy and happy and stumbly. I was peaking in the latter of those when my dad tossed my arm around his shoulders so he could hold me up.

He had driven there with Cindy, a genuine sweetheart who was totally different from the assortment of hard-drinking, chain-smoking, pool hall ladies my dad was usually attracted to. They'd go on to date on-and-off until she started liking him too much and he got scared. This was their first date. She waited in the car as my dad guided my staggering body down the sidewalk. As we passed a downtown alleyway, an angry-looking, muscular bald guy with tons of tattoos and a studded leather jacket walked in front of us.

"Oh, you're *tough*!" I said sarcastically as I pointed my finger in his face. Whenever my dad tells this story, he notes that this was the moment in which he felt his sphincter physically tighten up.

Tough Guy didn't instantly murder me, miraculously. My dad was praying that we'd just get to the car without incident. We were eventually walking behind two girls, and one of them was having a very dramatic conversation on her cell phone. It sounded like a petty argument, and the girl was drunk and very worked up about it. Apparently, I decided that this was the right time to reassure her about life in general.

"It'll be fine!" I loudly blurted out. "You're taking everything too seriously. Life always works out, it's fine. Everything's fine. It'll be *fine*."

I rambled a bit more until she had enough and turned around.

"Shut. The Fuck. Up," she said, as seriously as I'd ever heard anyone say anything.

This was around the drunkest I'd ever been, but I was adamant about going to the Red Balloon with my dad and Cindy on the way home. At first they agreed, but it quickly became apparent what a bad idea that was. Before we even ordered a drink, I felt the room spinning as I struggled to sit upright in a chair.

The next thing I remember is my father lifting me by the arms as a random bar patron took my legs. They carried me through the parking lot and hurled me into the back seat of my dad's car. Since Paul Ryckert is (understandably) incapable of leaving the Red Balloon without swinging through the Taco Bell drive-thru, he ordered entirely too much food before we hit the road. As he stopped at a red light on the way home, my body fell in a remarkably awkward position on the floor between the front seats and the back seat.

Dad and Cindy were unaware of this until they got me back to his house.

"Oh my god," I heard him say when he opened the back door. "You idiot."

Without the guy from the bar to help him, my dad struggled to lift my drunk body out of the backseat. Once he got me upright, he called on Cindy to help walk me up the stairs to his front door. I was nearly incoherent while I repeatedly thanked them for being so nice and helping me. As Dad and Cindy walked me to the door, I started uncontrollably farting each time I reached a new stair.

"Stop farting!" my dad yelled between laughs.

I did my best, but some rectal function had apparently passed out by this point. Another step, another fart. When we got inside, I laid down on the floor in the entryway. This didn't last long, as I instantly felt the need to vomit. My motor functions sobered up quickly as the feeling came on, and I scrambled on my hands and knees to the back porch.

There, I dropped to my knees and vomited. I dangled my head off the side of the porch in an effort to keep the puke from splattering on the wood. After I spent a couple of minutes adding to the expanding vomit pile, I realized that I needed to pee. It was dark, it was late, and the bathroom seemed insanely far away in the state I was in. While still kneeling, I unzipped my pants and started peeing off the side of the porch.

THREE STRIKES

It was a night that I had envisioned would be full of gloating and impressing former classmates. Girls I used to have crushes on would be amazed at how much more confident I'd become in ten years. Those jocks who used to punch me would be cursed with soulless corporate jobs, trying in vain to mask their extreme jealousy when they heard about my awesome career. I'd finally get confirmation that I had won in life, and they had lost.

Instead, all my high school insecurities came flooding back after lying dormant for a decade. During that time, I spent so long telling myself that everyone else was stupid and that I was the only one who had it all figured out. In reality, everyone else spent the reunion comfortably catching up with old friends and sharing fun memories, while I was confronted with stark reminders of my lack of a social life and my utter ineptitude with the opposite sex. For the first time, I truly realized how much I had kneecapped my potential for years by convincing myself that I wasn't capable of socializing with my peers or talking to girls.

Now I was here in Shawnee, farting on my dad's porch and attempting to steady myself as I pissed into a gargantuan puddle of my own vomit. But hey, there was still plenty of Taco Bell waiting for me inside.

Acknowledgements

I'd like to thank the following people for their support throughout the process:

- I wouldn't have even started writing this book if it weren't for Bianca. From suggesting the idea in the first place to proofreading it to creating the cover art, she's been by my side every step of the way.
- Thanks to Heather Varanini, Samit Sarkar, and Bryan Vore for looking over everything upon completion and offering their suggestions.
- My mother and father for tolerating me for all of the years described in this book. It probably wasn't easy at times.
- Jeff Gerstmann for his support of my side projects.
- Tim Turi for the great foreword.

Thanks for reading *The Dumbest Kid in Gifted Class*. For a collection of photos from the events described in this book, go to danryckert.com.